D0903831

TWAYNE'S WORLD AUTHORS SERIES
A Survey of the World's Literature

GREECE

Ruth Scodel, Harvard University

EDITOR

Xenophon of Ephesus

TWAS 613

XENOPHON
OF EPHESUS

By GARETH L. SCHMELING

University of Florida

TWAYNE PUBLISHERS

A DIVISION OF G. K. HALL & CO., BOSTON

Published in 1980 by Twayne Publishers,
A Division of G. K. Hall & Co.
All Rights Reserved

Printed on permanent/durable acid-free paper and bound
in the United States of America

First Printing

Library of Congress Cataloging in Publication Data

Schmeling, Gareth L.
Xenophon of Ephesus.

(Twayne's world authors series; TWAS 613: Greece)
Bibliography: p. 173-181
Includes index.
1. Xenophon, of Ephesus—Criticism and
interpretation. I. Title.
PA4500.X5S3   883'.01   80-15632
ISBN 0-8057-6455-0

Meinen Eltern
Tabea und Walter

Contents

About the Author

Gareth L. Schmeling is professor of Greek and Latin and chairman of the Department of Classics at the University of Florida. A graduate of Northwestern College (B.A.) and the University of Wisconsin (M.A., Ph.D.) in Classics, he has also taught at the University of Virginia.

At the University of Florida his research and teaching have concentrated on the literature of late antiquity, particularly on Greek and Latin imaginative prose fiction, works which are usually called novels. In 1969 he founded the Petronian Society, which has grown to include most scholars working on Petronius and the other ancient novelists. He has published a Latin translation, *Cornelius Nepos: Lives of Famous Men* (Lawrence, Kansas, 1971), an introductory study on the earliest Greek novelist, *Chariton* (New York, 1974), *A Bibliography of Petronius* (Leiden, 1977), and various articles in *Classical Philology, Latomus, Rivista di Studi Classici, Classical World, Giornale Italiano de Filologia, Classical Bulletin, Classical Outlook*, and *Studies in Comparative Literature*, together with a number of reviews.

Both at Virginia and Florida Mr. Schmeling has held faculty fellowships. He has received grants from the American Philosophical Society and the American Council of Learned Societies, as well as a one-year fellowship from the National Endowment for the Humanities. In 1977 he won the Rome Prize from the American Academy and spent 1977–1978 in Rome working on a critical Latin edition of the last ancient Latin novel, *Historia Apollonii Regis Tyri*.

Preface

Perhaps the closest ties between the ancient world and the modern world are the various genres of literature. Admittedly, we continue to worship at the shrine of Greek architecture, return to Plato as a kind of sacred touchstone, and encourage lawyers to sprinkle arguments with classical phrases. But our real contact with the ancient world is through literature, and the particular kind or genre of literature which Xenophon of Ephesus wrote is the novel or romance. The influence of this genre was widespread in the late Roman and early Christian Empire. Since the time when they were written, some examples of the genre have had sporadic influence on Western literature up to the present day. In the sixteenth, seventeenth, and eighteenth centuries a few of these ancient novels experienced a kind of revival or vogue, which coincided curiously with the origin or rise of the modern novel. In point of fact the ancient novels were seminal in the formation of modern prose fiction.

I confess that I cannot say with conviction that Xenophon or any other ancient Greek novelist is worth reading or has written a book of intrinsic merit in either content or structure, that is, the merit or worth of the philosophy of the content, or the literary quality of the structure or the craft. Among those who read in the area of the ancient novel, the consensus regarding literary merit is established for the Latin novelists Petronius and Apuleius, and for the Greek Longus and Heliodorus.

Then why do I spend so much time researching and working on Xenophon and Chariton? Because they are phenomena from the classical world; they are so radically different from the *standard* ancient Greek and Latin writers; they are by and large unaffected in style or content; they probably have some influence on the writings of the early Christian apologists and early modern novelists; the novels of Chariton and Xenophon are a storehouse of popular motifs and short stories, which probably reflect the kind of literature the middle and lower classes liked to read or hear read to them.

For the professional classicists the ancient Greek novels represent a level of social sophistication and literary perspective seldom, if ever, seen by those who pore over Sophocles, Vergil, and Cicero. The classicists who refuse to take into account the ancient Greek novels must necessarily fail to appreciate an important dimension of the world of ancient Greeks and Romans. How important that dimension is depends on each student's view of the ancient world, its people, and their influence on us. If the study of the ancient world is important only for some aesthetic appreciation of a past civilization, the Greek novels have little to offer. On the other hand, if the study of the ancient world is important because it bears directly on our lives, our time, and our own twentieth-century concerns, then I contend that the study of the ancient Greek novels is worthwhile. If in the pages that follow the reader does not discover some merit in the novel of Xenophon of Ephesus, I will have failed, not Xenophon.

The novel of Xenophon and those of the other ancient Greek writers are significant both for demonstrating the continuum of a literary form in the face of countless, dramatic political and economic upheavals, and for serving as a kind of litmus paper to record external stimuli.

Xenophon's work is the extant proof (contrary to Ian Watt's conclusions in *The Rise of the Novel* that the novel began in the early eighteenth century and contrary to Northrop Frye's statement in *The Anatomy of Criticism* that the ancient classical world gave us only three of our four generally accepted literary genres, epic, drama, lyric) that the novel goes back at least to the first century A.D., and, if Barns and Braun are correct in identifying proto-novels in the late Egyptian empire, something like another millennium can be added to this genre's history. An appreciation of this point could open up a whole range of perspectives to those interested in the history of the genre.

Students of literary history can observe in the ancient novel the birth, growth, evolution leading to a drastically changed format, and finally the resurrection of a purer form many centuries later. There is a continuum of both literary form and content which connects the ancient world to the modern and makes the study of the ancient relevant for the modern. There is relatively little new under the sun, and the literary continuum illustrates this.

If there is such a person as the general reader, this book is addressed to him. All Greek words, terms, and expressions have been translated into English; the section on Xenophon's language has therefore necessarily been kept brief. Fellow classicists will find much that is obvious, and I ask their tolerance. I hope, nevertheless, to have provided some useful explorations, not thorough analyses, for classicists. Of the students of the history of prose fiction, genre studies, and folklore I ask indulgence for having entered areas where I claim interest rather than competence.

There are many people who have tried to guide me in my study of ancient prose fiction: John Sullivan of the University of California at Santa Barbara, Gerald Sandy of the University of British Columbia, and Donald Levin of Rice University have provided solid criticism in the novel and other fields. Many thanks to B. P. Reardon of the University of California at Irvine, who invited me to participate in the International Conference on the Ancient Novel in Bangor, Wales, in July of 1976. I am grateful to Donald Levin, James O'Sullivan, B. P. Reardon, and Gerald Sandy for reading earlier drafts of this book; none of these is responsible for the errors and misinterpretations which remain. A very small payment on a very large debt is acknowledged in the dedication.

Finally, acknowledgment to Oxford University Press for permission to quote from Gilbert Highet, *The Classical Tradition*. Copyright © 1949 by Oxford University Press.

GARETH L. SCHMELING

University of Florida

Chronology

Ca. 100 B.C.	*Ninus Romance*.
A.D. 66	Petronius's *Satyricon*.
117–138	Hadrian, Roman Emperor.
Ca. 125	Chariton (perhaps as early as A.D. 50).
Ca. 150	Xenophon of Ephesus (perhaps as early as A.D. 125).
138–161	Antoninus Pius, Roman Emperor.
Ca. 175	Achilles Tatius.
161–180	Marcus Aurelius, Roman Emperor.
180–192	Commodus, Roman Emperor.
Ca. 180	Apuleius' *Metamorphoses*.
193–211	Septimius Severus, Roman Emperor.
211–217	Caracalla, Roman Emperor.
Ca. 225	Heliodorus.
Ca. 225	Longus.
285–305	Diocletian, Roman Emperor.
Ca. 300	*Romance of Alexander*.
Ca. 300	Romance of Apollonius of Tyre.
306–337	Constantine, Roman-Byzantine Emperor.
Ca. 400	*Romances of Troy* by Dictys and Dares.

CHAPTER 1

Introduction to Xenophon of Ephesus

I The Author

IF we know little about the ancient Greek novelists, and are suspicious of even that, we know least about Xenophon. Where Chariton opens his novel with an historical statement about himself and provides at least a meager reference for us, Xenophon is quiet. But where we have only doubtful external references to Chariton, the *Suda* (a late classical encyclopedia) records specific information about Xenophon and his work:

Xenophon, an Ephesian, historical narrator. [He wrote] the *Ephesiaca*, a love story in ten books about Habrocomes and Anthia. [He also wrote] *On the City of the Ephesians* and other things.

"*On the City of the Ephesians* and other things" are no longer extant, if in fact they ever existed; the *Suda* is not as responsible a piece of classical scholarship as Pauly-Wissowa's *Real-Encyclopädie*. This fact brings up another interesting statement in the above quotation: "in ten books." When the *Suda* defines the *Ephesiaca* as "a love story in ten books about Habrocomes and Anthia," there can be no doubt he means the extant work we are here considering. This extant work, however, has only *five* books. Reasons for this variance of numbers are not hard to come by: the *Suda* miscounted; only an epitome survives; the *Ephesiaca* was never really divided meaningfully into books (like Chariton's *Chaereas and Callirhoe*), which had some cogent purpose for their existence as books. Scholars have been and continue to be at no small pains to propose or dispose of the "epitome theory" of the extant work.

Might the problems of the quotation from the *Suda* be even more complicated than laid out above? It is quite possible that the *Suda* has confused the titles *Ephesiaca* and *On the City of the Ephesians*, and

15

created two works where there was in fact only one. Using the other Greek novels as points of reference, we discover a similarity in constructing the names for the novels. The name for Xenophon's novel was probably *The Ephesian Love Story of Habrocomes and Anthia*, and the *Suda* divided it into two titles: *The Love Story of Habrocomes and Anthia* and *The City of the Ephesians*. If this theory is wrong and there are two works, *The Ephesiaca* (*The Love Story of Habrocomes and Anthia in Ephesus*) and *On the City of the Ephesians*, the former is the piece of literature we will consider, and the latter is a kind of travelogue.

About the novel's author, Xenophon (a not uncommon name), we know precious little. He might have been a resident, or perhaps even native son, of Ephesus. The *Suda* alone claims that he was Ephesian; the only manuscript of the novel says nothing of the author's home. If the art of writing novels was not highly regarded in antiquity, it might have been wise for the literate writer not to use his real name. Xenophon of Ephesus then becomes a pseudonym. If it is a pseudonym, it is not a chance one, but rather a conscious selection to recall and to honor the earlier and more famous Xenophon, Xenophon of Athens (ca. 430–340 B.C.), who in his *Cyropaedia* wrote a proto-Greek novel. I must, however, in all these speculative proceedings, try not to stray too far from the only solid evidence, namely, the citation in the *Suda* and the medieval manuscript. Though neither is really reliable, we are constrained like drowning men to clutch at straws. The *Suda* and the manuscript agree in calling the novel *Ephesiaca* (*The Affairs in Ephesus*). The content of the novel does not bear out this title because little, if anything, except for the opening and closing pages, takes place in Ephesus. In conjunction with the reference to Xenophon of Ephesus and his *Ephesiaca*, the *Suda* also lists a Xenophon of Antioch, author of the *Babyloniaca*, and Xenophon of Cyprus, author of the *Cypriaca*. Gärtner and Reeve suggest that Xenophon of Antioch and his *Babyloniaca* are more believable historically because they do not fit the pattern of an author of a place writing about that place.[1] I believe that it is more logical to assume that all three together are historical, or all three are fictional. Of Xenophon of Antioch, Xenophon of Cyprus, and their writings, we have nothing.

There are some reasons for holding to the title of *Ephesiaca*: both the *Suda* and the manuscript call it that; the hero and heroine are residents of the city; and the novel concludes there, with the reunited couple living happily ever after. It is proper to ask whether or not

Xenophon lived in Ephesus. If a man named Xenophon wrote about a city, he was clearly an inhabitant of that place—so the *Suda* appears to reason. While it might be an accurate conclusion, it is incumbent on us to question an authority as doubtful as the *Suda*. Also, while it might be a small point, the residence of the author, since it is our only biographical information, is of great importance as we consider the nature of the novel. We must take it into account when we analyze the audience for whom the author wrote, and when we look at the background and training of the man who set down the words.

Though there is no hard evidence to contradict the *Suda*'s statement that Xenophon came from Ephesus, scholars have been suspicious for some time that Xenophon knew of Ephesus from secondhand sources only.[2] This does not in any way detract from the quality of the novel he wrote; it merely gives us a different understanding of the man who wrote it. (Some will reject this whole critical approach as the "biographical fallacy.") Scholars have looked in the novel for some evidence of a personal warmth or attachment of Xenophon to Ephesus, or of some statement with such specific references and details that everyone would have to agree that Xenophon had at least *been* in Ephesus. Nothing of the kind is available. All references to Ephesus are vague and could have come from contemporary guide books or from conversations with inhabitants of Ephesus. The opening scenes of Book 1, in which the procession of Artemis is described, are particularly vague in detail; it must have been one of the brightest and most spectacular festivals in Ephesus, where Artemis had, perhaps, her most powerful cult. It is strange that an inhabitant of Ephesus would not give more detail, whether he approved or disapproved of the festival, about the pageantry of the event. But what I find militating strongly against the appellation of Ephesian to Xenophon is disinterest in the city of Ephesus. An inhabitant of a city need not necessarily like his city; clearly many hate their own. It seems to obtain, however, that inhabitants usually have stronger feelings one way or the other about their own city than about another place. Xenophon goes on to describe with disinterest all cities; perhaps he had other goals than to write realistically about events and places; perhaps he was deliberately vague in order to give his novel a kind of fairy-tale landscape; perhaps he was not from Ephesus—he does not claim to be. In a 1926 article B. Lavagnini tried to argue that Xenophon offered no conclusive evidence that he was a native of Ephesus; Perry concurred.[3] I suspect that it is an issue which never occurred to Xenophon to settle.

II Date of Xenophon and His Novel

Dating Xenophon is at best a risky and speculative matter. Guesses range within such extremes that it might not be worthwhile to locate him at any specific spot between the extremes. The earliest possible date is the rule of the emperor Augustus (31 B.C.–A.D. 14) because we know that Augustus created the office of Prefect of Egypt, mentioned by Xenophon (3.12). The latest possible date is the fifth or sixth century because Aristaenetus, who knows the novel of Xenophon, lived then. But I believe that we should date Xenophon closer to the earlier extreme than to the later.

With some confidence we can date Chariton to the early years of the second century A.D. and perhaps as early as A.D. 50.[4] Xenophon's novel resembles Chariton's in many ways, even verbally, and should therefore be placed next to his rather than next to the last novel, that of Longus. The probable *terminus post quem* is the reign of the great Roman emperor Trajan (A.D. 98–117), in which the office of Eirenarch (Chief Peace Officer) of Cilicia was apparently instituted.[5] Xenophon mentions the Eirenarch (2.13), when the travels of his characters take them to Cilicia.

The *terminus ante quem*, or latest probable date, is A.D. 263, when the temple of Artemis at Ephesus was destroyed by the Goths. Xenophon writes of the temple as though it still stood intact. There is a small chance, however, that, since Xenophon clearly intended to divorce his novel from most historical references, he merely disregarded the fact that the temple had been destroyed, and wrote about an earlier and happier time. I believe the temple was still unravaged when Xenophon wrote. Xenophon describes a Roman Empire at a time of peace and prosperity when young married couples take honeymoon voyages to Egypt (1.6ff.) and merchants like Psammis ply the Eastern trade routes, guarded by soldiers and police. Such episodes reflect a stable empire. All of this evidence is, of course, internal and to be used judiciously. In his novel Xenophon refers to three cities by their old names: Mazacum, which was renamed Caesarea under the emperor Tiberius, A.D. 14–37; Perinthus, renamed Heraclea in the third (?) century A.D.; and Byzantium, rechristened Constantinople in A.D. 330. In the case of Caesarea Xenophon might have altered the name consciously to give his work an antique flavor, but in other aspects his approach is so unaffected and unsophisticated that I believe that he uses unaltered historical information.

I feel that a date of A.D. 125–200 for Xenophon is as reasonable a date as I can give, based on what is known at the present time.[6]

III *Xenophon's Manuscript*

The chances of a Greek manuscript, written in the first or second century A.D. surviving to the present day, are slim, practically non-existent. Wars, fires, general decay, vandalism, worms, pious churchmen, all have taken their toll. Overly zealous Christians in the years following the collapse of an effective Roman political government were hesitant to preserve anything which did not speak to the "otherworldliness" necessary for all true Christians. Preservation of ancient manuscripts, much less their duplication, was a costly business. In the West, Latin was the language of business and the Church. From the time of the demise of effective government in the West in the middle of the fifth century A.D. to the first stirring of what is called the Renaissance, the knowledge of Greek and the importance of Greek played an ever decreasing role. Only in a few isolated places like Ravenna or in a few cities with close Byzantine ties was there any use for Greek. This lack of interest in Greek, general opposition of the Church to fiction or frivolous works, and the difficulties of copying, all worked against the survival of a manuscript like Xenophon's.[7] In the Byzantine empire Greek, of course, was *the* language, and it is from works like Photius' (ninth century) *Bibliotheca* that we learn even the small things we know about ancient Greek novels. Photius was the Christian patriarch of Byzantium but was very interested in pagan literature. Though he does not mention Xenophon, he cites other novelists and provides brief summaries of their novels. The *Suda*, which is dated with some justification also to this time (tenth century), speaks of Xenophon and his novel but in no way indicates that his work is obscure or unknown to most. It is clear from Photius and the *Suda* that the ancient Greek novels had some audience, at least in the East, up to and including the ninth and tenth centuries. But the Byzantine empire fell in 1453 to the Turks, and with it the importance of Greek and the Greek classics of the past, and a great curtain descended between the ancient Greek world and ours.

With all of these animate and inanimate forces against it, it is amazing that even *one* manuscript of Xenophon is extant today: the Codex Abbazia Fiorentina 2728, Conventi Soppressi 627, from the thirteenth century, now in the Laurentian Library in Florence. The paper bridge over which Xenophon's work traveled from him to us is incredibly thin and often obscure. In the early 1800s the Florentine monastery Badia Fiorentina gave this manuscript to the Laurentian Library. The Badia Fiorentina had received the manuscript as a gift in 1425 from Antonio Corbinelli. It appears that the manuscript was written near Melitene on the Syrian-Armenian border. Angelo Poliziano knew about this manuscript and quoted from it in his *Miscellanea* of 1489. In the eighteenth century a copy was made of the *editio princeps*, and this copy (Codex Add. 10378) is now in the British Museum. The next person to show interest in Xenophon and his manuscript is H. Stephanus who discusses it in the Prolegomena to his 1561 *Xenophontis Opera Omnia*. Then in 1700 Antonio Salvini transcribed a copy (Codex Riccardianus 1172.1) of the Xenophon text which Antonio Cocchi used to prepare the 1726 *editio princeps*.[8]

In Conventi Soppressi 627 we find the only complete Greek text of Chariton, another novelist, dating to the time just before Xenophon. While four papyrus fragments found in the Fayum in Egypt are witness to the fact that Chariton's fame reached Egypt and that at least someone was interested in making copies of his work, no such evidence has been uncovered for Xenophon. The Florence manuscript is our only source for Xenophon. I feel confident, though, that had more papyri survived, we should be in possession of a number of Xenophon sources. Unfortunately behind the Florence manuscript all is darkness. The reader interested in the detailed information about Xenophon's manuscript would do well to consult Ben Perry's *The Ancient Romances* and A. D. Papanikolaou's *Xenophontis Ephesii Ephesiacorum libri V*.

CHAPTER 2

Analysis of the Ephesian Novel of Habrocomes and Anthia

THOUGH there have been serious questions about the completeness of *The Ephesian Novel*, and many scholars are convinced that our extant version is an epitome, I find the evidence to be circumstantial and frequently weak, applied as it is to a work which was not very carefully constructed by an author who, like his audience, was primarily interested in tales and adventures designed to amaze, startle, cause wonder, and stir simple emotions. For our purposes I will consider the novel complete. The reader will notice very quickly that Xenophon treats some episodes more fully than others. All of this leaves the finished product very uneven. Suffice it to say that Xenophon writes at length about things he likes and cuts short those he does not.

I The Path to Bliss Is Strewn with Obstacles: Love and Marriage Do Not Lead to a Long Honeymoon (1.1–1.16)

(Book 1.1) Genealogy is the first thing on the author's mind as he begins his novel:

> There was in Ephesus a man of the highest rank named Lycomedes, who had married a local girl called Themisto. Habrocomes was the name of their son, the handsomest youth in the world.

These opening words give the impression that a simple folktale will follow: "Once upon a time there was a. . . ." Apuleius begins the tale of "Cupid and Psyche" (*Metamorphoses* 4.28) with the very same formula: "There were in a certain city a king and a queen," and then goes on to describe Psyche. The novel *Apollonius of Tyre* also uses this formula in its opening words: "In the city of Antioch there was a

21

certain king . . . who had a beautiful daughter. . . ." The expected simple folktale does not follow in any of these cases.

In a few introductory lines Xenophon acquaints us with one of the two main characters, the hero (as it were) Habrocomes, tells us who his parents are, fixes the dramatic location in Ephesus, and describes Habrocomes' beauty (with the identical expression used by Chariton for Callirhoe in the opening lines of his novel). While the beginning of Xenophon's novel is intended to resemble Chariton's novel, which had preceded it in this genre, and by so doing to make the reader aware that he will get something similar, the contrasts to Chariton's opening lines are marked. Chariton introduces himself first, speaks about his employment and employer, tells where it is he lives, and then informs the reader that the ensuing story is a love story. The first character to be introduced by Chariton is Hermocrates, an historical figure who helped the people of Syracuse destroy the Athenian invasion force of 413 B.C. Chariton's novel thus has a firm dramatic setting and definite time. The heroine in Chariton's novel is Hermocrates' daughter, and the hero, the son of another leader of Syracuse. Though he writes an imaginative novel, Chariton operates within an historical framework, and in so doing imitates an earlier romance, the fragmentary, anonymous *Ninus Romance*.[1]

Xenophon breaks with this tradition, cuts his story free from historical bonds, and describes a world which exists for the most part in his imagination only. The lineage of the hero and heroine is set out because it is the ancient method of identification: so and so, the son or daughter of so and so, of Ephesus. In a world which does not use family names, street addresses, social security numbers, or passport numbers, such is the practice. Unlike Chariton, he does not give his own name, position, or city. Xenophon divorces himself and his background from his novel, and then divorces his story from historical ties, allowing it to float freely through time and space. This latter act is, of course, no help to the student of the ancient novel. Though Xenophon does not seem to have posterity in mind when he writes, the majority of ancient Greek and Latin writers apparently write for the ages. Horace's (65–8 B.C.) *exegi monumentum aere perennius* ("I have built a monument more lasting than bronze") is the typical emotional response of the ancient writer to his work. Xenophon's action might indicate that he does not take the end product of his writing seriously.

Habrocomes ("one with luxurious hair") and Anthia (or Antheia, "the one in bloom") are the most beautiful people in Ephesus, Asia

Minor, and perhaps in the world. Hägg has examined the names given to characters by Xenophon and offers this generalization:

> For most of the unimportant characters, he seems to have chosen the names quite at random among those in use in daily life, utilizing them for individualization but not for characterization. . . . One may perhaps venture the suggestion, however, that the impression which Xenophon's personal names made upon a contemporary audience—and which we are unable to experience spontaneously—was an impression more of realism than of literary invention.[2]

He notes that there are "33 characters (23 men, 10 women) who are given individual names", and that eleven go unnamed.[3] This is a high proportion of named characters for any work:

> Most of the personal names in Xenophon are to be found earlier in Greek literature as the names of mythical, historical or fictional characters. Six of them occur already in Homer, six more are met with for the first time in Herodotus, and, to take a late example, no less than fourteen are mentioned in the mythological handbook . . . of Apollodorus.[4]

The admiration of the citizens of Ephesus for Habrocomes' beauty only reinforces his own already high opinion of himself (C450; F575.2).[5] The subsequent overweening pride (*hybris*, C770; see also Q330 and L400–99) of Habrocomes drives him to consider himself beautiful and then, unfortunately, to disconnect this beauty from any erotic consideration. Because Xenophon develops nothing special out of this situation by way of a graphic analogue with the Narcissus myth, we should be able to conclude that he had very little concern either for such learned references and allusions, or for universalizing his story through the use of myth.

(1.2) Habrocomes worships beauty, virgin beauty as abstracted in Artemis, protectress of virgins (i.e., wild things), but despises Eros (C53.2), who uses beauty to attract people to each other. Habrocomes revels in his narcissism, and so offends Eros, whom he terms "a nothing," that the deity is enraged (A189.4), and determines to reduce the youth (sixteen years old) to nothing but erotic desires. This scene may be modeled on the one which begins the novel of Chariton, or perhaps on the "original" Greek novel, the story of Panthea and Abradatas in Xenophon of Athens' *Cyropaedia*, Books 5–7 (dated to about 400 B.C.). In the *Cyropaedia* the Persian prince Cyrus puts his friend Araspas in charge of guarding the beautiful young Panthea, wife of Abradatas, recently captured by Cyrus, until such time as Cyrus can enjoy her. Araspas thinks of this assignment as a small task, since erotic attractions (the powers of Eros and Aphrodite) are insignificant and powerless. But shortly thereafter Araspas is delivered to Cyrus for trial because of his attempted rape of Panthea, and he admits to Cyrus that Eros is a deity of diabolical power with whom he must reckon.[6] The intervention of the gods in Xenophon of Ephesus, however, is more explicit. In Chariton the future lovers met in a religious procession to the temple of Aphrodite; Xenophon uses the same motif to bring his future lovers together, but the procession now is in honor of Artemis. The occasion is the regular spring festival called Artemisia (T381.1).

Habrocomes leads the procession of young men, and Anthia (fourteen years old) that of the young girls. Xenophon foreshadows what will follow after the procession when he states:[7]

It is a custom for young men to find wives here and young girls to select husbands.

In a society where meetings between the sexes before marriage are infrequent and irregular, and where marriages between young people are arranged by their families, such processions and religious events serve a vital purpose for youths ripe for marriage (T381.1).

Xenophon pauses just long enough in his rapid narrative leading to the union of Habrocomes and Anthia to provide some rare and specific information about religious ritual in regard to the deity Artemis. While we know a good deal about ancient Greek and Roman religion, we know all too little about ritual and the exact nature and purpose of objects used in ritual. The inclusion of the procession dresses up the story of the meeting of the two future lovers. The procession is part of a literary motif which holds that individuals should meet for the first time and then fall in love at religious occasions (N202.1; N711.4). We find this motif scattered through classical literature (Callimachus' *Aitia* 3, "Acontius and Cydippe" (K2371.3); Parthenius 9.1 and 32.2). The procession also shows the general public's reaction to Anthia who is taken for the incarnate Artemis, and Habrocomes for (implied) Eros (H41). In a study called "The Graphic Analogue from Myth in Greek Romance", Grundy Steiner observes that only once is Anthia compared to a goddess, and that is to Artemis (Chariton compares Callirhoe to Aphrodite [1.1; 1.14; 2.3]; Apuleius compares Charite to Venus).[8] Little use is made by Xenophon of myth to help him universalize his characters and stories. By comparison Xenophon's model, Chariton, uses graphic analogue from myth to compare Callirhoe to goddesses at least eight times. Graphic descriptions give the reader an excellent idea of Callirhoe's beauty. There are some in the crowd who wonder aloud and foreshadow the possibility of Anthia's and Habrocomes' marrying. As in Chariton's novel, so here, the assembled citizens of the city act like the chorus in an ancient Greek drama, that is, they give both the author's inner feelings about his presentation and the first inkling of future events.

(1.3) At the end of the procession Habrocomes and Anthia get the chance to see each other at close range, and it is a case of love at first sight, a motif (N202.1; N711.4; T15) which, already in antiquity, was hackneyed.[9] Eros has his revenge here for Habrocomes' earlier disparaging remarks about his lack of power and afflicts him with wild desires. After Habrocomes' and Anthia's brief encounter before the temple, each goes his lovesick way home to a kind of miserable existence—familiar to all sixteen-year-old lovers. The tragedy of their love affair is proportional to their age: they should grow out of it, and the tragedy will prove to be a melodrama. A similar affair between Romeo and Juliet, on the other hand, is adult in every sense and played at the highest stakes. Perry has suggested that the teenage romance of Habrocomes and Anthia was written for a teenage audience.[10]

(1.4) Habrocomes makes one final attempt to withstand the onslaught of Eros, but Eros punishes him by keeping the object of his love removed from him. Anthia suffers the same pains, but as the passive partner she can make no overt moves toward Habrocomes.

(1.5) The chapter opens with a summary of Habrocomes and Anthia's respective positions and pain, which had just been narrated. We then get very brief glimpses of the lives of the two lovers—lives which are deteriorating and health which is failing: all in all a rather sentimental picture of lovesickness (T24.1). After much speculation the parents of Habrocomes, Lycomedes and Themisto, and the parents of Anthia, Megamedes and Euippe, finally realize the seriousness of the situation, as their children approach death. Separately and without contact between themselves, each father decides to consult the oracle of Apollo at Colophon to learn the cause of the illness. Neither Habrocomes nor Anthia had mentioned to his father that the reason for the grave illness was Eros—and from the anger of Eros the frustration of an unconsummated love. Apparently Habrocomes and Anthia had at this point never spoken to each other or about each other to their parents; the parents do not seem to have known each other. They might have learned of the love affair from the rumors and talk of the people of Ephesus who, as I have said, function as the chorus did in Greek tragedy, transmitting general knowledge to the audience who otherwise might remain uninformed.[11]

The description of the illness of the young lovers remains external and physical, not psychological. We see the outward symptoms generally, while the mental anguish does not seem to concern Xenophon. Words and concrete actions matter a great deal; inner stresses, strains, cross-currents which give little or no outward visible signs, apparently are unimportant. Physical appearances, however, do denote character (physiognomics): Habrocomes and Anthia are beautiful and consequently good.[12]

In mythology, fathers, worried about their lovesick daughters, are accustomed to consult oracles. In the Acontius and Cydippe myth (Callimachus, *Aitia* 3, used by Xenophon at 1.2 for a different motif) Cydippe is taken ill each time she is to marry someone. Finally, her father consults the oracle at Delphi who advises him that she should marry Acontius, the only act which can rid her of the sickness. He obeys the oracle and Cydippe recovers. In the "Cupid and Psyche" episode of the *Metamorphoses* (4.28ff) Apuleius pictures Psyche as lovesick and a distraught father as driven to the oracular Apollo to seek help. Xenophon's use of the same motif links his story to mythology. It is possible that many ancient novels no longer extant had some sort of conventional dream scene or oracular pronouncement at the outset of the story which advised the leading characters to do this or that, and which became the prime-moving domino in the plot. Never one to let a chance for burlesque slip by, Petronius appears to parody this convention by beginning his novel with an oracle (*Satyricon, Frag.* 44 [Ernout]).[13]

(1.6) The oracle at Colophon[14] mysteriously combines the separate requests for information from the two fathers and renders a single prophecy (D1712) in nine lines of dactylic hexameter (thus marked for special note. It was customary for the interpreters of the priestess of Apollo to render her prophecies in dactylic hexameter):

> Why do you want to know the cause and final outcome of
>   the illness?
> One disease afflicts both youngsters, and one remedy will cure both.
> Before the suffering is over I predict terrible experiences for them.

Pirates will pursue and chase them over the sea;
And they will wear the chains put on them by seamen;
A grave will be a bridal chamber for both, and there will also be
terrible fire (M341.1.1).
Then later by the banks of the Nile you will deliver up
Rich gifts to holy Isis, the savior.
After all their suffering, both will enjoy a happier fate.

Part of the suspense that Xenophon wants to build is destroyed by the last line of the prophecy. Had Xenophon withheld the prophecy until later in the novel, he might have increased the suspense, leaving the matter in doubt right up to the end. But Xenophon prefers (or does he believe his readers prefer?) instant gratification. Suspense, apparently, is not seen as a desirable stimulus on the emotions, and the subtle force of foreshadowing is consequently here lost.

The scene in which we see panic-stricken parents, who have no recourse to modern medical diagnosis, send off a frantic message to the oracle and plead for help is a touching one. The picture of the helpless parents watching their children slowly die is most moving. It is too bad Xenophon did not do more with the scene. Serious development is missing, but once we realize that this is a regular procedure, we can conclude with some confidence that Xenophon (or his readers) becomes easily bored by a plot which does not move rapidly from scene to scene, from one amazing event to another.

The real value of the response of the oracle, I believe, is to provide the reader with an outline of the plot of the story (M352; M358.1; M369.2). The response provides an acceptable roadmap which Xenophon carefully follows:

Lines 1–2	Books 1.1–1.9
3–5	1.10–4.2
6	3.7–4.2
7–8	4.3–5.5
9	5.6–5.15

It seems certain from this that Xenophon had either some general scheme in mind from the very beginning or that the architectonic unity of the novel form is so stereotyped that the same outline is appropriate to almost every novel. While there are surely many differences among the various Greek and Roman novels, a general outline, like the one found in Xenophon, would yield most plots. (1.7) The fathers of the two young people puzzle over the oracle for only a short time before deciding to encourage their children to marry. Compared with other oracular responses, this one, though not totally comprehended, seems straightforward. The fathers unfortunately do not see the future clearly and determine to send their children on a sea journey, whether or not such a journey is acceptable to the children. They are bewildered and passive, and their children, in accepting without challenge the order to go to sea, are, if possible, even more passive.

The frequent alternating between the story of the hero and then the story of the heroine, one set of parents and then the other, now finds another set in the sorrow-joy alternation. Fear of the future is set aside, and the city (we are asked to believe that the whole city is concerned with the impending wedding—to a sentimentalist the whole world is sentimental) and its inhabitants prepare for the wedding.

(1.8) In view of the brief and sketchy treatment given most scenes and episodes, the marriage is described in great detail and spread over two chapters. Like the earlier scene in which Xenophon described the ritualistic procession to the temple of Artemis, here also he goes to some lengths to picture the religious rituals of the wedding.

The description of the wedding is as complete as Xenophon's brand of decency will allow, and in fact it is the scenery which is described rather than the participants:

The golden bed was covered by a purple spread, and the canopy over the bed was made of rich Babylonian material embroidered on one side with figures of Cupids and Aphrodite . . . and on the other with Ares. . . .

This is the only other graphic analogue from myth in Xenophon, and it is evocative. In mythology Aphrodite was married to the crippled Hephaestus and had an extramarital affair with Ares—only to be caught *in flagrante* by Hephaestus. Why put such a scene over the marriage bed of especially chaste lovers? Does Xenophon know what he is doing? do dirty scenes produce fertility? passion? or is a little humor intended?

Using markedly similar elements Chariton had earlier described such a wedding and Catullus (probably 84–54 B.C.) had done so at an even earlier date. All of these narratives are, in addition, examples of ecphrasis. Not only is the whole wedding ceremony a literary set-piece, a motif, even some of the particulars like the descriptions of the wedding bed and its covering are traditional.

(1.9) All the action of this chapter occurs in bed. Though eager for love the youngsters are technically inefficient (J1744), but with determination overcome their lack of skill. The passive nature of Habrocomes becomes very evident, when we learn that he is spurred into lovemaking only by Anthia's chiding:

> Do I really look beautiful to you? Even though you are more handsome than I am pretty, do I stir you? Come my shy and bashful young man, take me without any more delay. Do not waste any more time. Dry up my tears of love with your hair and try to appreciate my eagerness for you. Let us make love now.

This mild form of verbal aggressiveness on Anthia's part and Habrocomes' corresponding retreat foreshadow later character delineation. The scene reminds us immediately of Lycaenion's personal instruction in lovemaking for Daphnis, who lacked any technical skill in sexual congress, a deficiency which frustrated Chloe until the end of the book (Longus' *Daphnis and Chloe*, Book 3).

Anthia prods her shy lover and mildly rebukes him for wasting time, for whispering sweet nothings at a time when action is called for. In defense of Habrocomes, however, I should add that immediate action on his part is necessarily retarded because Anthia refuses to end her lecture long enough for him to make any erotic overture. If he is too slow, she is too loquacious. Had she continued one line more, I would hazard that she perhaps had talked too much. Xenophon allows his young lovers to describe their own mating practices and does not turn the scene into one of authorial description: lovemaking is not a spectator sport.

Though the chapter ends with the consummation of their marriage, the vocabulary employed is restrained, nontechnical, unbiological, and metonymous. Longus uses more graphic images in *Daphnis and Chloe* (Book 3); when Petronius (died A.D. 66) had an opportunity to describe a similar scene, he did so with brutality; the recently discovered Greek romance *Phoenicica* of Lollianus (second century A.D.) contains a scene of deflowering. Another fragmentary Greek novel, the so-called *Iolaos*, is also made up of explicit and graphic sexual descriptions.[15] The erotic is thus treated very differently within the genre of the ancient Greek novel. The Latin novels of Petronius and Apuleius are very special cases. Xenophon goes to great lengths to avoid a biological discussion of relationships; Lollianus and the author of the *Iolaos* appear to wallow in such discussions. During the first few centuries of the Christian era, the whole spectrum of sexual and erotic scenes is experimented with and tested in the novel.

(1.10) The young couple and their parents are caught up in the festivities of the wedding and of the establishment of the new household, and the young couple is about to live happily ever after, except that Xenophon cannot possibly end the story here. It would be far too short. Xenophon, like Chariton before him, is going to give us two stories: Story One: Boy meets girl; love at first sight; difficulties in arriving at the altar; marriage and happy life. Story Two: Because of divine interference and jealousy in Story One the young couple must go on a long voyage, be separated as they were before they married, be reunited after many difficulties, and then finally be allowed to reconsummate the marriage. Story Two is in an expanded doublet of Story One.

The parents finally remember the oracle and its dire warnings. The decision to send the young couple abroad on a sea journey is described as an attempt "to mitigate the predicted evils of the oracle." We cannot be sure how Xenophon wants us to view the interference of the gods in the affairs of men because the act of sending the couple out onto the sea to Egypt is in fact the signal that at this point the prophecy of the oracle is now activated—not by divine intervention, but by a conscious act of concerned parents. At the end of Chapter 10 Megamedes prays aloud and begs that the couple be spared the extremes of evil but admits that some troubles lie in store (N251.4):

We are sending you on a terrible journey, but it is an inevitable one.

This is a clear statement that the parents understand the oracle and the misfortunes that lie ahead. It must be a sea journey because pirates and shipwreck were specifically mentioned in the oracle. And the ship must be sent to Egypt because, if there is any hope for a return, salvation must be found along the river Nile.

Megamedes' statement that he would die if anything bad happens to the couple is, of course, anticipatory and prophetic. In Chariton's novel the parents are alive at the end to welcome their children home. Xenophon departs from his model and loses some of the symmetry available to the story by not having the parents there to greet their returning children, as they had said farewell at the start.

Very elaborate provisions are made for the sea voyage, including great quantities of supplies (these items are frequently repeated and become part of the travel motif): "All kinds of clothes, vast amounts of gold and silver and sundry items." These are the kinds of supplies that attract the attention of pirates. Only rich graves are robbed and rich ships plundered. By stocking the hold of the ship with gold and silver the parents of the young couple ensure that it will be seized.

A curious thing happens because of Xenophon's careful itemization of all of the people and things that go on board the ship bound for Egypt. The reader is, as it were, invited to go along on the journey, and is made to feel himself a part of the group of travelers. Excitement about traveling has always been infectious, and it was probably so in the ancient world. The opportunity for the ancient reader (who probably traveled very little and then close to home only) to go to far off places with exotic names is almost reason enough for him to continue to read the novel to the end.

(1.11) A scene shift finds the young couple huddling together on board ship, delighted to be together, but fearful that their happiness will not last. Of all the terrors which the oracle predicts that they would have to suffer, no mention is made of a separation. As they leave Ephesus for their first destination, the island of Samos, Anthia and Habrocomes enumerate, as it were, the facets of their sticky situation. Xenophon describes their feelings; he does not allow his actors to show them: "They feel sorry for their parents, already miss the city of Ephesus, live in dread of the fulfillment of the oracle, and are afraid of their voyage." But they are together. A day-night-day interval formula is used to continue the action and get the boat south of the island of Samos. The passage of time is marked by such formulae as "after having dined and when night came, they resumed their journey." As Hägg points out, Xenophon uses this formula to indicate the passage of time, but does it so very irregularly that we are unable to keep any accurate measure.[16] The control of time is not something that concerns Xenophon.

The subject of the first reported conversation of the young lovers on their honeymoon is their possible separation:

You are more precious to me than life. I pray that we will stay together forever. If the gods so ordain that we must be painfully separated, let us pledge to each other eternal chastity: you will never have another man, and I shall never take another woman. (M149)

Anthia picks up Habrocomes' remarks as a kind of challenge and responds by outpledging him:

Do you think that I would live long enough after being separated from you to marry someone else? Separation from you would mean immediate death. . . . If I am separated from you for even a short period, I will die. (M149.2)

Habrocomes increases the terms of his pledge and makes his vow equal to hers.

The apprehension over separation shown by the young couple serves two purposes, one of which is immediate. It shows the depth of affection of one lover for the other and gives some hint of a growing relationship. Without some such indication the reader could easily be left with the impression that their whole affair has no depth. The suddenness of their love affair and marriage leaves little time for growth and development. The second purpose for raising the possibility of separation is to foreshadow the event, to communicate the apprehension of the lovers, and to prompt the readers to expect a separation in the near future.[17]

(1.12) After the ship docks at Rhodes, Anthia and Habrocomes go ashore and walk through the city, attracting crowds wherever they go. The young couple is not average: their beauty reminds *all* the people on Rhodes of the beauty of the gods, a beauty which they have never seen except in their imaginations or in statuary (F575.1). It is thus possible for us to get an impression of what they look like: they look like familiar statues of Apollo or Artemis, i.e., perfect types of perfect bodies with no distinguishing marks except a kind of divine beauty. What of her eyes, nose, and mouth? is she tall, perhaps on the slender side? Does Habrocomes have wide shoulders, narrow hips, and powerful forearms?

One of the items which a reader of Xenophon will want to observe is the implicit comparison of people with statues. The graphic analogue of heroine to goddess is really heroine to statue. In those rare instances in which Xenophon apparently has some desire to be descriptive, he does a fairly thorough job. It seems that, for whatever reason, Xenophon is interested at least in geography. Whenever Anthia, Habrocomes, and Hippothous travel, Xenophon places them in a specific geographical setting. Xenophon has a fairly clear picture of a map in his mind, for he does not have the travelers double back on themselves (as Apuleius does in the *Metamorphoses*). As characters travel from one site to another, as Anthia and Habrocomes do in their abortive trip toward Egypt, Xenophon directs them on the shortest possible route, ticking off the islands visited by anyone going south from Ephesus. Word of the visit of two creatures as lovely as the gods stirs the interest of everyone on Rhodes, and they gather round to worship the beauty of the gods. The inhabitants desert work, children, shopping, and everyday chores to run after the latest rumor, as though some messiah had appeared on the scene. Anthia and Habrocomes, however, do not do anything, speak, act, or perform. They simply stand there while the *whole* city declares a holiday. This kind of sentimental exaggeration is not confined to works of fiction (Apuleius, *Metamorphoses* 4.33), for we can find similar examples of exaggeration in biographers like Cornelius Nepos (ca. 100–25 B.C.), who claims to be writing fact (*Atticus* 4: "The whole city of the Athenians escorted Atticus as he left town. . . ."").

Is Xenophon merely imitating Chariton, the beauty of whose characters attracted crowds, or is it simply Xenophon's method of emphasis through extreme exaggeration? Instead of describing the beauty itself of Anthia, for example, Xenophon describes other people's reactions to it. He appears to be more interested in the audience's reaction to the beauty of Anthia than in a delineation of it. It is, of course, very likely that a meaningful description of Anthia's beauty, i.e., those specific lines, features, colorings, and contours which in proper proportion make one woman beautiful and another less than pleasing, is beyond Xenophon's ability.

In the temple of Helius, the sun, the young couple set up a votive offering to Helius, the chief deity of the island of Rhodes. Though Habrocomes and Anthia have just arrived from Ephesus, whose state deity is Artemis, goddess of the moon (among other things), they dedicate a votive to the local state deity. It is good to point out with R. E. Witt and others that both Artemis and Helius are syncretized with Isis in the minds of many in the ancient world.

The votive offering set up in the temple of Helius will appear again at the end of the story, where we can expect to find a recognition scene. In Greek Middle Comedy, the New Comedy of Menander, and in the Latin plays of Plautus and Terence we frequently see mothers and fathers giving children objects of some kind, by which they will be identified as their own children in the last act of the play. While Xenophon will later employ the votive in a way that differs from the use of traditional recognition tokens, he will use this temple setting, common to both Anthia and Habrocomes and suggestive of happier times when they were together, as a prelude to the recognition scene. Anthia's return to the same temple and recognition of the same offering will alert the audience that the recognition scene is near.

All the people of Rhodes (again an exaggeration for emphasis) escort the young couple to their resupplied ships, and they head south toward Egypt on a direct route. This is, of course, the longest and most dangerous part of the journey, but as they knew from the oracle, a necessary journey to the river Nile and salvation at the hands of Isis. It is at this juncture that events must take a turn for the worse and the dire predictions of the oracle come true, or else the young couple will arrive in Egypt at the Nile to be rescued by Isis without undergoing any ordeals. A logical progression leads the young lovers into trouble: the wind dies; the ship sits idle; the crew becomes drunk; the pirates can strike a now defenseless ship. At the same time Habrocomes has a dream (D1812.3.3) in which a woman of goddesslike proportions appears to him; the ship is set afire and only he and Anthia are saved. The audience is now forewarned about future events.

Xenophon handles the dream scene very well; he has the dream forewarn Habrocomes of impending evils without telling the reader exactly what will happen next. Habrocomes' menacing nightmare can be explained as the working of his subconsciousness on the predictions of the oracle.

(1.13) The Phoenicians, as often in ancient literature, are type-cast into the role of pirates,[18] and the physical appearance of the pirate leader Corymbus is actually described: "young, stocky, mean, and his hair was long and uncombed." At this time an opinion about Ephesians is expressed by the pirates through Xenophon: "They were contemptuous of the Ephesians because they knew they would not fight back." If Xenophon is from Ephesus it is a strange thing for him as storyteller to say. If Corymbus had said it in direct discourse, one might conclude that it was merely his Phoenician opinion.

The ships full of drunk and lazy Ephesians fall quickly to the desperate Phoenicians, who lay waste the ships and kill all the passengers except for Anthia and Habrocomes and their personal slaves (R12.3). We are presented with the motif of the sole survivors, a motif which probably goes back to Odysseus' surviving a shipwreck and washing ashore in Book Six of the *Odyssey*. The reactions of Habrocomes and Anthia are noteworthy for their clear demonstration of that pair's unmitigated pusillanimity. No attempt is made to flee, to hide, or to defend themselves—or even to kill themselves. Habrocomes and Anthia are not mere passengers on the boat but are in a very real sense responsible for the craft and the welfare of its other passengers. It is reasonable to have expected that the main characters show some sense of responsibility; they do not. They appear to float free of any involvement or commitment to anything except themselves. It is difficult to grasp both the author's feeling toward such characters and the intent or effect he wishes to achieve by so describing them. What tone does Xenophon intend to present to his audience? It would be strange indeed if he intended to give the impression or impart the tone which he does.

The only request that the young lovers make of the pirates, who they seem to have suspected would seize their ship, is that they be sold to the same slaveowner and not be separated. We meet again that irrational fear of separation, at which the oracle did not even hint:

> Keep all our goods and make us slaves, o master.
> Do not kill us since we willingly submit to you.

After such a statement by the young lovers to the pirate leader, the reader is at least slightly amazed to learn in the next chapters that Anthia and Habrocomes are indignant when the pirates take them up on their pledge to "submit to you."

(1.14) The abject surrender of Anthia and Habrocomes does put a temporary stop to the slaughter of the Ephesians. Corymbus orders the halt, not out of compassion but because violence will ruin the treasure he hopes to take. Once the valuables have been transferred to his ship, he sets fire to all else, thus ridding himself of too many eye-witnesses and bulky, only semiprecious property.

The scene that follows could be made into a Hollywood epic of vast dimensions with small talents. Xenophon narrates the next episode with the intent to portray in graphic detail a scene which would remind the reader of a critical battle in epic or a moment of high drama in tragedy:

After Corymbus transfers Habrocomes and Anthia, several costly slaves and all the valuable cargo, and realizing that he can not safely take on board everything, he sets the ship afire (R244). The scene is terrible to behold with some Ephesians carried off by Corymbus and others awaiting certain death on board a burning ship. These latter people hold up their hands and cry out loud: "Master and mistress, where are they taking you? In what country, in what city will you live?" A couple shouted, "Those die lucky who die before being thrown into chains or before they become slaves." In all the confusion and terror the young lovers are taken away in a pirate ship while those on the Ephesian ship die in the flames. Habrocomes' old and respected tutor (curiously unnamed) leaps into the water and by swimming tries to catch up to the fleeing pirate ship. With tears running down his face, he shouts for Habrocomes: "I am an old man and your tutor. Will you leave me here? Where are you going? I would prefer that you yourself end my life and bury me here because I cannot live without you." Realizing that Habrocomes is lost to him forever, the tutor quietly slides under the waves (P361.1). Habrocomes tries to reach out to the old man and pleads with the pirates to return and pick up his tutor. His pleas are in vain, and three days later they arrive in the Phoenician city of Tyre.

As Gärtner has pointed out, Xenophon has an inordinate amount of difficulty with this episode.[19] Instead of a scene which elicits pity, the combination of events and speeches strikes the sensitive reader as grotesque. Individual units are emotional enough by themselves, but set out in a logical sequence they entice the reader to smile. As soon as the pirates attack, Anthia and Habrocomes forget about the duty owed to their comrades, servants, and noble station in life. In surrendering they grovel and plead for slavery, anything in exchange for their lives. Some of the servants jump into the water to avoid a burning ship, others are burned alive on board ship, but all are concerned only for the fate of their masters, who they hope will be killed quickly and never suffer the ignominy of slavery. None of the Ephesians, drowning in the sea or roasted on board ship, shows any concern for himself. While they pray for death for their masters instead of slavery, their masters plead for slavery—anything instead of death.

The appeal of Xenophon to his readers misfires; instead of stirring pity, he arouses only a feeling of aversion to the grotesque. Perhaps I am making too much of Anthia and Habrocomes' desertion of their servants in the face of menacing pirates. In addition I cannot explain the heroine and hero's desire for slavery over death, while their servants pray for their masters' death before slavery. Furthermore there is no reasonable explanation for Xenophon's treatment of Habrocomes' tutor, unless the reader can be persuaded to credit Xenophon with a fine sense of the grotesque.

As it turns out Corymbus does not dock the ship in Tyre itself, but a short distance away at pirate headquarters, where he turns over the booty to Apsyrtus, the chief pirate. It is then, just before the chapter ends, that we learn that, like many others, Corymbus has fallen in love with Habrocomes (T463).

(1.15) Corymbus did not tip his hand and show Habrocomes his true feelings while they were at sea because he feared immediate rejection so soon after the seizure of his boat. He observed Habrocomes' love for Anthia and probably suspected the suicidal condition of the young lover's mind. Once in the pirate camp and thus again in his own element, Corymbus feels that his chances to win Habrocomes have improved, and he begins his attack on Habrocomes gently. In his highly charged emotional state Corymbus quite naturally turns for help to a friend, in this case Euxinus. On learning of Corymbus' problems, Euxinus is extremely sympathetic because (as chance would have it) he has fallen in love with Anthia.

Xenophon then presents us with a double–Miles Standish motif: Euxinus persuades Corymbus to speak to Anthia about him, and Euxinus agrees to plead on behalf of Corymbus.

A fly—or rather a pair of flies—is about to drop into the ointment of these two pirates: Manto, Apsyrtus' daughter, falls in love with Habrocomes, and Moeris, Manto's husband, develops a powerful attraction for Anthia. A graphic diagram lays out the situation from Book 1.1 to Book 2.14:

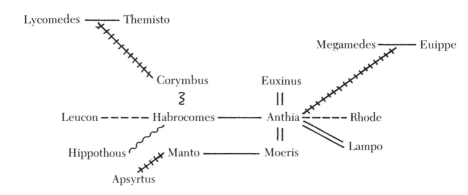

———— married

===== attempted heterosexual affair

∿∿∿ attempted homosexual affair

– – – servants

++++++ father, mother to son, daughter

Both Hägg and Gärtner point out that Xenophon likes things in pairs:
a pair of lovers each with a pair of parents; the pair of lovers have a pair
of servants; a pair of pirates fall in love with the hero-heroine pair;
then a married couple develop a strong attraction for our dramatic
protagonists; and before long we see that a pair of homosexuals have
tried to attach themselves to Habrocomes.[20]

As our hero or heroine confronts new admirers, each confronts new
trials; a newly proposed affair always has an attendant conflict or trial;
they come in pairs. With each trial for Anthia there is one for
Habrocomes, and a need for proving that the old love still exists. Pairs
of admirers bring pairs of trials, but all are resolved in oaths of
faithfulness and open expressions of love: one pair of circumstances
generates a corresponding pair of responses. In addition to protecting
themselves from other people and preserving themselves exclusively
for each other, the young lovers follow an almost Christian ideal of
guarding their *sophrosyne* (an abstraction for something like virtue).
In her illuminating study on the subject called *Sophrosyne: Self-
Knowledge and Self-Restraint in Greek Literature*, Helen North
offers detailed information about the history of the word (and con-
cepts behind the word) *sophrosyne* from the time when it meant an
all-encompassing value system to the Greek novel, when it means a
simple sexual purity:

If Greek literature after the close of the classical period yields no startling
development in the concept of sophrosyne, it nevertheless offers a wealth of
allusions in poetry, prose and inscriptions. . . . Sophrosyne is nearly always
interpreted as the control of appetite, usually erotic . . . (p. 243).
Sophrosyne is the primary virtue of women in Greek inscriptions, often the
only one mentioned, or the only moral virtue amid a list of physical qualities. . . . But sophrosyne is by no means limited to women. . . .
(p. 255) [21]

(1.16) Having developed the strategy of agreeing to speak in each
other's behalf to the young couple, Euxinus takes Habrocomes aside
and Corymbus speaks to Anthia. Euxinus adopts a very rational
approach to Habrocomes and outlines his options:

Fate has made you a slave, though once you were a free man. You are
understandably upset, but there is one man who is more than willing to help
you if only you will return his love. Corymbus is now your master. That is a
fact, and the proper view of reality should show you that only Corymbus can
help you regain your former wealth and status as a free man. He loves you and

asks only to be loved in return. The alternative to what could be a very amiable situation is not very pleasant. You find yourself in a strange country; you are the captive of a band of pirates. Your wife cannot possibly be of any good to you here, but your new master can.

Euxinus' speech is very convincing to someone not personally involved with Anthia. His is a rational approach, however, and can have little influence on a relationship which is in this case totally irrational. The attraction between Anthia and Habrocomes is anything but intellectual. An examination of his speech (above) also discloses internally contradictory statements. While Euxinus describes Corymbus as someone in love with Habrocomes and thus worthy of his love in return, he reminds Habrocomes that Corymbus is a pirate, someone who has killed before and will kill again. Rather than minimizing the violent and criminal side of Corymbus to Habrocomes, who is surely portrayed as soft, delicate, I might almost say effeminate, Euxinus threatens.

While Euxinus is pleading with Habrocomes, Corymbus is praising Euxinus to Anthia, telling her that Euxinus has only honorable intentions of marriage and no thoughts about an affair or forcing himself on her. He adds that Euxinus is her master.

The whole affair with Corymbus and Euxinus will soon prove superfluous to the main thread of the story because Apsyrtus, the chief pirate, takes the young lovers as his own share of the booty from the robbery. It is strangely similar to Agamemnon's seizure of Achilles' booty of a young woman in the *Iliad*. As is Xenophon's habit, he does not develop a stronger plot from such an episode. Earlier in the story Xenophon had the opportunity to make use of the angry-deity motif as the efficient motif of the novel, but dropped it after a few pages. In the *Iliad* Agamemnon's seizure of Achilles' young woman causes the anger of Achilles, which then becomes the efficient motif of that work. What Homer could do, Xenophon cannot.

Book 1 ends on a very unstable note.

II   *Separation, New Affairs (2.1–2.5)*

(Book 2.1) Anthia and Habrocomes seem to have special freedom to move about the pirate camp, and, after meeting with the amorous but restrained (perhaps too restrained for ancient pirates) pirates, they return to their private (!) quarters. As soon as they enter their room they bemoan their fate and cry out for their parents. Considering the ages of the lovers, we are not surprised at the total surrender to emotions. Habrocomes is able finally to control himself and is the first to speak:

Now that we are in the hands of brutal pirates and a long way from home, what outrages lie in store for us? The prophecy of the oracle is coming true. Eros is taking his revenge on me for belittling his power and has caused Corymbus to love me and Euxinus you. Our good looks are our problem. Have I remained chaste up to this day only to satisfy the lust of an amorous pirate? What kind of life is it to be the concubine, to give up my status as a man, and to lose Anthia? I swear by that chastity that I have preserved until now that I will remain so and that I will kill myself before Corymbus can take me. (T210)

Death is, of course, the perfect haven from all such attacks, and Habrocomes chooses the passive way out of his troubles (R169.16). He can be faithful in death and never have to face temptation. He concludes his speech in a shower of tears, and Anthia speaks. She does not complement Habrocomes' speech but rather delivers her own, as though he were not there and she had not heard his words. The pattern of alternating instead of complementing/adding/filling-in/contrasting/comparing obtains throughout the novel. Xenophon appears to be more comfortable with holding now one thread, now another, and even a third. He refuses to weave an integrated fabric for us:

Our marriage vows will soon be tested, and soon we will know the meaning of slavery. Some stranger is trying to convince me that he is a better lover than Habrocomes. May the gods keep me from loving life so much that I give in to him. Let us renew our pact, Habrocomes. Let us die and live with each other in the next life.[22]

This is one of the many references to their marriage vows: death before unfaithfulness (M149.2). Habrocomes, fearing separation from Anthia and rape from Corymbus, vows to kill himself; Anthia, fearing slavery and rape, pledges to end it all in suicide. The idea that there is only one wife for one husband, and faithfulness and chastity to one spouse, whether alive or dead, appears early in Greek literature. I need but mention Penelope, the long-suffering wife of Odysseus (who did not always share his wife's values). But the model on which Xenophon bases his heroine, who is prepared to die rather than be unfaithful, is probably Panthea in Xenophon of Athens' *Cyropaedia*, who did in fact commit suicide.[23] Anthia and Habrocomes frequently threaten suicide, but neither one carries out the threat. In Chariton's novel there are similar promises of suicide which likewise never occur. Chariton's heroine Callirhoe, when confronted by the necessity to marry a second man (her first husband, Chaereas, is still alive), does not honor her vows of faithfulness because she discovers she is pregnant. She is the only heroine in the Greek novels who is even technically unfaithful.

(2.2) As it turns out, the next surprise awaits not our young hero and heroine, but rather their pirate lovers. Like Agamemnon in the *Iliad*, Apsyrtus chooses the best part of the booty for himself. On a visit to the pirate camp from Tyre Apsyrtus immediately sees the real value of Anthia and Habrocomes, and demands them for himself. Corymbus and Euxinus are understandably outraged, but it is clear that they have no intentions of contesting the decision with their pirate chief. Apsyrtus is an anomaly in this novel because he is the only young (relatively) man who has Anthia in close proximity and does not fall in love with her. He sees only piles of gold and silver when he looks at her, and in this respect is a realistically delineated character.

In addition to Anthia and Habrocomes, Rhode and Leucon, the two personal servants of the protagonists, are also taken by Apsyrtus for his personal booty. To Xenophon's mind a pair of lovers requires a pair of servants. Xenophon will need them briefly twice more for his devices, and he must therefore include them in the story each time a move is made. It seems that these are the kinds of details an epitomizer would drop, since the presence of servants at all times could be assumed.

(2.3) Xenophon conveniently removes Apsyrtus, who would be an obstacle in the next episode, from the scene in Tyre and sends him inland into Syria on business. Other ancient novelists (e.g., Petronius and Apuleius) move their characters into required positions by sending them on business trips. The practice is common also in contemporary novels. Even though he is a pirate who has desperate killers, plunderers, and generally immoral thieves working for him, Apsyrtus holds to a surprising array of middle-class tenets of morality. It is interesting to note that pirates like Corymbus and Euxinus are ruthless murderers who at sea destroy people and things without remorse. But as soon as they return to camp (a symbol of civilization? does the sea represent a wilderness on which men are free of the constraints of civilization, their society, and their particular morality?

and the pirate camp symbolize order, restraint, and a place where normal rules of conduct obtain?), they do not force themselves upon the helpless Anthia and Habrocomes.[24]

With Apsyrtus away on business, his daughter Manto, a lovely young woman (but not as lovely as Anthia) with strong sexual desires, develops a powerful attraction (N202.1) for the godlike Habrocomes, whom her father had brought into the house:

Manto's cravings for Habrocomes are uncontrollable. Since she knows he has a wife and harbors no illusions about competing with her, and because she can talk to no one without her father discovering her plans, she becomes exceedingly depressed. In fact, her desire becomes even hotter.

We see here shades of Potiphar's wife and Phaedra (see also Apuleius, *Metamorphoses* 10.2ff). It is the first convention in the Potiphar's Wife motif (K2111). Manto's fear of her father presages the outcome of this episode. Since I contend that Xenophon writes for a fairly unsophisticated audience, the use of this uncommon literary motif must be explained. As an educated man, Xenophon probably had read about Potiphar's wife and Phaedra and incorporated the motif here. It is not necessary that the audience appreciate the use of this specific motif, but simply appreciate the story. The use of the motif in the story allows for an interesting—might I say marvelous?—twist to the story, the literary history of which the reader need not know in order to enjoy.

The unstable triangle created by Manto's desire to have Habrocomes finds no stable resolution in Manto's proposed plan. She approaches Rhode and asks her to intercede on her behalf with Habrocomes. Rhode has no options open to herself, since she is now a slave two times over, and Manto reminds her of that situation. Manto, of course, could have forced Habrocomes' compliance, but Xenophon rarely explores the power or options available to master over subjects. In Chariton's novel Dionysius uses a servant woman, Plangon, to convince Callirhoe that she ought to marry him, and later the king uses Artaxates for the same purpose. Such use of servants as go-betweens was very popular already in New Comedy.

With promises of good things if she helps and threats of dire consequences if she fails to help, Rhode seeks the advice of her sexual partner and fellow servant, Leucon (as in Chariton, Xenophon's go-between servants come in pairs):

We are ruined, since Manto, our new master's daughter, has developed this strong passion for Habrocomes, and plans to take our old master from us. She threatens to harm us if she does not get Habrocomes. We have a real dilemma: we are courting terrible danger if we refuse to cooperate with a barbarian woman; even if we wanted to, it would be impossible to convince Habrocomes to leave Anthia.

It is important to note that Rhode and Leucon, two servants who Xenophon clearly indicates have their own erotic concerns, appreciate the problems inherent in having two sets (three, counting Manto) of masters. The novel's protagonists do not seem to be as aware of their servants' problems, as the servants are of theirs. A glance at relationships between masters and slaves in New Comedy shows that there also the slaves are better equipped for dealing with life's problems than are the masters (J1111.6; J1114; P361). For her part, Rhode is concerned not to arouse either the anger or the jealousy of a "barbarian woman." There is something wild, unpredictable, and irrational about "barbarians" as compared to people from Ephesus, i.e., Greeks. Xenophon continues a kind of bigotry toward non-Greeks, which Chariton also espoused.

(2.4) Habrocomes meanwhile is concerned with nothing except thoughts of Anthia. Our hero is described as a kind of lost pilgrim, drowning in self-pity, when Leucon arrives and addresses Habrocomes and Anthia:

Friends, we have a new problem which defies solution. O Habrocomes, one of our masters, Manto, the daughter of Apsyrtus, has conceived a deep passion for you, and you know that it is a fearful prospect even to think of rejecting a barbarian woman in heat. You can do as you please, but please do not sit there motionless and thoughtless and leave us to the tender mercy of pirates. Think about all your responsibilities.

Habrocomes' reply is given in anger, evades the point of Leucon's address, and misses the burning issue confronting them all:

You traitor! You are worse than these barbarians. How could you even mention Manto's name in Anthia's presence. I am a slave now also, but gentlemen do not discuss the subject of a lady in public. Manto can torture me because she has power over my slave's body, but she cannot make me mistreat Anthia.

Anthia speaks last; she is concerned only for Habrocomes:

I love you, Habrocomes, and am confident that you love me. But I plead with
you not to make yourself the object of a barbarian woman's rage. Give in to
her desire for your body. I will leave and kill myself. Just kiss me before you
bury me, and promise to remember me.

I have paraphrased all three brief speeches, each of which illustrates
so well the character of the speaker. Leucon is aggressive for a slave,
plainspoken, and accustomed to face issues; Leucon addresses Habrocomes as simply one of the slaves of a new master. The slave comes
off very much the superior (J1114). It is difficult all through this novel
to find out what is masterly about Master Habrocomes. (If I may be
permitted a brief digression and a reference to P. G. Wodehouse, I
would like to observe that in many of the comedies of Wodehouse the
bumbling hero, Bertie Wooster, is saved by the quick thinking of his
servant Jeeves.)
(2.5) The heat of passion is so great in Manto that she can no longer sit
back and wait for an answer from Rhode. She writes Habrocomes a
letter, the second of a *pair* of attempts to win him over (T338):

TO HABROCOMES: FROM YOUR SERVANT
I love you and can no longer restrain myself. You will surely find this action
unbecoming a young girl, but I beg you not to reject my offer which is as good
for you as it is for me. If you agree, I will convince my father, and we can
dispose of your wife. You will not regret it. If you reject me, I will inflict such
punishments as you cannot imagine, on you and on your comrades who
support you.

References to barbarian anger are probably justified, if the above is
the nature of barbarian love letters.[25] Perhaps I am being unfair and
too harsh. These could easily be the first blunderings of malice in
loveland. When she writes her letter to Habrocomes, we see the
second convention in the Potiphar's Wife motif (K2111).

Habrocomes receives Manto's letter, stores it, and replies that no
torture could make him her lover. The only thing that bothers him is
the implied threat to get at him through violence to Anthia. The rage
of a heathen which we are led to anticipate, because of all Xenophon
has said about it and her, now comes to the forefront, when Habrocomes writes back to Manto rejecting any and all offers. In her rage
Manto thrashes about, not knowing immediately where or how to
avenge her pride. "It is the psychological portrayal of the irresolute
heroine so notably painted in Euripides' *Medea* and in Seneca's
drama, and so frequently imitated in the Greek romances."[26]

The motif employed here is that of the scorned woman, who, not having received any love, accuses the man of rape. When Apsyrtus returns from business in Syria, Manto tears her hair and robes, and charges Habrocomes with assault. She incenses her father by claiming that Habrocomes misused the kindnesses that Apsyrtus had shown him. She leaves off her tirade against Habrocomes by saying that, if Apsyrtus does not mind if slaves use her, she will kill herself (K2050). The young girl's threats seem to know no bounds. The threats of this scorned woman are similar to those of Euripides' Medea, the book of Genesis' Potiphar's wife, and Stheneboia. This is the third convention of the motif (K2111).

III *A Father's Pride Crushed (2.6–2.12)*

(2.6) Some few pages ago Apsyrtus had exerted his authority to wrench Habrocomes out of the clutches of Corymbus and to save his lovely body for a future slave market. His anger is now so great that all of that passes out of his mind, and revenge fills it. He has an added concern: on his business trip to Syria he found and brought back for Manto a husband, named Moeris. Should Apsyrtus fail to make a large show of punishing Habrocomes, Moeris might easily feel that he was getting damaged merchandise not worth a lot. After having cursed Habrocomes for assaulting his master's daughter (a slave's attacking a free woman was considered in the ancient world a serious and capital crime), Apsyrtus adds that he will get no pleasure from it, and furthermore he will be made an example to all other slaves (correction officials have been wrong about the rehabilitation of criminals since the ancient world).

Though Xenophon apparently likes to run through most scenes quickly, he relishes for some time a description of the torture (R51.3) of Habrocomes: his clothes are stripped off and hot branding irons are applied; whips are used; his skin is ripped in such a way that it will leave scars; he is bleeding badly when they hit him with chains and burn flesh here and there; other nameless tortures are used. When Anthia begs Apsyrtus to stop, he reminds her that what Habrocomes did, was also done to her. I suppose he expects her to thank him for teaching Habrocomes a lesson. This scene is similar to the movie about the Old South in which the sheriff whips the young black man for his alleged flirtation with a white woman, and tells the black man's wife, who is watching, that this will make him a better husband.

(2.7) Habrocomes regains consciousness in a dark cell and observes his bloody limbs in chains. Since Anthia is not there, he fears the worst and, had numerous guards not stood in the way, would have killed himself. This prison scene is set in stark contrast to the happenings above ground, the week-long festival of the marriage of Manto and Moeris. Apsyrtus' violent retaliation against Habrocomes is the fourth convention in the motif (K2111), and we now simply wait for the fifth.

Anthia is not immobilized by events as much as her husband, and assumes an aggressive role by bribing and otherwise persuading guards to let her see Habrocomes. Since Moeris is taking Manto back to Syria to live, Apsyrtus sends along rich presents of silver, gold, and clothes (the traditional triad of supplies in ancient Greek novels; the clothes are usually Babylonian fabric—see 1.8 and the wedding bed, and also similar scenes in Chariton), but, more importantly for our story, to Manto he gives Anthia, Rhode, and Leucon (Q437; R61). Anthia gets one more opportunity to steal into the cell and see Habrocomes. It is the last time they see each other until the last reel of the movie:

I am going to Syria as a present to Manto, and you will stay here and die miserably in this prison, with no one to care for your body. Whether I live or die, I promise to remain faithful to you.

Anthia has changed her original contract (1.11), in which she promised not to live a single day if separated from Habrocomes. The realities of dying now confront her, and she does not like what she sees—nor does Xenophon, who cannot end his novel here.

This chapter (2.7) marks a major seam in the story, because after this Xenophon must report a narrative made up of two separate threads: first he traces the thread of Anthia's adventures and travel, and when he brings that to a place where he can tie some kind of temporary knot, he goes back and picks of the thread of Habrocomes' travel. But as Bryan Reardon has so perceptively pointed out recently:

. . . love and travel: the point of having a love theme at all is surely that it should be permitted to develop in some way. And it cannot very well if the couple are separated by hundreds of miles . . . all it does is vegetate.[27]

(2.8) Finding himself alone, separated from Anthia for the first time, Habrocomes cries out for his father and mother, and wonders at the terrible situation in which he exists. It is interesting that Xenophon has him call out for his parents and not for Anthia. My own reading of this passage offers the reminder that Habrocomes is only sixteen years old, away from home for the first time, has had his first severe physical testing (torture), and now wishes he were home, where everything was good.

In a state of fatigue Habrocomes falls asleep and dreams (D1812.3.3):

His father, dressed all in black, roams over the land and sea, and, finding him in prison, frees him. He sees himself then metamorphosed into the shape of a stallion, traversing land after land in pursuit of a mare. As he comes upon the mare he changes back into his previous shape. After the dream he rises from the ground and feels better for the experience.

Even had he remembered the oracle which predicted he would in the beginning suffer gravely, he could take no comfort from it in regard to his separation from Anthia. A dream is significant in classical literature because, like oracles, dreams come true; and both oracles and dreams are frequently misunderstood (Heliodorus 1.18–31). In the first part of the dream in which he sees his father, dressed in black, wandering in search of him and finally finding and rescuing him from prison, we probably are given a foreshadowing of the death of Habrocomes' father. Habrocomes is rescued numerous times but never by his father, and this part of the dream must remain dark to us. His transformation into a stallion who chases and catches a mare is an obvious foreshadowing of the time when he will have Anthia back. The only surprising thing about this metaphor is its explicit sexual nature, something to which Xenophon does not often resort.

(2.9) With Habrocomes in prison, Anthia is taken as a slave to Syria by Manto and Moeris. Manto acts quickly now to get revenge, and, since she suspected Rhode all along of having aided Anthia, she sells Rhode and Leucon as slaves to foreign slavetraders (Q437; R61).

For Anthia Manto conjures up an exquisite form of revenge. She calls one of her husband's farmhands, a smelly goatherd, and orders him to take Anthia for his wife (L113.1.0.1). This episode is analogous to the motif in which a parent marries off a haughty daughter to a poor man as a form of punishment (H465; Q499.7). We see this in Euripides' *Electra*, Herodotus (1.107), and *Thousand and One Nights* (Ali Nour); in Apuleius' *Metamorphoses* (4.31) Venus, outraged that humans think Psyche more beautiful than she (Eros in Xenophon 1.2), orders her son, Cupid, to make Psyche fall in love with the basest of men.[28] If Anthia offers any resistance, the goatherd is to rape her. Manto has done her worst to Habrocomes and now is working on Anthia. By force she is taken to the goatherd's hut, and quickly learns what Manto has devised for her. At this point in the story an amazing thing happens. Anthia drops to her knees, pleads with the goatherd to honor her chaste state, explains who she is and how she came here. He is persuaded by her and does not even touch her (T350)! If this were a contemporary novel, we would now begin to be amazed by a scene of explicit sex. Xenophon causes the same kind of amazement in the reader by doing the opposite of what we had here expected. Had Xenophon allowed me to watch the goatherd agonize over his decision, I could applaud more easily his reactions to her pleas. Instead of a conflict of interests among emotional people, a passive acceptance of a situation by two creatures more like dolls than living and breathing people, is offered us.

Anthia will repeat, with interesting variations, this performance of preserving her chastity. There is a strikingly similar theme in Euripides' play *Electra*, and a century or two after Xenophon we see this motif appearing again in the influential Latin novel *Apollonius of Tyre*.

(2.10) As chance would have it, Apsyrtus is cleaning out Habrocomes' old room and comes across Manto's letter to Habrocomes, the contents of which convince him that the youth is innocent. This is the fifth convention in the Potiphar's Wife motif, the discovery that the woman (wife or daughter) in the case is guilty (K2111). It is a nice touch on the part of Xenophon to have Apsyrtus find the letter and by his own actions recognize what his daughter did and by his own volition free the injured Habrocomes. The scene, however, makes me wonder about the intelligence of our hero, who had the evidence to refute Manto all along but did not make use of it. For her part, Manto made no effort to retrieve it.

Apsyrtus makes Habrocomes a free man, promises to find him a suitable wife now that Anthia is gone, and places him over the management of his estate, like Joseph in Egypt. This action is the last convention from the Potiphar's Wife motif (K2111).

Xenophon then brings the readers up to date about the affairs of Rhode and Leucon, telling us that they were sold (Q437; R61) to a kindly old man in Xanthus in Lycia (an area in southern Turkey, north and east and very close to the island of Rhodes, where the novel will end). Already at this point in the novel Xenophon has Rhode and Leucon in position to help reunite the lovers.

(2.11) Retribution for her evil deeds is swift in coming to Manto, not divine retribution like the kind that real heroes suffer, but good old human lust. While making the rounds of his property near Antioch, Moeris also visits the goatherd-husband of Anthia and falls in love with her. After some time emotions get the best of Moeris and he bribes the goatherd to deliver Anthia up to him. The goatherd is now neatly caught in the middle between Manto and Moeris. He chooses to side with the female of the species, the more deadly, and reports to Manto what Moeris is planning. The use of servants as intermediaries between lovers, or between people who hope to persuade someone to be a lover, here records its third occurrence. Pledging even worse terrors for Anthia, Manto awaits the next time Moeris goes off on out-of-town business (as Apsyrtus did) and strikes at Anthia. The previous occasion on which Manto resorted to questionable acts occurred likewise at a time when male authority figures (Apsyrtus-father and Moeris-husband) were absent.

Manto orders the goatherd to take Anthia out into the forest and kill her. As the goatherd is about to stab her, Anthia asks only that, since Habrocomes is already dead, he bury her in the usual ritual fashion, insuring her a happy afterlife with Habrocomes. Xenophon stops the action at this point to develop a personality around the goatherd, who reasons with himself about his position. If he does not kill Anthia, Manto will kill him. But he admits to fearing the gods, and furthermore he cannot bring himself to end the life of such beauty. The gods must be honored and beauty preserved (N857).

As the goatherd sells (Q437; R61) Anthia to Cilician traders, she calls down the blessings of her patron deity Artemis on him. The Cilician traders add her to their other merchandise on board ship and set sail. But the boat breaks up in a storm, and the shipwrecked merchants and Anthia are captured/rescued (R111.8) by the outlaw Hippothous.

(2.12) Xenophon very cleverly brings Habrocomes back into the story by having Manto write her father a letter, stating that she had sold Anthia as a slave because of continued treachery. The contents of the letter are made known to Habrocomes by Apsyrtus because (I am guessing here) he still wishes to redress wrongs done by his family. Habrocomes, with at least some hope of finding Anthia alive, deserts Apsyrtus' household to search for her (H1385.3). Had Manto admitted the truth to her father, that she had ordered Anthia killed, Habrocomes might never have initiated his search. The truth comes to Habrocomes via Manto's lie. Poetic justice rules Xenophon's world thus: Lampo lies to Manto but protects Anthia; Manto, believing the lie to be truth and confident (because of hybris) that she is cleverer than anyone else, twists the lie and unwittingly reports the truth; the lie of the noble goatherd yields truth, while the lie of the evil woman ruins only the liar. This is the best example of irony in Xenophon.

IV   Enter the Rogue, Hippothous (2.13–2.14)

(2.13) The scene now shifts again and we find Hippothous and his band about to hang Anthia and throw javelins at her as a human sacrifice (S260.1.3; S263) to Ares, god of war and destruction, and god of these men. Evidence for human sacrifice as a regular practice is rare in the Greek and Roman world, and its appearance in ancient prose fiction is probably intended more to amaze than to inform (Heliodorus 1.31; 10.7; Achilles Tatius 3.12–15; Lucian, *The Ass* 24). The instance of human sacrifice in Achilles Tatius is graphic, to the point of being nauseating, and creates an atmosphere of the marvelous, the erotic, and the violent. Narrative of Anthia's sacrifice is so condensed that the reader has no chance to become fearful for her life, to hold his breath as the first javelin is thrown and then to feel relief when it misses the mark. Nor does Xenophon leave Anthia hanging about and switch the narrative back to Habrocomes, an artistic procedure intended to cause anxiety in the reader. In the novel of Achilles Tatius, Cleitophon the narrator tells about the capture of Leucippe (3.12) as a virgin sacrifice; he then switches the narrative to relate his own doings before returning to the actual sacrifice (3.15). Though Achilles Tatius and Cleitophon know (it is a narrative of past events) that Leucippe was not actually sacrificed, Cleitophon goes on to describe a sacrifice which, he tells the reader, was a sacrifice of Leucippe. Cleitophon tells this episode from the limited point of view he had when he saw the sacrifice, not from the point of view of the narrator who knew the outcome.[29] By manipulating the point of view at this juncture, Achilles Tatius makes of Cleitophon an unreliable narrator, but one capable of keeping the reader in the dark and creating a surprise ending. Xenophon's narrative is not so sophisticated.

The *deus ex machina* who rescues (R111.1.2; R116) Anthia from all this is Perilaus, chief law-enforcement agent for Cilicia. As is Xenophon's wont, he has the rescuer arrive just in the nick of time and rescue Anthia from her previous rescuer (R111.8). This is a scheme which modern movie makers use with such expertise and anticipated regularity. Perilaus kills most of Hippothous' band

and captures a few, but Hippothous alone escapes. Lone survivors and lone escapees from danger are frequent in classical literature (Z356). This *deus ex machina* for Anthia turns out to be her next ardent admirer.

By the time Perilaus reaches his home in Tarsus in Cilicia, he is completely devoted to Anthia. We learn quickly that Perilaus is unmarried, with no children, rich, and powerful. Matched off against a poor, defenseless, ill-equipped child, Perilaus wins a promise of marriage from Anthia. Her early refusals are followed by compliance, when she begins to fear that he might turn violent. For a young girl who had just a short time earlier pledged eternal faithfulness and suffering even unto death rather than to betray Habrocomes, she gives in very easily. She does, however, obtain a thirty-day delay in the marriage through some unnamed excuse (K536.1; T151.2; T315.1). The pretext is probably some religious taboo in which Perilaus believes. I offer this explanation because a little later in the novel she uses that mode, and we know that the episodes built around Anthia and her admirers repeat themselves.

(2.14) With Anthia waiting out the thirty days until her marriage, Habrocomes pushes his horse on into Cilicia in search of her: this is a fairly representative example of the way Xenophon switches from one narrative thread (Anthia's) to another (Habrocomes'). He gives a kind of summary statement as he leaves one of the two strains, and then follows with an introductory comment on the other. One way to view Xenophon's method, a mode which deemphasizes the switching, is to see the progress of the story (from 2.8 on) as a kind of race, in which Habrocomes is trying to catch up to Anthia. Wherever she was last, he is now; when she leaves a place, he arrives.[30]

Immediately upon his arrival in Cilicia, Habrocomes, like some kind of homing pigeon, heads straight toward the camp of Hippothous. Near the camp Hippothous meets him, and the two ride their horses down the same road:

"I can see," said Hippothous, "that, though you are young, you are already a man. Your appearance tells me that you have been wandering for some time and that you have been sorely mistreated. Let us ride out of Cilicia and go up to Cappadocia and Pontus. I hear that the people there are happier."

Though the last information about Anthia pointed to Cilicia, Habrocomes now simply gives up the search for his lost wife and follows Hippothous. Guided by the vague hope that he might somehow

mysteriously bump into Anthia in the no-man's-land to the north, he
adopts an apparently irrational search pattern. I say apparently irrational because he might have accompanied Hippothous for other
reasons. His present actions, if explained as a search for Anthia, are
irrational, or, at best, unintelligible. But he does not seem irrational,
and his actions are otherwise straightforward and direct. Since
Xenophon's novel is a fairly short work, it is dangerous to interpret
cloudy events from the clearer items; but if it is the only evidence the
reader has, he uses it. We will learn shortly that Hippothous is
homosexual (in fact bisexual), and a man of fine sensitivities. I would
like to suggest that when Hippothous (the older man) meets Habrocomes (a youth) on the road in Cilicia, they strike up a very natural
homosexual relationship, temporary in nature, and aberrant from
Habrocomes' natural instincts, but not from Hippothous', as the story
will illustrate. Habrocomes is under unusual stress at this time and
has in fact given up hope of finding Anthia. His former confidence is
gone and replaced by nothing. As George Devereux has pointed out,
a Greek young man goes through a stage where he is the *erōmenos*
(loved one) of an older man, but that this "was viewed by the Greeks
as a stage in the child's development toward masculinity." [31] Further, I would like to suggest that Xenophon makes little of this
encounter because he supposes that every reader will understand
what is happening.

V   *Death, Birth, Marriage, Death:*
Not the Usual Rites of Passage (3.1–3.12)

(3.1) As Hippothous and Habrocomes make their way from Cilicia
north toward Mazacum in Cappadocia, Hippothous begins to formu-
late a plan to rebuild his robber band and to plunder the countryside.
He knows the territory, the language, and gets on well with many
people. [32] After resting for some time from the long trip, drinking and
eating some good food, Hippothous drops the tough exterior of a
brigand and begins to cry. Questions directed at him by his new
friend elicit this reply: "It is a long story. I really should call it a
tragedy." Hippothous' choice of words is very telling: story (*diēgēma-
ta* in Greek) means a narration in full but also means the kind of story
that we might designate as fiction. By his description of Hippothous
as a dangerous villain and then by changing him into a sobbing lover,
Xenophon is giving us every indication that behind the tears of
Hippothous there is a good story. His word tragedy (*tragōidia* in

Greek; cf. Apuleius, *Metamorphoses* 10.2) is the technical word for a production of a tragedy that appears on stage. Tragedy here is not used in our modern popular idiom to mean an accident, or some terrible event. Xenophon through Hippothous means to tell us that the story which follows can be properly presented only if done on a stage. Chariton (1.4; 4.4; 6.3) refers to a part of his novel as a drama fit for the stage. Tragedy and drama in the ancient world imply the use of graphic images, tense scenes, emotional stress, and plots which are mythical, stranger than truth. Hippothous puts Habrocomes on notice that he is about to hear a story closer to fiction than to everyday reality.

(3.2) For the first time in this novel the main thread of the plot is dropped; the action that was begun with the first words of the story is set aside. We are presented here with an interpolated tale, a story within a story. What we will learn from Hippothous' narration is a bit about his background and an explanation of how he became a robber. The story he is about to tell us is important because it offers a change of pace, a relief from the long, drawn-out problems of Anthia and Habrocomes, and is part of a literary convention among ancient novelists (e.g., Petronius and Apuleius).

Hippothous tells Habrocomes that he comes from Perinthus on the Sea of Marmara, south of Byzantium, where his family is part of the nobility. When he was a youth (he is now probably middle-aged), he fell in love with a young man named Hyperanthes (T463), whom he had seen in the gymnasium (shades of Plato). At a festival in Perinthus Hippothous finally got a chance to tell Hyperanthes of his love, and Hyperanthes responded, beginning with kisses and fondling. Though the affair began well, it quickly incurred the jealousy (*phthonos*) of one of the gods (A189.4). Hippothous feels that it was the work of some god or other that an older man named Aristomachus came just at this time from Byzantium to Perinthus, also fell in love with Hyperanthes, and bribed the lad's father into making him his tutor. Both from ancient sources (e.g., Plato and Petronius) and modern (e.g., classical operas) we know why men chose to be tutors to the young. Aristomachus took Hyperanthes back to Byzantium with him after a time, and Hippothous followed. But the latter found little to please him there because there were so many guards around the boy. Returning to Perinthus, Hippothous sold all his property, turned everything into cash, and bought a dagger. As had been planned previously, Hippothous returned to pick up his beloved, by force if necessary. By chance he happened to find him in bed with Aristomachus, and in a fit of jealous rage stabbed the so-called tutor. Hippothous and Hyperanthes fled the scene of the murder, retreated to Perinthus and caught the next boat south into the Aegean Sea (R225.2). Everything was going well until the boat came near the island of Lesbos, where a severe storm wrecked the boat and threw the young lovers into the sea. Hyperanthes was not strong or a swimmer, and, though helped to shore by Hippothous, died at sea (N318). After a ritual burial Hippothous placed an inscribed tombstone on his grave. He did not go back to Perinthus, but joined a band of itinerant robbers, finally establishing his own band in Cilicia.

Hippothous tells this story in the first person and dwells on his great love for his boyfriend and on the sense of loss he still feels. No attempt is made by Hippothous to hide his life of crime; in fact he presents his career as the leader of a group of brigands so nonchalantly that he might have been describing his job in a factory. One is law-abiding and one is not; but this is not seen as a difference of any consequence. There are no internal standards that the characters apply, nor are there any externally imposed values. The kind of chaste love that exists between Anthia and Habrocomes is assumed to be applicable to all lovers both homosexual and heterosexual and seems to constitute the only constant value recognized in Xenophon's novel. Hippothous states that he turned to a life of crime because he needed some way to make a living, and because he was depressed by Hyperanthes' death (he thought a life of crime would be good therapy?). He makes no excuses to explain away his antisocial behavior.

Xenophon pictures the troubles of Hippothous and Hyperanthes as a love affair very much like Anthia's and Habrocomes', but one in which everything goes wrong instead of right. Hippothous' story is, as it were, the same as Habrocomes', but frequently a mirror image; the mirror in this case reflects evil instead of good.

Habrocomes and Anthia	*Hippothous and Hyperanthes*
1A. Parents are prominent citizens of Ephesus	1A. Parents are prominent citizens of Perinthus
2A. Pair meet and fall in love at religious festival	2A. Hippothous sees boy in gymnasium but they fall in love at religious festival
3A. Habrocomes opposes Eros who forces lovers together	3B. Lovers' affair is broken up by unnamed, jealous deity

4A.	Anthia apparently has no other suitors (Xenophon varies his story from his model, Chariton)	4B.	Hyperanthes (Anthia's passive counterpart) has one other suitor
5A.	Parents are honorable and support marriage	5B.	Hyperanthes' father sells him to an older man
6A.	Lovers separated by pirates but remain faithful	6B.	Lovers separated by an additional lover
7A.	Anthia (passive) defends herself in a cave and kills would-be rapist (4.5)	7B.	Hippothous (active) murders Hyperanthes' lover
8A.	Anthia and Habrocomes are shipwrecked but always survive	8B.	Hippothous and Hyperanthes are shipwrecked once and Hyperanthes dies (it is probably significant that a homosexual lover is killed and buried on the island of Lesbos)
9A.	Anthia and Habrocomes set up monument on Rhodes by which they recognize each other at end of novel	9B.	Hippothous sets up monument to Hyperanthes on his grave
10A.	Lovers live through trials and happily ever after	10B.	Hyperanthes does not live through trials and story has sad ending

(The letter "A" in both columns indicates similar actions or outcomes; an "A" in the left column and "B" in the right means opposite actions.)

Though the story of Hippothous is an interpolated tale and does not help the progress of the main plot, it does cause the reader to slow down, to consider an affair that turned out very badly, and to ponder whether a like fate is in store for Habrocomes. The death of Hyperanthes brings an ingredient and a facet of emotional appeal to the whole novel, which could only be achieved by introducing and then disposing of a secondary character.

(3.3) After Hippothous has finished speaking, Habrocomes takes his turn. His narrative lasts for only a few words (the reader already knows his story and needs no background), when it is cut short by Hippothous:

Where are my parents, my country, and above all, my Hyperanthes? Habrocomes, you will see your beloved again, but I will never get Hyperanthes back.

Hippothous then shows Habrocomes a cutting from Hyperanthes' hair, the only memento he has. (Xenophon uses a lock of hair in a recognition scene for Anthia in 5.11.) The pathos of the scene in which Hippothous is standing before Habrocomes and holding a lock of his dead lover's hair is intensified first by the knowledge that the story almost had a happy ending and secondly by the realization that Habrocomes' affairs are not yet settled, and they too could end in sadness.

After a short interval Hippothous tells Habrocomes about the way in which Perilaus had attacked his band of robbers. He notes that he forgot to say that they had previously captured a pretty, young girl about Habrocomes' age who also had come from Ephesus. This curious omission had led the way into Hippothous' long (for Xenophon) interpolated story about Hyperanthes. Had Hippothous mentioned immediately the incident of the young girl, he would never have had a chance to tell the story of his own sad love affair.

Habrocomes' homosexual fascination (T463) for Hippothous is simply a temporary aberration in place of his lasting attraction to Anthia. As soon as Habrocomes learns that his wife was in Cilicia and was definitely alive just a few days earlier when Hippothous held her, he makes preparations to go south again:

My Anthia! You have seen my wife. Where can she have gone? to what country? She cannot have gone far and probably is still in Cilicia. Let us return and get her. Before the soul of Hyperanthes I beg you not to wrong me but to help me find Anthia.

Habrocomes indicates here that he is breaking off the homosexual relationship with Hippothous (active partner) and begs him not to wrong him because of this. If Hippothous really likes him, he will consent even to helping him find his wife. If I am mistaken and there is no homosexual relationship between the two, the passage above will still require an explanation. Why would Habrocomes ask his companion, who has been entirely peaceful, not to harm him, and why swear by the soul of Hyperanthes? And why desert Cilicia in the first place? No, I believe that my interpretation is the most simple and is implied by the sequence of events.

(3.4) As it happens, an elderly physician from Ephesus named Eudoxus is shipwrecked at this time, befriended by Perilaus and sent by him to Anthia to make her feel less homesick. Though he can give her no current news from Ephesus, his mere presence cheers her, and she befriends him. After he comes to know her better, he tells her that he left a wife and children in Ephesus and begs her to help him return there. The stories of these two people from Ephesus are in many ways the same: the most obvious is that they both wish to return home to Ephesus, but, because of shipwreck or unfavorable deities, they are prevented (Odysseus motif).

(3.5) Preparations for a great state wedding are proceeding apace, but Anthia, though gorgeously arrayed in bridal clothes, weeps almost constantly—a fact of which Perilaus seems particularly ignorant:

Habrocomes has been faithful, but I am about to do unjust things to him. He had to suffer imprisonment and torture and is probably dead—but still faithful. I am going to be married and go off to Perilaus' wedding bed. But, Habrocomes, wherever you are, please have confidence that I will not betray you. I will remain your chaste bride until death. (M149.2)

Faithfulness for Anthia is a matter of sexual abstinence from all others. The emotions surrounding it are likewise simple and one-dimensional. Her strong desire to remain chaste and faithful is in fact a death wish, for only in death can the two of them escape temptation and be sure of chastity forever. Xenophon clearly implies a life after death and for lovers a life together after death.

As the threat of her marriage grows closer with every passing hour, Anthia hits on a plan to join Habrocomes (T323). Taking Eudoxus aside and exacting a pledge that he will remain silent but grant her every wish, Anthia tells Eudoxus that Habrocomes is dead and that, in order to rid herself of all temptations to betray his faithfulness, she needs from him a strong poison (N343.4).

Anthia wins Eudoxus over to her viewpoint by promising that, if he provides a poison, she will give him the funds to return to his family in Ephesus. A nice girl like Anthia should have given him the funds to go home without any *quid pro quo*. Eudoxus is requested also to seek out Anthia's parents in Ephesus and to tell them that she and her husband have perished. She then loads him with great quantities of silver and jewelry to ensure his aid. We have before us all the ingredients of an euthanasia episode as it might be staged for a Tuesday afternoon soap opera.

Eudoxus considers his chances of getting home, pities the girl, and stares at all his new money. He agrees to bring the poison, but, faced with its actual, physical preparation, cannot go through with it. Instead of poison he delivers a powerful drug, but it is not lethal (cf. Apuleius, *Metamorphoses* 10.11; K512.4). While he embarks on a boat for Ephesus, Anthia considers the appropriate time to drink the supposed poison.

(3.6) Anthia cannot delay important decisions much longer. It is now night (Xenophon's way of making the reader aware of the passage of time) and her bridal chamber awaits. Crying, holding the potion close to her bosom, walking to the bridal bower to the accompaniment of wedding songs, Anthia screws up her courage. This whole scene reminds her of her marriage to Habrocomes, which had occurred not all that long before. She recalls her vows of chastity (again) and because she believes Habrocomes is already dead, acquires the resolve to drink the poison and join him (N343.4; P214.1; T311.2.1; T326). In an almost relaxed mood she enters the chamber, asks for a drink of water to quench her thirst, and drinks the poison (M341.1.1). Calling upon Habrocomes and death to rescue and receive her into a happy afterlife, she falls asleep almost immediately.[33]

Sometime after Xenophon had published his novel there appeared the very influential (anonymous) Latin *Apollonius of Tyre*, a novel much in the mold of Xenophon's work. In *Apollonius of Tyre* (chapter 26) we find also the appearance of a physician from Ephesus who does the opposite to Eudoxus and restores the chaste and virginal Tarsia back to life from death. These two episodes are merely variants of the same *Scheintod* (apparent death) motif (Type 990;[34] N694), a motif used in Chariton's novel, and to be used in *Romeo and Juliet*. There is a separate motif (V65.3) which describes a wedding chamber as a tomb (Greek *thalamos=taphos*). Antigone in Sophocles' play of the same name (lines 891ff) calls her tomb, where she kills herself, her wedding chamber (*O tymbos, O nympheion*) because, with Haemon her beloved now dead, she can be united with him only in death. Through literary history this motif (*thalamos=taphos*) returns: in Petronius' *Satyricon* (111–12); Apuleius' *Metamorphoses* (4.34; 8.11); Achilles Tatius 1.13, 3.10; Heliodorus 2.29, 10.16; *Romeo and Juliet*; and Verdi's *Aida*.[35]

(3.7) Perilaus enters with great expectation the special bridal chamber of Anthia, but becomes immediately detumescent at the sight of
Anthia lying still on the floor (K1317). Perilaus' servants and friends
gather around and grieve over the dead girl (V65.4.1).
   Perilaus comes close to cursing Anthia's bridal chamber, which is
in fact a tomb. The wedding or honeymoon as a funeral is a motif
which the oracle had predicted many pages ago. Xenophon changes
the point of view of Anthia's apparent death from Anthia, who chooses
death rather than unfaithfulness, to Perilaus who sees in this death
Anthia's escape to Habrocomes in the underworld. Neither point of
view sees reality; only Xenophon and the reader understand the
situation. Perilaus cries out that Habrocomes will be happy now
because his bride has come to meet him in that afterlife where lovers
can finally be at peace. How Perilaus found out about Anthia's earlier
life or about Habrocomes is a mystery—especially to the reader, who
is accustomed to knowing all. Perilaus has Anthia dressed richly and
placed in a gold-filled tomb (R53.1; S123.1) somewhere outside the
city (i.e., outside the realm of civilization). She is carried to her tomb
on the eve of her second (third, if we count the goatherd) marriage.
The *Scheintod* (Type 990; E50; E68; E162.0.1) is not uncommon in
classical literature.
(3.8) We can only imagine the surprise of Anthia when she awakens in
her pitch-black tomb and realizes what has happened. In a way she
must be seen for what she is: a neurotic and seared young woman
cheated out of death by the only friend she thought she had, a fellow
countryman. The picture of Anthia sitting on her sarcophagus awaiting death via starvation recalls to mind the famous Widow of Ephesus
(K2213.1) story in Petronius' *Satyricon* (111–12), in which the widow,
having made up her mind to die in her husband's tomb, refuses to eat
or drink. Like the widow, Anthia is rescued from the tomb by armed
men before she can starve herself (R212.1.1). Did Xenophon borrow
from Petronius or did they both borrow from a common store? The
version found in Petronius' *Satyricon* is the most popular use of the
motif. Where Xenophon is ideal, Petronius is cynical. In the *Satyricon* we find a young widow determined to die on her husband's tomb
in an underground vault. A soldier, guarding criminals recently
crucified, sees her light in the tomb, goes to her, convinces her she is
following the wrong course, and seduces her. Meanwhile, back at the
site of the crucifixion, relatives have removed one of the bodies from a
cross. The guard, whose passion was greater than his patriotism, is

about to kill himself because he knows what his superiors will do to him, when the widow drags out her dead husband and hangs his substitute body on the cross. She could not bear to lose both a husband and a lover on the same day.

Anthia is rescued, like her model Callirhoe in Chariton's novel a half a century or so earlier, by a band of grave robbers (N650). Xenophon had foreshadowed the grave robbery by having Perilaus heap gold around the presumably dead Anthia. Anthia's speech to the grave robbers is almost a parody of what it might have been:

Gentlemen, whoever you are, take all of the riches here but leave me alone. The two deities, Love and Death, watch over me as I pray to them. I beg you not to drag me into the light of day. I wish to stay here.

This sounds a bit like the A. E. Housman lines on a fragment of Greek tragedy. As one would expect, her polite speech does not impress the grave robbers, who seize her and take her with them on board a boat to Alexandria.

(3.9) The ship lands at Alexandria, where Anthia is to be sold (Q437; R61); meanwhile, back in Tarsus, Perilaus learns that the tomb has been robbed and the body stolen. At the same time Habrocomes and Hippothous are back in Cilicia, near Tarsus, and questioning everyone they meet about Anthia. Meeting with no success, Habrocomes retires to the robbers' camp and, as he is about to go to sleep, an old woman named Chrysion begins to tell a story to those around the campfire. The story is that of Perilaus and Anthia, how he had rescued her from brigands, how he had prepared a state wedding, and how she then had killed herself. It would be worthwhile to compare the very famous "Cupid and Psyche" story from Apuleius' *Metamorphoses* (4.28ff), which is told by an old woman and runs along lines similar to those in Xenophon.

Hippothous recognizes enough of the story (H11) both to know that Chrysion is talking about Perilaus' raid on his camp and to remember that Habrocomes has identified the young woman of the story as Anthia. Habrocomes, who also hears the story, is so passive (as usual) that he cannot deduce the simplest things from it. He finally absorbs the import of what has happened, understands that Anthia is dead, and asks about her tomb. Chrysion replies (with an ancient version of "first the good news and now the bad"):

I have not yet told you the worst thing that took place. Perilaus gave her a nice funeral, too good and too rich. It attracted grave robbers who stole the beautiful girl's body.

(3.10) Habrocomes is understandably crushed, after having searched so long and then to be left without even Anthia's body. Is he secretly pleased that the report is she died chaste? It would make living with Anthia in the afterlife much easier. That anyone could be so base as to lust over the body of a dead woman and steal it appalls him. This is strange because he will not be appalled by the same act in 5.1. Now he is even more determined to die—as soon as he finds Anthia's body. For a man who has sworn so often to die, he is finding it a hard thing to do.

In the middle of the night Habrocomes deserts Hippothous and his men and races out to find Anthia's body. He boards ship and heads for Alexandria in Egypt, while Hippothous and his men make plans to pillage in Syria and Phoenicia.

(3.11) Anthia is in Alexandria and Habrocomes on his way there. Just as she leaves, he arrives, following closely on her trail. Anthia leaves a trail in Xenophon's mind; I am sure of that. But how does Habrocomes know it? Of all the ships going to hundreds of ports in the Mediterranean, why does Habrocomes pick the one going to Alexandria? No character in the novel and no reader can see any trail because the grave robbers give no indication of where they are headed. (Perhaps I should suggest that the epitomizer of Xenophon's novel has left out part of the story—a handy crutch and a very appealing solution, if you first accept the theory that the novel is merely an epitome.)

Anthia is well cared for in Alexandria that she might bring as good a price as possible at auction time. A visiting, wealthy merchant named Psammis from India buys her (Q437; R61), for he has fallen in love with her at first sight like everyone else. She stops his first sexual advances and refuses to have any contacts of any kind with him. Exactly how the frail, little slave holds off her lusting owner is unclear, but she did it, and did it with words. She convinces Psammis that at birth she had been consecrated to Isis (T322.4) for an unspecified number of years, at the end of which she could marry (K536.1; T151.3; T315.1). At the present time she is still sworn to Isis and will be for another year. She does threaten Psammis by stating in very precise language that anyone who misuses a maiden sworn to Isis will

suffer terrible punishment. In an aside Xenophon adds: "Barbarians
are naturally superstitious." We now know that Xenophon believes
barbarians have never seen a woman as beautiful as a beautiful Greek
woman (2.2), that barbarians have terrible tempers (2.3), and that
they are superstitious (3.11).

Anthia has now successfully protected her chastity in two very
difficult situations. I pass over some minor threats. Her only defense
is her ability to defend herself with words. Her voice acts like a
charm, exactly like her body. I would hazard a guess that Xenophon
sees her as a kind of witch, a priestess, someone with special powers
to make men go wild or to control them. It is clear that her words
carry a magical force over men who could be controlled by nothing
else.

Though it is a matter parenthetical to our main discussion, the story
of an Indian buying Greeks in Alexandria for transport back to India is
interesting. There is a small amount of evidence to show that, while
this may not have been widespread, the export of young Greek
women to India through Alexandria to serve wealthy princes as
concubines was nevertheless frequent enough.[36] The episode is intended to appeal to the reader who knows of Alexandria and India
only as exotic and fairytale places. And among Xenophon's readers or
listeners are probably young girls who will lie awake at night out of
fear (or hope) of finding themselves one day alone in Alexandria with
an Indian prince.

(3.12) While Anthia is fighting off the advances of Psammis, Habrocomes is fighting for his life near Alexandria, where his ship is
wrecked. Judging from the number of shipwrecks in the ancient
world as a percentage of the number of sea voyages, I am surprised
that people did not give up the whole business of ships and walk.
Once on shore Habrocomes and his comrades are attacked by local
and unfriendly shepherds, tied up, carried off to Pelusium in the
eastern Egyptian Nile Delta, and sold as slaves. Earlier I observed
that Xenophon portrays the cities as areas relatively civilized but the
countryside and high seas as wild and the domain of evil men. Here
we see that even simple shepherds and thus inhabitants of the countryside are not above robbing a disabled ship and selling the crew into
captivity. Already in the ninth century B.C. Homer seems to know
about the existence of fierce herdsmen and others who live in the
country whom he terms *boucoloi* (*Odyssey* 11.293). These *boucoloi*
are country brigands by the second century A.D. when they appear in

the novels of Achilles Tatius (3.9; 4.7; passim) and Heliodorus (1.6; passim).

A military veteran named Araxus buys Habrocomes, but treats him more like the son he never had. Bitch (Greek *Kyno*), Araxus' wife, falls in love with him immediately (N202.1) and treats him like her mate (the mate of a female praying mantis). Compared to Bitch, Manto is a fun-loving young lady. The attraction Bitch feels for Habrocomes can be described as nothing less than a primordial urge, the estrus instinct of a female gone mad in heat. Bitch is crude and crass, and every other word she uses to Habrocomes denotes sex. Since Xenophon does not share with us a description of Bitch's physical state, we can only guess about it. It appears that Habrocomes shrinks from both her appearance and her character. And thus (as Peter De Vries in *The Vale of Laughter* [1967] has so neatly express-ed it, "That a woman isn't appetizing doesn't mean she isn't hungry") Bitch simply tries harder. After several rejections she begs him to take her, in return for which she will free him, and murder her present husband (S60; K2213). A proposal like this is bound to offend a sensitive young man like Habrocomes. He thinks over her proposi-tion and calculates the damage his desire for chastity has already done to Anthia and to himself, and he consents (T338; U66). His consent at this point amounts to nothing less than a confession beaten out of a prisoner-of-war. Habrocomes must surely have felt like a prisoner of some kind of war.

That very night Bitch kills her husband (cf. Apuleius, *Metamor-phoses* 9.26ff and other episodes of adulteresses) and in her blind rage races off to Habrocomes, who is so shocked that he cancels his previous agreement, saying that he could not sleep with a murderess (K2213.3.2.2). This jolts Bitch out of her state of high sexual excite-ment and brings her back somewhere near the real world: she has the dead body of her husband on her hands. To clear herself and to get sweet revenge on Habrocomes, she waits until he leaves, and then rushes into Pelusium and tells everyone, including police officials, that Habrocomes has killed her husband so that he could have his way with her (K2050). This is a variation of the Manto episode and of the Potiphar's Wife motif (K2111). Habrocomes is promptly arrested and sent in chains to the governor of Egypt in Alexandria for the murder of Araxus. The establishment in the ancient world did not deal kindly with slaves who had murdered their masters, since the establishment was made up of masters who had numerous slaves.

We see Habrocomes led into Alexandria in chains as Anthia is led out in bondage by Psammis. This episode is nothing more than a doublet of the earlier Manto-Habrocomes episode. In Xenophon's bag of literary tricks there are clearly a finite number of items, and we see that he has begun to ring more changes on a theme than to develop new themes.

VI   *Hero and Heroine Defy Death (4.1–4.6)*

While Book Four of Xenophon's novel is short and contains the most marvels, it is a static book in that the story does not make any spatial progress.

(4.1) We learn first about three actions of Hippothous, whom we had left near Tarsus in Cilicia. After he gathers a gang of thieves and murderers, he moves to Syria, pillaging and killing. We know that he is not totally evil because wherever he goes he inquires about Habrocomes. From Syria he moves on through Phoenicia to Egypt and finally to southern Egypt, where he locates his permanent headquarters near Coptus on the great trade route to Ethiopia and India.[37] Xenophon uses the first chapter of Book 4 to bring Hippothous back into the picture and to set him in a position where he can once again rescue Anthia. The usefulness and charm of the rogue-hero Hippothous is noted and plagiarized by Heliodorus in his character Thyamis.

(4.2) Habrocomes is sent under guard to the governor of Egypt for prosecution on a charge of having murdered his master. The governor is very busy (as are all governors) and passes sentence on the evidence of written accusations by the people in Pelusium: Habrocomes is to be taken out to a designated spot high above the Nile River and crucified. The belief that Anthia is dead makes him despondent and passive to everything going on around him. Xenophon probably borrows this scene from Chariton, where (4.3) Chaereas is about to die on a cross but is saved when his comrade Polycharmus brings news of a pardon. It is, of course, possible that scenes of abortive attempts at crucifixion come from a common store of motifs, where Greek novelists shop. In addition to its use by Chariton and Xenophon, the motif is found also in Iamblichus' *Babyloniaca*—a summary of this lost novel is preserved in Photius' *Bibliotheca*, 94. Habrocomes is left for dead on his cross just as Anthia had been left in her tomb. He rises as she rose. Once on the cross he looks up toward the sun and then down at the river Nile.

For many pages the gods have not played any significant role in the action of the story. Xenophon has employed quite normal agencies up to this time to rescue or entangle his protagonists. Now, however, he has Habrocomes in such a predicament that the *deus ex machina* is necessary. Habrocomes prays to the sun:

If I have done anything wrong, punish me with a terrible death. If, however, I have been falsely accused by a nymphomaniac, I ask that the holy Nile not be polluted by my innocent body and that it not be responsible for having executed an honest man.

After this prayer (D 906) a strong wind arises and hurls Habrocomes, cross and all, into the river, which carries him out into the Delta, where he is recaptured by guards. Brought once again before the governor of Egypt, who is now more than a little upset by the whole matter and the strange story he has heard, Habrocomes is condemned to die at the stake. And once again his prayers work a miracle, for the Nile rises from its banks and extinguishes the fires just as they are about to consume him (A1017.2; D915; D1382.8; D2151.2; D2151.2.2; F932.8; R117).[38] And one more time he comes before the governor, who, thoroughly perturbed, sends him to prison.

Xenophon uses chance happenings of all kinds to govern the lives of his characters, and, up to a point, readers will believe in the agency of chance. But external, divine intervention is of a different order from random (melodramatic) events which are seen as internal matters. The audience is asked to adjust now to the supernatural. Much of what appears to be miracles in other ancient Greek novels turns out later in the same novels to have reasonable explanations. Not so these two rescues of Habrocomes.

(4.3) We have three threads at present in our novel: (1) Habrocomes; (2) Anthia-Psammis; (3) Hippothous; but everything more than two threads represents an unstable situation in Xenophon. Consequently, the reader can expect something drastic in the plot to restore the old order.

Psammis is leading a caravan loaded with gold, silver, clothes (the same three items which accompany every traveler in Xenophon), and, of course, Anthia, when, as a kind of answer to her prayer to Isis, Hippothous attacks the caravan and kills Psammis (R111.8). The caravan had gone as far south as Ethiopia when it was destroyed. Strangely, neither Anthia (who calls herself Memphitis) nor Hippothous recognize each other, though this is the second time Hippothous has rescued Anthia (R169.5.1), and between those two events he has come to know Habrocomes. The bandit-murderer has assumed the role of catalyst for the action of the story and also the role of rescuer of Anthia. He clearly rivals Habrocomes for the role of dominant male character.

(4.4) With the first serious inquiry into the matter, the governor of Egypt learns the real story, frees Habrocomes, and orders Bitch crucified for the murder of Araxus (Q211). But no deity comes to her rescue: whatever supernatural forces manage the affairs of men, they apparently have some sense of right and wrong and some obligation to reward the good and punish the bad. It is to be understood that Hippothous atones for his evil deeds by rendering great service to the young lovers. The poetic justice of Xenophon does not hold him accountable for murder.

(4.5) Hippothous takes Anthia as his part of the booty in his raid on Psammis, and places Anchialus, who promptly and according to pattern falls in love with her, in charge of guarding her in a cave (R53.1). It is a common motif in ancient literature that the guardian of a young person falls in love with his ward (Eumolpus in Petronius' *Satyricon*, Araspas in Xenophon's *Cyropaedia*, and Juvenal's famous quip, *sed quis custodiat ipsos custodes* [*Satire* 6.031–032], "But who is to guard the guards?"). Because he sees Anthia every day and his lust grows accordingly, it is simply a matter of time until he forces himself on her. She responds by protecting herself with a sword and running him through (T320.2). Terrified about her future, she sits with the body until the change of the guard.

Regardless of the social implication of her actions and the role of a suppressed woman fighting off a would-be rapist, the mere fact that the heroine kills anybody is news in a Greek novel. Except for reports of heroes like Chaereas in Chariton's novel, heroes do not normally kill people—and heroines even much less. Sinonis, the heroine of Iamblichus' novel *Babyloniaca*, stabs to death a man she has enticed into her room. Xenophon does not intend to have his readers marvel at Anthia's action; he intends by this to shock them.

(4.6) As it happens Anchialus was a friend of Hippothous, and, though he admits to Anthia's need to protect herself, he is extremely upset by the death of a friend from Cilician days. In the ensuing debate among the thieves over the proper punishment for Anthia, there are suggestions for crucifixion and exposure to animals. There is a strikingly similar scene to this one in Apuleius' *Metamorphoses* (6.31), where the suggested punishments are identical.[39] Hippothous has a pit dug and, having placed two killer dogs in it, throws Anthia in (Q415; R53.1). This is the third instance of the same motif (R53.1). The first was her burial in a tomb by Perilaus, the second her imprisonment in a cave by Hippothous, and now this. The form of the confinement is always similar. The guard at the pit, Amphinomus, because of his earlier exposure to Anthia falls in love with her and, when no one is watching, feeds the dogs and her.

VII   *The Final Hardships. All's Well That Ends Well (5.1–5.15)*

On the sea voyage to Italy bad storms drive Habrocomes to seek cover in Syracuse, where he is rescued by Aigialeus, a poor but honest fisherman, who shares his meagre food and clothes (P271.2). I am reminded here of a similar story in *Apollonius of Tyre* (chapter 8) in which the old, poor Hellenicus, who is probably a fisherman, comes to the aid of Apollonius. After a time, Habrocomes tells Aigialeus the whole story of his unfortunate experiences, which elicits from the fisherman an equal response. As he speaks, the reader confronts his second interpolated tale:

I was born not in Syracuse but Sparta in Greece, where my family is wealthy and powerful. There I fell in love with a girl named Thelxinoe, and at a religious festival with the aid of some deity we were intimate for the first time. We continued this relationship for some time, pledging faithfulness, until some deity felt we were too happy. Thelxinoe's parents arranged a marriage for her with Androcles, but she was able to delay the wedding on a pretence of illness. Finally on the scheduled wedding night, she and I escaped by boat to Sicily (R225.2). Though very poor we lived here quite happily until some time back when she died. But it is really not so bad. I have mummified her body after the fashion of the Egyptians, and so I am still able to kiss and make love to her. To you she probably looks old and wrinkled, but I remember her as she looked the first time we made love. Come and I will introduce you to her.

If Xenophon's reader was dozing up to this point, he is wide awake now. There is nothing like a little necrophilia (T16.2; T211.4.1; T466) to stir one's interest.[40] (I remember in high school reading stories of necrophilia, Mika Waltari's *The Egyptian* and Faulkner's short story "A Rose for Emily," and then discussing these for hours. It is a topic of some interest among young boys.) Habrocomes does not bolt out of the house immediately to avoid living with a senile lunatic. Rather, he settles in for a long stay and envies the lucky Aigialeus:

Anthia, my unfortunate wife, will I ever see you again—even if it is only your corpse? Aigialeus here has found comfort in the corpse of his wife and proves that love does not cease when one gets old. I have traveled all over, and I have learned nothing about you, Anthia. O Apollo, in your oracle you foretold a happy ending. Please bring that to pass.

At this point Habrocomes would settle even for Anthia's corpse. This is a much different opinion about Anthia's corpse from the one he expressed in 3.10, when he learned that grave robbers had stolen Anthia's (presumably) dead body. At that time he was in a state of disbelief that anybody could lust after a corpse—albeit a lovely one. After saying that he could live with less than a living Anthia, he recalls for the first time the last line of the oracle's prophecy in 1.6. Xenophon may be signaling the end of the novel here when he has Habrocomes plead for only the body of Anthia; he has reached the nadir of despondency.

To retreat, for a moment, and return to Aigialeus' interpolated tale, a review of it will illustrate that it has the same structure as Hippothous' tale, only the names (and sexes) of the characters have been changed. And both Hippothous' and Aigialeus' tales are patterned on the larger story of Habrocomes and Anthia. All three stories have the young couple falling in love or experiencing their first intimate relations at a religious festival. They all experience love at first sight, and all three couples are the victims of deities who are jealous of their happiness. In the case of Hippothous and Aigialeus the parents of their lovers give them to someone else. The net result in all three plots is that all must make sea voyages: Hippothous' lover dies at sea; Aigialeus finds joy across the sea; Habrocomes and Anthia, once reunited, sail home together. Xenophon has precious few plots, but has learned somehow to incorporate a number of variations.

(5.2) The destruction of the city of Areia by Hippothous attracts the attention of the government in Egypt, and an official named Polyidus is dispatched to bring this pillaging to an end.

But what of Anthia? She is very much alive; Amphinomus has extracted her and the dogs from the pit, taking care to make sure the dogs are safe and have food to eat—a curious detail that Xenophon has time to handle.

(5.3) Because of the size of Hippothous' raid on Areia and its destructive force, the governor of Egypt sends Polyidus together with a large contingent of soldiers to track down the gang. Polyidus finds Hippothous a short distance from Pelusium in northeastern Egypt, and a bloody battle ensues. The discipline of trained soldiers tips the scale and leads finally to a rout. Hippothous is, of course, the only one to escape. The motif of the lone survivor is made possible, because Anthia has conveniently been left behind (Z356). Although this episode is surely a simple doublet of the scene in 2.13 where Perilaus attacked Hippothous and seized Anthia, Xenophon extends the narrative by separating Hippothous and Anthia and allowing Polyidus to deal with them separately.

(5.4) In an attempt to seize the elusive Hippothous, Polyidus begins a search of the countryside until he reaches as far south as Coptus. Xenophon tells us that Polyidus took some of Hippothous' former fellow thieves along to help identify still other thieves. Though by this device Polyidus captures only one more outlaw, Amphinomus, this capture leads directly to Anthia's return to the story (R111.1.2), and her rescue from her previous rescuer (R111.8; R116).

The inevitable now occurs: Polyidus falls in love with Anthia on the long trip north to Alexandria. Through an almost casual aside Xenophon informs the reader that Polyidus has a wife in that place. It is an ominous note, and it sets the stage for the next love triangle. But even before they arrive at Alexandria, Polyidus' advances cause Anthia to flee and take refuge in a sanctuary of Isis (R325). The religious awe in which Polyidus holds Isis causes him to agree to respect Anthia, if she will leave the temple and accompany him.

Continuing on the journey to Alexandria, they stop in Memphis, where Anthia worships in the temple of Apis, famous for oracles, an attraction which brings Anthia there to learn her future. She seems completely to have forgotten the first oracle. In one of the most interesting details provided for us by Xenophon, we learn about the rituals of the oracle at Memphis (D1712). The individual desiring the prophecy of the oracular Apis enters the temple, makes his request of the deity, and then leaves. The message of the oracle is delivered through children acting as a medium and standing at the front of the temple. Anthia goes through the prescribed course, and, on her reappearance from the temple, hears the children cry out: "Very soon now Anthia will find Habrocomes."

(5.5) Polyidus' wife, Rhenaia, is aware of her husband's newest war booty, and quite reasonably hates Anthia before meeting her. We think immediately of Agamemnon's bringing Cassandra home to Clytemnestra, and of Heracles' inviting Iole to share his house with his wife, Deianira.

Rhenaia is quick to protect her home and bed from all outsiders.

The very first time Polyidus is out of town on business (the same device was used in the episode in which Manto mounted her attack on Habrocomes) she strikes at Anthia. The fury of Rhenaia is incredible. After many curses she attempts to disfigure (R51.3) the loveliness of Anthia, which is causing all her troubles (S160.2). She tears off Anthia's clothes, scratches her, shaves her hair off (P672.2; Q488), puts heavy chains on her, and then tells her own faithful slave Clytus to sell (Q437; R61) her to a whorehouse in Italy. Her closing words to Anthia are: "Maybe in a whorehouse you can satisfy your urges!" Rhenaia rescues Anthia from Polyidus, who had just rescued her from Hippothous (R111.8). While at Tarentum in Sicily, Clytus is selling Anthia to a local pimp, back in Alexandria Rhenaia is explaining to Polyidus what happened to Anthia. Polyidus believes his wife when she says that Anthia ran away, because she had done the same to him. (5.6) There is just a hint in Xenophon's Greek that the parents of both Habrocomes and Anthia had become so despondent about the loss of their children that they committed suicide (N344). For the first time we learn that the parents of the couple had hired investigators to find out what had happened to them.
(5.7) Finding herself in a brothel and in fear of imminent selection, Anthia delivers a monologue:

More troubles—as if my earlier problems with prison and robbers were not enough. Do I now have to prostitute myself? I curse my beauty, which has got me into this. But why am I complaining in vain when I could be planning (T323) some way to keep my hard-won chastity?

Just as the bidding for Anthia's favors begins, she falls into an epileptic fit. The realization that before him on the floor lies a diseased woman destroys even the most ardent lover's desires. Recognizing the effect this sight will have on customers, the pimp removes her from his establishment before anyone can digest fully what had happened. (In similar fashion at 3.7 Anthia had destroyed the plans Perilaus had for a sexual relationship.) Anthia later explains that when she was very young, she came upon the grave of a man who just died; someone leaped out of this grave, held her captive until morning, and, when he finally released her, struck her on the chest and gave her epilepsy. Her story convinces her pimp, but certainly amazes the readers (among whom are married males thanking the gods that their wives are not as good at telling impromptu stories). In *Apollonius of Tyre* (34) the young virgin Tarsia, finding herself an inmate in a whorehouse and playing upon the emotions of her customers through the narration of her sad life's story, retains her chastity. Plautus' (254–184 B.C.) young women preserve their chastity in brothels in *Casina, Curculio,* and *Poenulus.*

The reader knows that Anthia does not have epilepsy. Just before the sudden onslaught of her seizure, she had informed the reader that she intended to devise some means to preserve her chastity. The epileptic fit then comes as no surprise—unfortunately for the reader who, in this predictable novel, needs a few surprises. Leucippe, in Achilles Tatius' novel (4.9), also goes mad, but there the reader is caught by surprise because Cleitophon, the narrator, did not tip his hand to the reader. Nor does Cleitophon lessen the "suspense of uncertainty" about Leucippe's eventual recovery by indicating there is any cure. Cleitophon, in fact, goes on to relate other events, leaving Leucippe for ten days in her mad state and the audience in suspense for nine chapters (4.17). Cleitophon as narrator limits his point of view for this episode to what he knew as an actor in the real-life drama.[41] The audience is left in the dark and the object of Achilles Tatius' irony. Xenophon never excludes his reader from any secret. Each of Xenophon's main characters, Habrocomes and Anthia, knows one-half of everything; Hippothous also knows approximately one-half of everything—but it is a mixture of Anthia's and Habrocomes' knowledge.

(5.8) While Habrocomes is working as a stonecutter in Nucerium (Italy), Anthia (in Tarentum) has a dream (D1812.3.3) in which a strange woman steals Habrocomes away. She rationalizes Habrocomes' alleged sins by attributing them to acts done under duress. In her present state of being by day an ostensible whore exposed to eager men and by night a sleepless and tormented woman, she again threatens suicide.

(5.9) In Taormina on Sicily Hippothous, always crafty, scheming, the only survivor, marries a wealthy but old woman (U66), who mercifully dies quickly, leaving him her vast fortune. As soon as the need to be heterosexual passes, he reverts to form and takes a young man named Cleisthenes for a traveling companion (T463). He journeys up to Tarentum to buy things befitting a member of the young, rich set and to search for Habrocomes, just as Anthia's pimp puts her up for sale (Q437; R61) in the local slave market. While walking by the slave market, Hippothous recognizes Anthia as the woman he had condemned to death in the pit in Egypt, and rescues her (R169.5.1). Why he did not recognize her in Egypt, since she had been his captive in

Cilicia (2.11–2.13), we never learn. Though Anthia does not for her
part recognize him, she expects him to know her, since, she says, her
sufferings are known all over. This is a stock theme from ancient epic.
For some reason, however, Hippothous does not put together the
whole puzzle and connect her with Habrocomes. He proves his
bisexual nature by falling in love with her (T15.1), causing her finally
to blurt out the whole story including the fact that she has a husband
named Habrocomes (H11, T320.1).

(5.10) Habrocomes finds that his delicate nature is not suited for
stonecutting, and decides to return to Ephesus and search for Anthia
on the way. On the first leg of his journey he stops in Sicily and learns
that Aigialeus is dead. This is not, I believe, superfluous information,
but is intended to bring a satisfactory conclusion to the necrophiliac
episode in 5.1: husband and wife are together at peace in the next
world. After more sea voyages (as the novel winds down towards its
inevitable conclusion, the main characters no longer have shipwrecks; as the novel wound up toward its turning point, almost every
sea voyage ended on the rocks) Habrocomes returns to Rhodes,
where he and Anthia had stopped on their honeymoon.

We left Leucon and Rhode (5.6) on Rhodes, where they now are
joined by Habrocomes. Of the four threads of the fabric of our story
(Habrocomes, Anthia, Hippothous, Leucon and Rhode) we find that
two have been woven with two others, leaving us with only two. Out
of a sense of piety (P361) Leucon and Rhode set up an inscribed votive
offering for their old masters next to the golden offering their masters
had dedicated on their earlier visit. In his searching for Anthia
Habrocomes stumbles on his servants' votive and is deeply moved,
especially when he sees his own and Anthia's earlier votive nearby
(H80–149).

Leucon and Rhode approach their votive and notice the stranger
weeping there. A series of trite questions and answers follow, but no
one recognizes the other. While this seems very improbable to us,
such scenes qualify as regular motifs of ancient tragedy and comedy.
For some reason in many places in ancient imaginative literature,
whenever friends, lovers or what have you are reunited after a period
of separation, they do not recognize each other until they have gone
through a prescribed ritual of questions and answers: Odysseus is
recognized and accepted only after having answered successfully
questions put to him. This ritual probably goes back into the dim past
of man when heroes ventured outside the tribe and had to be recerti-
fied before being readmitted.

(5.11) Hippothous feels that he owes it to his old friend Habrocomes to take his wife back to Ephesus. Accordingly he sets sail for Ephesus, but stops for a visit on Rhodes. The two threads are almost one. In Rhodes the populace is celebrating the summer, quadrennial Halieia, a festival for their state god, the sun (Helius), which Anthia, Hippothous, and Rhode and Leucon attend. Anthia visits the temple of the sun and to commemorate this visit cuts off several locks of hair and places them on a notice inscribed: "To the Sun Anthia dedicates her hair[42] for the sake of Habrocomes."

As Xenophon brings his novel toward its conclusion he takes his characters back to places already visited to see things done at the very beginning of the work. This dedicatory rite of hair on the altar leads quickly to anagnorisis. The same result was precipitated by cut hair in Sophocles' *Electra* and in Aeschylus' *Choephoroe*.

(5.12) Now Leucon and Rhode enter the temple of the Sun and immediately come upon and recognize Anthia's hair and votive (H75; H80–149). I cannot help but be amazed that in recognition scenes, one party recognizes objects of the other party such as hair much more quickly than he or she recognizes the person from whose head it comes. Though Habrocomes now has real reason for hope to find Anthia, he does not go out the next day with his two servants to find her.

Because of bad weather Anthia and Hippothous can not set sail for Ephesus and so return to the temple, where Leucon and Rhode recognize and embrace her (H14). To fill out the motif to its usual length, Anthia does not admit to recognizing them until after they give out their names and remind her who they are. Quickly they announce that Habrocomes is alive and is in fact in their house (N737; N741). Anthia wants them to tell her all about Habrocomes, but expresses no desire to see him. Xenophon is stretching this thing out as far as it will go.

(5.13) It is almost humorous to look at the scene before us. Xenophon, his readers, the main characters in the story, and all the inhabitants of Rhodes know that the novel has come to an end—except for Habrocomes. It is a kind of poetic justice that the passive, and sometimes uninterested, Habrocomes should be the last to discover that his months of travel and searching are almost at an end.

(5.14) Together and alone for the first time since the early pages of the novel, Anthia and Habrocomes climb into bed and make their innocent confessions. Such concluding scenes as this and the one in Chariton's novel may look back to the final pages of the *Odyssey* and the reunion of Penelope and Odysseus. They have absolute faith in each other's chastity and ask for no proof of faithfulness (chastity ordeals are used by Heliodorus and Achilles Tatius).[43]

(5.15) The six main characters all depart for Ephesus the next day, and, landing in Ephesus a few days later, rush off to the great temple of Artemis, where they give many thank-offerings. No mention is made here of Isis. The novel begins and ends with Artemis, the patron deity of Ephesus. Xenophon states that the special thank-offering to Artemis is an inscription in her temple which lays out in detail all the adventures of Habrocomes and Anthia (cf. Apuleius' *Metamorphoses* 11). By adding this note to the narrative Xenophon may be implying that his novel has an historical foundation and thus is worthy of record. The anonymous author of the Latin novel *Apollonius of Tyre* tells us that a record of Apollonius' adventures is kept in the temple of Artemis in Ephesus.

CHAPTER 3

The Language and Style of Xenophon

XENOPHON writes prose fiction, to which we assign the term "novel." The academic Greeks seem not to have had any name for the form because they did not consider it a serious form:

> There is next to no comment to be found on the form at all, in fact. The Greek Académie appears to have regarded prose fiction as a thoroughbred racehorse might regard a camel, with puzzlement and disdain.[1]

> No ancient Ars Poetica ventured to admit it to the Select Society of Literary Nobility; no ancient Philologia provided it with a *carte d'identité*. Subsidised by a papyrus dealer, the child found its way in the world even without papers. It was surprisingly long-lived and had an immense number of descendants.[2]

Like today's literature, the ancient world's literature had a classical/academic level and a popular/pulp level.[3] The Greek novels, including Xenophon's, belong to the latter kind. But unlike the classical and academic literature which demands a social circumstance, as at the theater, or a long formal education, as in rhetoric and public speaking, or an attachment to national destiny and purpose, as in epic, or leisure time for contemplation, which the wealthy have for delving into esoteric poetry, the popular literature of Xenophon is written for a single person to read in a private setting, and no greater purpose intended than simple entertainment. None of the popular literature is to be committed to memory like the lines of Homer or passages from Sophocles. But while camels cannot display the form of thoroughbreds, they are generally more useful—except to the horsey set.

Turner's comments that the language of Xenophon is so inornate that he "gives the impression of being almost illiterate," and that "the style . . . is referential to the point of being slipshod," make a good starting place.[4] The tradition of style in Greek antiquity showed little concern for the direct relationship of words to things, and preferred by far to dwell on the external embellishments of description brought to bear by the application of rhetoric. Xenophon is often attacked for being inarticulate, inaccurate, and clumsy, when it would perhaps be better to say that his language is too exclusively denotive (as opposed to emotive). The language of Xenophon is referential and the stuff of which realistic literature is made. Unfortunately for Xenophon realistic/referential language is applied to an often fantastic plot; this misapplication of one style/level of language to a different style/level of plot surely offends a natural decorum of literature. Literary sensitivity of subject to style is missing. The referential language of Xenophon calls for realism in content, but the plot runs directly counter to the premises. John Dennis noted that "no sort of imagery can ever be the language of grief. If a man complains in simile, I either laugh or sleep." One of Xenophon's failures is that in his search for a vehicle of realism through an avoidance of imagery, he cannot locate the language of grief.

Xenophon provides only rare descriptions of people and places. We have no idea of the physical appearance of his characters or of the places they visited. I assume the sea and sky are blue, the plants green, the cities radiant in white marble. Beautiful is the adjective applied to the protagonists, but it is so loose and so hollow. From the small to the large: scenes are barely developed—about all we are ever offered in an episode is a skeleton—before we are taken into another scene. In addition to such scenes we are given shallow people, characters of one and one-tenth dimensions, except for some of the minor characters like Aigialeus. Events are piled relentlessly upon other events, and, as Hägg shows us, while we can easily keep the order and sequence of events straight, we cannot appreciate the distance or irony (if any) between events.[5]

Xenophon is not an original author, but one who prefers to borrow from others. His chief source is his immediate (extant) predecessor, Chariton. In his 1973 Teubner Greek edition of Xenophon A. D. Papanikolaou provides the reader with a special running list of verbal borrowings of Xenophon from Chariton—and they are considerable. Gärtner and Hägg have also done a considerable amount of original work in identifying Xenophon's sources.

In addition to the usual problems which confront any work of literature as it proceeds on its way from the second to the twentieth century, there is the question of whether or not we possess an epitome of the original or the original. A large body of scholars, following Bürger,[6] believes that many sections of the work have been epitomized, while others have been left to stand intact. This is not only an ingenious scholarly observation. It is a godsend to help explain away (without really explaining) many of the problems associated with Xenophon's style and language. It is a source of last resort to unanswered questions: the text is an epitome of the original and represents not what Xenophon wrote but what a clumsy epitomizer substituted. In his study of hiatus (the gap that occurs when a word ending with a vowel is immediately followed by a word beginning with a vowel) in Greek novels, M. D. Reeve explains why in parts of the novel Xenophon allows hiatus but in other parts avoids it: the parts that contain few instances of hiatus are those written by Xenophon, while a high incidence of hiatus indicates epitomized sections.[7] The student reading Xenophon in Greek can use this as a rule of thumb for identifying real and forged Xenophon. I find it hard to believe that Xenophon paid any attention to a refinement like hiatus. He paid little attention to all other refinements. Again, for the student reading Xenophon in Greek and using Papanikolaou's edition there is an indication in the *apparatus criticus* for every suspected epitomized part. This sort of thing is probably a very interesting scholarly pursuit, but I cannot affirm that in Xenophon's case it could be productive. I do not mean to dismiss the epitome theory out of hand, because I too find it can offer an explanation of sorts in cases like Book 3.12. In this episode Bitch has offered to kill her husband, marry Habrocomes, and give him her husband's estate. Bitch is easily the ugliest and meanest of all of Habrocomes' temptations, and he finds it almost easy to stand up to her and refuse. But then all of a sudden and quite without cause he consents to her proposals. When she kills her husband and then offers herself to Habrocomes as though she were some little virgin schoolgirl who had never before done this sort of thing, he is horrified. This is a bit extreme even for Xenophon, who is fond of skeletons without flesh.

Another simple indication I can list here as illustrative of the style of Xenophon is his use of similes, compared to the other Greek novelists (Scobie has made the numerical analysis):

Heliodorus, 120 similes
Achilles Tatius, 110
Longus, 107
Chariton, 49
Xenophon, 4

While it is dangerous to make too much of these figures, we can safely make at least one observation: Xenophon is so inornate that he "gives the impression of being almost illiterate."

The language of Xenophon is simple, straightforward, denotive, and can be read easily by someone who can handle the New Testament. It resembles the old graded reader which offered the schoolboy a controlled vocabulary, which he was expected to master. Dalmeyda, Gärtner, Mann, and Hägg have made detailed studies on Xenophon's Greek, and from their observations I offer a selection which I hope will indicate something about Xenophon's language.

There are repeated words and expressions or words and expressions so similar to each other that they seem mere repetition, which in Homer we call *formulae*. To someone reading Xenophon today these repeated phrases spell monotony; to someone in the ancient world *hearing* this novel read to him (because he can not afford to buy it) these repeated phrases allow him to become familiar with and close to the story. Such *formulae* are "gold, silver, clothes and a supply of everything else," used (three times) for journeys; "the most important people of the area" (six times); "she (or he) was distressed" (seven times) and "no longer able to endure" (five times); after Polyidus has been introduced to the reader he is later referred to as "*that* Polyidus," even though there is only *one* Polyidus in the story—it is as though his first name were That and last name Polyidus; "having finished a voyage of many days they arrived . . ." (once for every voyage in the novel); the expression "on the one hand he/ she . . . on the other hand she/he" marks every alternation from one thread of the story to the next, and, though monotonous, helps to bring order to a novel of too many episodes.

The basic structure of Xenophon's writing is the simple sentence, a declarative clause without involved syntax. The language is almost paratactic instead of syntactic and resembles a style I associate with students learning to write in a foreign language. There is never any doubt about what Xenophon means by what he says. Instead of building an involved sentence, one with innumerable clauses, Xenophon uses adverbial expressions or participles. To accompany his simple and basic vocabulary and his straightforward grammar, he also delivers a simple message (5.1): "they enjoyed the things because of which they had married." In a novel like Xenophon's, which is concerned primarily with the erotic, the contemporary reader will be amazed to discover upon reading that there are no obscene words or expressions. These facts add weight to statements that the intended audience for Xenophon's novel was (1) literate teenagers, (2) students, (3) housewives.

Until the last few years the greatest and most enthusiastic spokesman for the value and quality of ancient Greek novels was Elizabeth Haight. Her enthusiasm clearly got out of hand when she began to discuss the language of Xenophon: "The style of this gem of a novel is finely cut, clear and beautiful in its pure Atticism." [8] Xenophon's Greek is simple, not gemlike or finely cut; it is clear and for the most part Attic Greek. The district in and around Athens is called Attica, and the name has been transferred to the dialect of Greek spoken there. Since the three great Greek dramatists and Aristophanes, Plato, Xenophon of Athens, Aristotle, Demosthenes, and many others wrote in Attic Greek, this dialect became the most important and influential. When anyone speaks of reading Greek, chances are he means Attic Greek. Xenophon does not write pure Attic, but rather a later form of Attic which allows for influence of the Koine: the use of the subjunctive mood where Atticists would use the optative; avoidance of the dual; carelessness about reflexives; very loose use of the genitive, dative, and accusative cases to indicate time—something not in "pure" Attic; failure to augment the pluperfect tense; and non-Attic variations in standard declensions.

None of the above should be construed as negative criticisms. I have collected these observations simply to suggest to the Greekless readers the kind of language Xenophon wrote. Supporters and detractors of Xenophon usually do not base their criticisms or praises of him on the nature of his language.

CHAPTER 4

The Structure and Nature of Xenophon's Writing

I Introduction

THE story of Xenophon ends, as it were, where it began. At the end of the story the lovers are reunited, and they begin again to lead a peaceful life together. Everything between their first chance meeting at the temple of Artemis in Ephesus and their reunion near the temple of Isis on the island of Rhodes is a stormy prologue to the normal life that they will lead from now on. At the very beginning of his novel Xenophon, unlike Chariton, does not introduce himself or his subject matter, but plows immediately into his story, which he relates in painful and unerring chronological order. In his novel Longus tells us in the opening pages that a painting of Love so inspired him that he felt constrained to write a reply to that painting, and that reply is his novel. Achilles Tatius in his novel reports at the outset that, some time ago, when he was in the city of Sidon and was gazing at an erotic picture, a young man came up to him and told him about the many adventures which had befallen him and his lover before they were married. Achilles Tatius' novel is then the story of these lovers. Among the Latin novelists we see that the first part of Petronius' *Satyricon* is missing, but that Apuleius spends the first several sentences introducing the setting for his *Metamorphoses*. And finally, one of the last extant ancient Greek novels, the *Aethiopica* of Heliodorus, opens *in medias res*, retraces its steps back to the beginning, and then proceeds toward the denouement.

Many novelists provide some sort of introductory material, if only to say something to give credence to the story, like "I saw this with my own eyes" or "a reliable friend told me" or even "a distraught lover related a very sad tale." Xenophon offers us nothing of this kind, but he does, I believe, like Achilles Tatius, say something very clearly and simply about the origins of his novel. In the opening lines of his novel Achilles Tatius recounts the following:

> While I was strolling around the city and inspecting in the temples the gifts offered to the gods, I spied a picture. . . .

When Anthia and Habrocomes return to Ephesus at the very end of their long journeys, they record in written form all of their adventures and dedicate this inscribed record as a gift to Artemis. The technical term for such votive gifts is *anathema*, and that is the word used by Xenophon to describe the kind of inscription-gift given by these lovers to their goddess.

The conclusion of Chariton's novel finds the heroine thanking Aphrodite in her temple, while the hero retells the whole story of the novel to the inhabitants of the city of Syracuse as they sit assembled in the theater (Chariton had earlier described his work as a drama fit for a theater). The story behind Chariton's novel is thus at least the kind of thing well known to people from the theater.

It seems worthwhile to hazard a guess that each novelist to a varying degree feels some kind of requirement to suggest whence he got his story. Achilles Tatius tells us that he was "inspecting in the temples the gifts offered to the gods . . ." among which gifts, I believe, he sought the kind that Anthia and Habrocomes had placed in the temple of Artemis, i.e., a detailed story of love, adventure, and final salvation by the deity in whose temple the inscription is placed. There must have been a goodly number of such gifts with short inscriptions giving the reasons and history of the gift. A compilation and ordering of such inscriptions would, I suggest, make an excellent ancient novel.

II *The Structure and Nature of Xenophon's Writing*

A. An Overview

In commenting on Glazunov, the Russian composer, the British critic Gerald Abraham notes:

> A Glazunov symphony is just an uninterrupted flow of melodious ideas. . . . But nothing ever happens to these ideas (although) climaxes are arranged. . . . There is no growth. . . . Moreover, practically every one of Glazunov's symphonies sounds like the others.

Although every comparison limps, this description of a Glazunov symphony can be applied to Xenophon's novel. The episodes in the plot fill out the plot without meaning anything. The plot in Xenophon is simple, and the reader is taken up no dead-end streets in order to amuse the writer. Anthia and Habrocomes meet at a religious festival, fall in love, and, through the interference of an oracle, are married by concerned parents. They are separated, and each one goes through a series of adventures, finally to be reunited in the last reel. The outline of Xenophon's novel is strikingly similar to that of New Comedy, and probably identified as such by some of the readers.[1]

Scarcella has developed an overall and unifying approach to the structure of this novel, which is more anthropological than literary.[2] After pointing out the obvious, that the whole novel is framed by festivals to Artemis (1.2 and 5.15), and that the geographical progression through the novel from the East to the East, via the South, West, and North, constitutes a "ring composition," Scarcella develops an imaginative essay on artistic control in Xenophon. He sees in this novel a "geometric pattern" which serves as the outline of the story: Anthia and Habrocomes move from left to right on horizontal/parallel narrative lines which begin to converge when they begin to fall in love, and which run closely parallel as soon as they are married (1.1–1.8). The period before the marriage is seen by Scarcella as a nonintegral or preliminary part of the story which sets the stage for the main story, the marriage-separation-reunion (1.8–5.13). The main story is pictured as a narrative-time circle, which Anthia and Habrocomes (as parallel lines) leave after their reunion. Once in the narrative-time circle Anthia and Habrocomes (as parallel lines) continue to move from left to right until the first episodes with Euxinus and Corymbus. In the narrative-time circle each episode concerning Anthia is pictured as a high point on a graph which falls back to the horizontal narrative line between episodes; each episode concerning Habrocomes appears as a low point on a graph which rises back to the horizontal narrative line between episodes. Six high points on Anthia's part of the graph are matched by five low points on Habrocomes':

Euxinus (1.15)-Moeris (2.1)-Perilaus (3.11)-Psammis (3.11)-Polyidus (5.4)-Pimp (5.5)
Corymbus (1.14)-Manto (2.3)-Apsyrtus (2.5)-Bitch (3.12)-Governor (3.12)

Each episode (a high or low point) appears as a departure from the horizontal narrative line, which serves as a kind of norm. Though the episodes of Anthia and Habrocomes take each one in opposite directions momentarily, the conclusion of the episode brings them back toward the narrative time line. The episodes should be seen as disjunct parallel lines which, not as economically as straight lines nor as interestingly, carry the narrative line forward toward the reunion. At 5.13 and the reunion the narrative lines of Anthia and Habrocomes become closely parallel as they were in 1.8. With the end of their adventures, which are always narrative episodes, Anthia and Habrocomes leave the narrative time circle to live happily everafter.

Though the structure of the novel has a clearly defined beginning, middle, and end, and, as Scarcella has demonstrated, is nicely patterned and balanced, the reader does not observe a similar development, appreciation or understanding on the part of the characters in the structure. By 1.8 in the novel Anthia and Habrocomes have gone through a kind of beginning, middle and end with their discovery of each other, lovesickness, and marriage, and will develop no further from 1.8 to the end of the novel. The structure develops, but the characters do not. Such an imbalance does not help the novel. In his 1949 *Hero with a Thousand Faces* Joseph Campbell claimed that many myths, sagas, legends, and epics have a developmental structure, which Scarcella now claims for Xenophon.[3] Heroes, however, according to Campbell, should develop along with the structure, and, when they return home at the end, are not only themselves better, but they bring boons for their families and cities (e.g., Lucius in Apuleius' *Metamorphoses*). The structure Xenophon adopts for his novel almost encourages him to delineate characters which, because of their experience in many episodes, grow through learning to become kinds of heroes. The static quality of the character development of the novel's protagonists is in conflict with its structure.

The final and exhaustive recapitulation at 5.14, in which Anthia and Habrocomes, now reunited, exchange stories of their adventures, imposes a nice bit of structure on the novel.[4] For in this recapitulation Xenophon has his lovers respond to the predictions of the oracle at 1.6 and relate how each item in that prophecy came true. Adventures promised by the oracle in the beginning of the novel are accomplished in the middle section of episodes, and then told in summary form at the end of the novel in a recapitulation. The effect of a final recapitulation, which corresponds to an introductory oracle, is to place the central episodes within a frame.

As soon as the lovers have been married, the plot achieves a kind of climax which can be reached again or exceeded only by separating the lovers and then reuniting them, and then repeating the procedure. Heliodorus does this with some skill. Between the first union and the final reunion the novelist can insert any number of episodes; when he thinks the reader has had enough, he brings it all to an end. Because the middle of the structure is elastic, but full of marvelous episodes, the beginning and ending are prone to be weak.[5] Xenophon concentrates his inventiveness on the episodes; he stumbles into them at the beginning of the middle section and gets out of them at the end of the middle section, as best he can.

Of the five extant Greek novelists only Chariton and Xenophon arrange to have their lovers marry before they are separated. The climax of the novel then cannot be a marriage; it must be a reunion. Reardon feels that Xenophon makes a structural mistake by placing the marriage at the beginning of the novel, which then forces Xenophon to tie the separated lovers together by means of a clumsy "common factor," Hippothous. "For all the difference it makes in Xenophon's novel his Anthia could have been unmarried and virgin."[6] I believe, however, that Reardon is mistaken here. The structure is both sound and reasonable: good stories can be full of episodes in which married lovers are separated but strive mightily to effect a reunion; the motivation of separated husband and wife to find each other is just as strong, if not stronger than that of virgin lovers; emotional forces necessary to find someone whom one has had but lost are surely as basic as those necessary to find someone whom one has never totally had. The climactic reunion of Odysseus and Penelope is surely as satisfying as making "marriage the consummation of the story."[7] Though the lovers are separated Xenophon keeps always before his reader the hope of their final reunion by attaching to Habrocomes' name words connected with "searching" and to Anthia's name words of "regret/longing."[8]

It is apparent to all discerning readers that Xenophon has problems with setting his story in motion, and, when he ends it, there is no internal reason for ending it just there. Xenophon's problems are not structural, as Reardon believes, but rather motivational. There is nothing inherently wrong with an author's using an oracle to activate his plot and then, by means of a series of connected episodes, to bring the story to an end. The general structure of this novel is acceptable, but the frequency of chance items coupled with the paucity of strong cause and effect renders the story unsatisfactory.

The parents of Anthia and Habrocomes are reasonably happily married and urge their children to assume the same state; Apsyrtus is or was married and, recognizing the violence of his daughter's sex drive, secures a husband for her who is to calm her down (2.5); once Manto and Moeris cease chasing other partners, they settle down, we may assume, to a normal, i.e., prosperous, marriage; Leucon and Rhode are married and prosperous; as long as Hippothous is "married" to Hyperanthes and then to Cleisthenes, he is portrayed as happy and law-abiding; Perilaus, as a responsible government official, acknowledges the value and respects the conditions imposed by marriage; Bitch breaks up her marriage and is executed for having done so; the married state is continued by Aigialeus even though Thelxinoe is dead. Xenophon equates prosperity, happiness, and normalcy with marriage. Until married, Anthia and Habrocomes are in an unstable state; marriage, in fact, prevents their death. The structure of many of the individual episodes is dependent upon the belief that marriage is worth preserving. Xenophon's novel is concerned with the difficulty of married partners preserving their marriages (see Rhenaia's handling of Anthia in 5.5.), not with single persons looking for a suitably seductive mate (as in New Comedy). The institution of marriage is alive and well in Xenophon. Thus the structure supports the ideas Xenophon sets forward.

Because Xenophon separates the married lovers, he is able to put twice as many episodes into his novel. The best part of Xenophon's novel, and the part he obviously felt at home in, is the episodes. Attention can be focused and sharpened on Anthia's plight, if Habrocomes is not present, and vice versa. The episode with Euxinus and Corymbus (1.14 ff) and the first part of the Manto episode, both of which occur before the separation of Anthia and Habrocomes, are clearly not as successful as the later episodes. Xenophon seems to feel he is writing for an audience with a short attention span and thus does not remain very long with any episode before he moves on to the next. Again, the structure supports the idea.

Once Xenophon has designed a structure in which the lovers are first married, then separated in long travels which involve them in various adventures, the love part of his love-and-travel novel has no real presence. The love exists only in the memories of the two lovers: ". . . the point of having a love theme at all is surely that it should be permitted to develop in some way. And it cannot very well if the couple is separated by hundreds of miles. . . ." [9] To rescue the situation, Xenophon brings onto the stage Hippothous, who not only functions as the rescuer and messenger of the lovers, but is in his own right the best delineated character in the novel. The picaresque episodes in which Hippothous appears provide an excellent foil for the passive and restrained sections of Habrocomes. The addition of a common factor character like Hippothous allows Xenophon to enlarge the number of central figures to three and to tell of the adventures of a different kind of character. Though Hippothous has a function as a go-between in the travels of the lovers, this should not be viewed as a necessarily weak function (as Reardon views it; in a way, Dionysius serves a similar function in Chariton). Xenophon is following in a long literary tradition of New Comedy by using go-betweens for separated lovers; Leucon and Rhode serve the same function. Chariton had earlier used a go-between. The use of go-betweens invites the participation of the audience, who associate with such characters because they and the go-between know more than the young lovers.

Many scholars agree in calling Xenophon's novel crude. I also, but not because the structure is weak. The novel is crude because the leading characters are weak (almost shadowy); the characters do not develop, grow, or learn; too many episodes develop from nowhere and go nowhere; the range of emotions is severely restricted. There is in the content of the work little substantive appreciation of the wide range of human aspirations. The level of the Greek language and the intellectual capacity necessary to grasp what is said are low. This is not the studied *simplicitas* of a Petronius; it is, rather, a low order of simpleness. Given Xenophon's structure, a skillful writer could produce a first-rate novel. Hence, I disagree with the statement regarding Xenophon's novel that "adventure militates against love." [10] In Xenophon's case adventure explains and exposes the love of Anthia and Habrocomes for each other. In the opening pages Xenophon has the young couple so lovesick that they almost die. By any standard this is a fairly intense love. As early as Book 1.8, Xenophon has his lovers in bed locked in an erotic encounter. Unlike modern writers, Xenophon can go no further in this vein. The ancient genre will not allow it. *Ad nauseam* the lovers *profess* under oath their love. Yet another avenue was still open to Xenophon by which he could have his leading actors *prove* their love: episodes in which that love is tested by would-be rivals. Most of the episodes fall into the category of "love and faithfulness tempted." Xenophon uses the episodic structure to pile up proofs of the love of Anthia and Habrocomes and at the same time to add elements of adventure. In Xenophon love and adventure are mutually supportive and supported by the structure.

B. Point of View

Several points of view are theoretically possible in a novel, but three are generally present: the narrator/author, the characters, and the audience. When there exists "disparity of understanding" among these points of view the result is irony:

Our pleasure in narrative literature itself, then, can be seen as a function of disparity of viewpoint or irony. Because we are not involved in the action represented, we always enjoy a certain superiority over the characters who are.[11]

The bulk of Xenophon's novel is presented to the reader in the third person; the interpolated, first-person narratives of Hippothous and Aigialeus and the direct speeches are exceptions. Though our author (unlike Chariton) does not introduce himself and comment on the kind of story he is about to tell us, he imitates the approach of Chariton and makes the author the third-person narrator. The most successful sorts of prose fiction in antiquity, Apuleius' *Metamorphoses* and Petronius' *Satyricon*, are both first-person narratives.

Xenophon does not pretend that he is interpreting a traditional story known in some form in Ephesus, or relating the product of his own research, or telling an eye-witness account (Achilles Tatius says he got his story directly from Cleitophon who was an eye-witness). Xenophon does not claim to be inspired or to have special blessings from the Muse. He appeals, instead, directly to the reader to appreciate his novel on whatever level he can.[12] If this novel is complete and intact as Xenophon wrote it, the viewpoints of Xenophon and the intended reader are clear. The appeal of Xenophon's novel must come from the novel itself and its aesthetic qualities. While it is not probable, it is possible that Xenophon had a didactic intent in writing; the kind of intent writers like Petronius and Lucian could parody.

Xenophon and the reader share an omniscient point of view. Since the two viewpoints are the same as regards the past and present state of the action and characters, the reader can experience suspense only for future episodes and appreciate irony only in the disparity of understanding among the characters. There is no disparity of understanding between author and reader. The separation of the young lovers opens up the plot to frequent disparities of understanding, the most common being the belief that the other lover is dead. The reader feels superior in his knowledge that both are alive and finds cause to hope for the future. A good example of irony occurs at 2.6, where Apsyrtus is deceived into believing that his daughter Manto has been assaulted by Habrocomes. All the other characters and the reader know the truth. The poignancy of the irony occurs only after the separation of the lovers, when Apsyrtus stumbles on the truth. To achieve even small instances of irony Xenophon seems to need to have the lovers separated. His irony is clearly dependent on the structure.

There is irony among the characters in the episodes where Perilaus believes Anthia dead and the governor of Egypt tries to execute Habrocomes, but these are unimportant when compared to the lovers' belief that each other is dead—an irony which almost causes two suicides. Xenophon does not develop any disparities between himself and his reader, as Heliodorus does at 1.30–31. In Heliodorus the audience is not led to believe an untruth; it is told one which only later is explained. It would have been more subtle had Heliodorus seduced the reader into concluding something which had not really happened. Heliodorus becomes that rare bird among ancient writers, an unreliable narrator. When Anthia pretends to have epilepsy (5.7), only the pimp is taken in by the ploy. The reader is told that Anthia is merely using it as a device to save her chastity. In the novel by Achilles Tatius we see the author meet Cleitophon, whose story the author relays to the reader as though told by the character. When the novel ends Cleitophon is still talking, and the author seems to have disappeared. At 3.15 Cleitophon describes how certain robbers sacrifice his beloved Leucippe, but Achilles Tatius imposes at that time a dramatic point of view on Cleitophon who otherwise would have known (and told the readers) that Leucippe had not been killed. It is a clever manipulation of the point of view by Achilles Tatius.[13]

Unlike Achilles Tatius, Xenophon never appears in the text of his own novel. Authorial comments (as in 4.5) are extremely rare, as Xenophon keeps a cool distance from the action. His habit of summarizing even psychological developments strikes the modern reader as perhaps too distant, too unrelated, and from too lofty a perspective. It is difficult to suffer with Habrocomes, since the reader often does not learn of his sufferings from his point of view.

As I have pointed out earlier, Xenophon has a special fondness for pairs. This extends even to his pairs of viewpoints. Hägg demonstrates that as soon as more than two viewpoints are possible, because of the addition of new characters, viewpoints are dropped or combined, but the total is always two.[14]

C. The Oracle: Foreshadowing and Structure

The employment of an oracle to initiate the action of a novel is a nice, artistic touch. It is unfortunate that Xenophon did not handle it artistically. When the parents of the lovers consult the oracle, all they know is that their children are sick and probably dying. The answer they get from the oracle (1.6) is a plot outline for the whole novel. Revealing the contents of the oracular response before any of the adventures takes place is a little like telling the punchline of a joke before the joke.

Placement of the oracle so early in the story is perhaps an instance of faulty structure. It is true that publication of the first part of the oracle is necessary to activate the plot (*deus ex machina* motif) and cause the lovers to begin their journey. The oracle also includes the information that a common cause afflicts both young people, and thus it is a necessary part of the sequence leading to marriage. The last line of the oracular response is unnecessary at this time. To enhance the structure it might have been more appropriate to include it in a second oracle later in the novel. Since in classical literature oracles must come true, some of the suspense that the novel might otherwise have created is lost because of the last line. The parents of the young couple clearly understand the last line of the oracle and are delighted with it. Like their children they forget it, and then in the end die because they believe all is lost (5.6). Gärtner suggests that their deaths might have been suicides. These are, however, small points when compared with the real damage done to the credibility of the ordeals of the protagonists. No one really quite sympathizes with the extremes of some of the ordeals, though there must exist in the reader a minimum of acceptance that the lovers are actually suffering. The last line of the oracle destroys that. If Anthia and Habrocomes and the reader all know that they are treading water until the last page, the reader has no emotional bond with the heroes.

In his *Aethiopica* (2.35) Heliodorus has an oracle provide a look into the future of the young lovers, but he does so only after the novel has progressed some distance. The oracle sketches out future events in the most enigmatic terms, designed to baffle all those who hear it. This dark oracular prophecy does not do away with most of the tension concerning the denouement, as it does in Xenophon. In fact, the enigmatic character of the oracle's words heightens the interest of the reader.

Though the oracle at 1.6 is clumsily placed in the larger structure, in the smaller Xenophon uses it economically. The prediction of the oracle that Anthia and Habrocomes will be captured by pirates is reinforced by Xenophon's (dramatically external) comment that the words of the oracle were beginning to come true (1.12) and shortly thereafter by Habrocomes' dream about burning ships. At 1.13 the pirates mentioned in the oracle appear on the scene and plot to attack the ship, killing those who resist and selling the rest. In the very next chapter Xenophon has the pirates carry out what they had threatened.[15] Had Xenophon developed his entire novel with the care and economy used to set up this section of one episode, the whole novel might have hung together.

In his analysis of narrative technique Hägg catalogues the occurrences of forebodings, a small group of rather obvious hints as to what the future holds in store. In addition to the oracle at 1.6 there is a second one at 5.4, and in addition to the dream at 1.12 mentioned above, there are others at 2.8 and 5.8. Almost from the first pages of the novel Xenophon employs the device of foreboding, in most cases somewhat ambiguously. Eros threatens (1.2–1.4) dire consequences and Anthia and Habrocomes fear separation—all for some unspecified time in the future. Each time Anthia is taken by a new captor, Xenophon gives some hint of foreboding that something is about to happen. But his hints are not always reliable, a situation which aggravates the already capricious appearance of the plot: Anthia is given up to pirates who do not ravage her (1.14), to a goatherd husband who does not violate her chastity (2.9), to a kind of priest who does not sacrifice her (2.13), to a physician who promises but then does not poison her (3.5), to killers who do not kill her (4.6), and finally to a pimp who does not use her (5.7). Xenophon arouses the emotion of fear but allays it with a happy resolution before that emotion can be fully exploited. The result of these rapid resolutions of frequent forebodings is a cluttering of the story with minor episodes and a diminution of the importance of the overall structure and final resolution at 5.13.

D. Alternation

One of the marked features throughout Xenophon's work is the constant alternation of scenes between Habrocomes and Anthia and later among all sorts of people. First a short scene with Habrocomes, then Anthia, then back to the first, then to the other, etc. No scene with either one is ever really very long, and thus it is not necessary to resort to flashbacks to fill in the intervening scenes. Sometimes, however, flashbacks would be preferable to the constant switching back and forth between scenes to pick up every little change that occurs in the life of our hero or heroine: a flashback could deal with a whole series of events concerning one character before switching back to the other. The alternation does much to destroy the even flow of the story and to force the reader to impose an external sense of continuity on the episodes.

It is interesting to speculate why Xenophon would write this way. The first answer would be a lack of basic skills. This is a neat, simple answer, but in view of the skill shown in handling other problems and procedures, it is, I think, not the best answer. Anyway, Xenophon models much of his novel on that of Chariton, who did not alternate short scenes with the same frequency. It seems clear that he does exactly what he wants, and that is to make the alternating a kind of two-part dialogue, in which alternately each of the lovers speaks and is answered, or speaks to the last things said in the previous section. It is a clumsy attempt by Xenophon, but a noble one and perhaps worthy, in an improved form, of imitation. Moses Hadas has called attention to the parallels between Xenophon's rapid scene changes and the ever-changing scenes in today's motion pictures:

The moral premises are very like those which govern the production of American moving pictures: vice is never made attractive, and virtue is always rewarded. There are other patent affinities with the cinema: patterned plots, rapidly shifting scenes, the interest in the spectacular, such as shipwrecks, courtroom scenes, and the courts of foreign potentates, and the constant tendency toward the melodramatic.[16]

Such frequent scene changes are still part of the storehouse of gimmicks used by writers, of which the best example is the work of P. G. Wodehouse. And a good instance of this device appears in *Summer Lightning*:

And meanwhile, if we may borrow an expression from a sister art, what of
Hugo Carmody? It is a defect unfortunately inseparable from any such
document as this faithful record of events in and about Blandings Castle that
the chronicler, in order to give a square deal to each of the individuals whose
fortunes he has undertaken to narrate, is compelled to flit abruptly from one
to the other in the manner popularized by the chamois of the Alps leaping
from crag to crag. The activities of the Efficient Baxter seeming to him to
demand immediate attention, he was reluctantly compelled some little while
back to leave Hugo in the very act of reeling beneath a crushing blow. The
moment has now come to return to him.[17]

Wodehouse is, of course, a master craftsman and uses his devices
very cleverly, and, by explaining to the reader that he is using a
clumsy coupling method, raises an otherwise weak means of transition to a level of humor. By laughing at himself he compels us to laugh
with him.

Greek language has a fondness for parallel action or alternation.
This is expressed by *men . . . de*, two particles which might be
rendered "on the one hand . . . on the other hand." I do not know
what percentage of sentences in Greek literature utilizes this device
of symmetry, but it is a sizable percentage. It appears that either the
Greek mind or the language, or both, has a powerful attraction for
this technique of alternation, parallelism, symmetry. It is there in the
language, and Xenophon extends its use to the larger structure.

Once Xenophon has determined to write a novel of love and travel,
and once the two lovers have been geographically separated, he is
compelled to write a *men . . . de* novel. It is impossible to know
what element influenced Xenophon more strongly. In the middle
section of the novel (2.8–5.13) which contains the episodes of the
lovers' separation, Hägg reports that there are thirty-two "narrative
shifts," eighteen of which occur immediately between Anthia and
Habrocomes. Xenophon's love of symmetry is revealed by his allot-
ment of the same number of narrative units to both Anthia and
Habrocomes: eleven.[18]

Though these alternations are patently necessary to the plot,
Xenophon makes no attempt to soften the transitions. In fact, he uses
set phrases when he shifts from one character to another and stresses
the point of transition as though it were some kind of epic *formula*.
Xenophon's structure of alternation offers him a golden opportunity
to build on the emotion of suspense in his novel: he could leave one
character in a precarious position as he switches to another character,
in much the same fashion as television "soap operas" operate. As he

does, however, in the sections of foreboding, Xenophon resolves each unit before he brings on the parallel.[19] Anthia's sections conclude after her chastity has been assured; Habrocomes' after his resolve to continue to search. The alternation is handled so nonchalantly that it appears to be a function of the language rather than a conscious literary device.

E. Recapitulations

Ancient classical literature like eighteenth- and nineteenth-century classical music recognizes and uses a device called recapitulation. From the earliest Greek literature to the end of the classical world we find this device.[20] Upon returning home after twenty years, Odysseus recounts for his wife Penelope the highlights of his adventures since he saw her last (Homer, *Odyssey* 23. 310–41). From 800 B.C., when Homer wrote, until the first century A.D., when Chariton wrote, we can find extant examples of recapituation. Chariton recapitulates his past adventures near the end of his novel (8.7–8) because, like Homer, he is compelled by dramatic necessity. While the reader of Chariton has been dragged through each event, the friends and relatives of Chaereas and Callirhoe, the protagonists of Chariton's novel, back in Syracuse are ignorant of their adventures and desirous of hearing about them. In order to keep his novel at a distance from himself and at the same time internally consistent, Chariton has Chaereas recapitulate his adventures.

The modern reader does not much appreciate recapitulations in fiction because for him it is simply a rehashing of material he plowed through only several hours before. When encountering recapitulations in epic (I assume people still read epic literature), modern readers identify the device as "a mark of the epic." Since epics were recited by traveling bards (so the reasoning goes), the listener needed recapitulations to substitute for his inability to refer back in the text to something covered yesterday. Chariton uses the epic device as he does a couple of dozen quotations from Homer: to associate his work with epic and to mark his writings as literarily allusive.

Recapitulations are recognized by Quintilian (*Institutio Oratoria* 6.1) as useful devices in summations of speeches, a practice which continues to our own day in courtrooms. We recognize it for what it is in ancient epics, but appreciate it in ancient courtrooms because the custom has not changed. There are also recapitulations in ancient novels, a usage which unsettles us because it is extremely rare in

modern prose fiction. In Xenophon (see chapter 2 above) there are
frequent recapitulations, produced by Habrocomes and Anthia at
regular intervals throughout their separation, as they complain about
their unhappy fate. Like Chariton, but in much briefer fashion,
Xenophon's two young lovers provide a reconciliatory recapitulation
of their past adventures, each filling in for the other what he/she could
not have known. Habrocomes and Anthia later make the ultimate in
concrete recapitulations (5.15), when they set up an inscription re-
cording on some permanent material the history of their adventures.

Though other ancient novelists do not offer as many or as formal a
group of recapitulations as Xenophon, Chariton (3.8; 8.7–8), Achilles
Tatius (5.18), and others do, from time to time, sum up affairs. We
might ask why? The intent of these recapitulations, which usually
recount suffering, is, on one level, to affect the reader's emotions by
juxtaposing in rapid fire disaster next to disaster. Because of the large
number of episodes and because, for much of the novel there is a
bifurcated plot, recapitulations serve, on a second level, to keep the
involved incidents straight and clear. Hägg suggests several more
reasons for the recapitulations: [21] the material in the novels is completely new to the reader (unlike drama) who is accustomed to meet
stories about which he knew at least the general outlines; the audience for the novels was not a learned group, perhaps more listener
than reader; the audience may have heard the novel in serial fashion
(not likely, as Hägg admits, since Xenophon does not let any episode
end in suspense, a procedure which would have brought the audience back for more).

Many of the recapitulations appear "forced" into the narrative,
extraneous, and unnatural. Generally they are not justified by the
action at hand or the needs of the characters. One recapitulation,
however, stands out as structurally sound and integrated into the
action. At 3.9 an old woman named Chrysion tells the story of Anthia
and Perilaus to those sitting around Hippothous' camp. It is a natural
setting, which the reader has visited before, and it is natural that
someone should tell a story just at bedtime. This recapitulation not
only surveys past events for the reader, but also brings to light for
Habrocomes and Hippothous new information which they will need
to continue their search for Anthia. The device here is doubly infor-
mative. A similarly natural recapitulation is found at 2.12 where
Lampo, confronted by Habrocomes, narrates the life of Anthia,
Manto, Moeris, and his own "marriage" to Anthia. Nothing new is
added to the narrative by this recapitulation, but its presence at this

point brings Habrocomes up to date and gives him a reason to continue to search —a search which continues the story.

F. Narrative Techniques

In 1971 Tomas Hägg published the most comprehensive and searching inquiry into narrative technique in Chariton, Xenophon, and Achilles Tatius. In the fashion of a brief survey I would like to mention a few of the more important conclusions and results of his study. By "more important" I mean those results which characterize the whole of Xenophon as opposed to those for a short episode or minor character.

Something which becomes obvious quickly to the reader of Xenophon is the passivity of the characters. By natural inclination Anthia and Habrocomes are passive, and Xenophon brings this into sharp focus by adding helplessness to passivity and surrounding his young lovers with stronger characters who constantly must come to their aid. In addition, by means of narrative technique, Xenophon frequently keeps his leading characters from speaking for themselves. He is fond of reporting what each character does and thinks, rather than permitting him to express his own feelings directly to the reader. Hägg calculates that in Xenophon direct speech accounts for only 29 percent of the novel (44 percent in Chariton).[22] Time and time again Xenophon summarizes in chronological order, supplying specific names of the actors and the countries they visit, the thoughts and actions of his characters. Too often Xenophon "tells" us; his characters do not "show" us.

Long sections of Xenophon's romance are dominated by pure "summary." . . . There are, it is true, occasionally some large blocks of "scene" with a large percentage of direct speech—notably the monologues or dialogues. . . .[23]

Xenophon's predilection for summarizing turns him from concentrating on selected (seemingly insignificant) details and observations which frequently enlighten the reader as to the basic nature of the characters involved. A few illustrative details about Anthia and Habrocomes would have brought the reader into closer contact with the two than all the representational deeds and words managed.[24] Xenophon describes neither people or things. Hägg observes that Xenophon draws a picture for his readers of only one object, the canopy over the bridal bed (1.8), and the reader is so surprized to find even this one description that he considers it a "digression." [25] We know nothing about the little habits of Anthia or Habrocomes, the little things Anthia keeps in her case of toiletries, or the kinds of clothes the young lovers like: "Gossip is more interesting than fiction—even to the literati." [26]

Xenophon provides little background scenery or local color. Modern travelers upon sighting a Greek temple frequently attempt to wax poetic; Xenophon, though he takes his characters into numerous temples, is (strangely) silent about their appearance, history, or visitors. The parade to the temple of Artemis, which is one of the rare bits of "tableau" offered by Xenophon, takes place at the very beginning of the novel and is, consequently, deceptive because so little will follow. [27] The wedding episode (1.7–8), the attack by pirates (1.14), and the necrophiliac love affair (5.1) represent the best attempts at local color.

Like an uninterested newspaperman Xenophon gives the reader the bare facts of the story. He refuses to offer his own commentary on events, but does allow from time to time his characters to step forward and comment. During these commentaries the progress of the story stops, for the direct speech of the characters never introduces new material. In monologues of bitter complaint the characters lay some few of their psychological stresses open to view by the reader, but many more of these are served up to the reader in summaries by the author.

III   *Survey of Xenophon's Roots*

The real proof of the literary pudding is in the eating thereof. It is perfectly proper to look at the recipe the cook says she followed, to take into account the ingredients she used, to examine her intentions to make a certain kind of pudding, and her care in preparing it—or her carelessness. But the prime fact for judging will still be the pudding itself. The tasting, the eating, the experience is what finally counts. [28]

The origins of the ancient novel are unknown and likely to remain so. In this section I intend to offer only a brief survey of the theories about the origins of the ancient novel and some biographical information about these theories, and then to conclude with observations about the importance of New Comedy for the novel. I do not know how important a study of the ancient novel's origins really is; surely not as important as a study of the text. All too often scholars writing on the novel are in fact historians of its origins; my faults are in a way opposite those. A look into the novel's origins will call down on our heads the New Critics' charge of "intentional fallacy" and "biographical fallacy."

There are many theories about the novel's origins, and at the very outset I will reveal my prejudices by stating that I believe (with B. P. Reardon and others) that New Comedy had a significant influence on the writers of the extant Greek novels. Before I list some of the more widely accepted theories on the origin and development of the form of the novel, I would like to list a series of disclaimers:

Such forms (as the Greek novel) . . . never come into being as the result of an evolutionary process. . . .[29]

What the old form (any forerunner of the new novel) supplies is not motivation or causation, or inspiration, but only a loose structural pattern and building materials. . . .[30]

The analogy of biological evolution is false and misleading . . . because it ignores the human will . . . to create new forms . . . in response to its own spiritual or intellectual needs.[31]

Thus Rohde devoted, irrelevantly, some 275 pages of his great book on the Greek romance to what he called *Vorläufer*, these being the authors of Alexandrian erotic poetry on the one hand and, on the other, those who . . . had written about travel in strange lands; because the principal parts of romance . . . were supposed to be love and travel. Formula: Divide the mature literary product into parts and say all you can about the previous history of each.[32]

Rohde's "great book," *Der griechische Roman*, first published in 1876, remained for years preeminent in the field until discoveries of papyri disproved his dating system of the novels and discredited much else. The popularity and influence of Rohde's work was demonstrated in 1976 by an international conference on the ancient novel, held to commemorate the centenary of its publication. Rohde compiled a lot of information, but as Perry says (see above quotation), much of it is irrelevant to the origin of the novel. The novel is more than a literary "concoction by sophists" of travel and love elements.[33] He fails to take into account the "spiritual or intellectual needs" of the age and its audiences and also the creative forces behind the authors.

In 1896 Schwartz placed the novel in a literary setting without actually speculating about the origins of the form.[34] He did, however, seem to indicate that the writing of history had some influence on the development of the novel. Certain works like the *Ninus Romance*, the *Romance of Alexander*, and Xenophon of Athens' *Cyropaedia*, which mingle history and fiction, added to works like Ctesias' (fl. 400 B.C.) *History of Persia* and *History of India*—which are frequently called "tragic histories"—appear to have some influence on Chariton's novel, which sets itself up as a kind of (fictionalized) history of two young lovers from Syracuse. The lovers are otherwise unknown from history, but the young woman's father is a famous general. Novelists, it might be said, used certain elements of historiography to make their new genre more acceptable. Novelists, in the beginning at least, so this theory goes, thought to cloak themselves with the respectability of historiography and biography. In overly simplified form, the novel evolves (some would say degenerates) from historiography and from historiography's stepchild, biography. Xenophon of Athens' *Cyropaedia* (*Education of Cyrus*) only masquerades as historical biography, when in fact it is fiction with didactic overtones. The intent, however, is not, as it is with Xenophon of Ephesus, to entertain the reader. Exactly how history and biography are subverted to novels is not explained by the proponents of this theory. From an interest in information and teaching there is a big leap to entertainment.

In the case of the *Romance of Alexander*, Martin Braun[35] argues that the legend and romance of Alexander evolve *into* history not *from* history:

> From its beginning as legend it rose to the level of uncritical history and thence to romance. Since much of ancient history was uncritical, the legend and the romance of Alexander were taken for history. This theory is all the more acceptable if Braun is right when he says that the legend grew up around, and belonged spiritually and socially to, the common people, who did not differentiate between history in the written form and literary fiction.[36]

John Barns is also interested in the influence of historiography on the Greek novels, but he believes "that the Greek romance developed . . . in Egypt rather than in Greece." [37] The hero of the *Dream of Nectanebus* is involved in episodes of love and of travel, as is Habrocomes. The *Dream* appears to come from second century B.C. Egypt, and was translated from demotic Egyptian into Greek. Barns suggests that the romance is imported into Greece from Egypt where it had had a considerable previous history "before one example was translated into Greek." [38]

J. W. H. Atkins, writing in the *Oxford Classical Dictionary*, seems quite secure in claiming that *progymnasmata*, "exercises . . . in schools of rhetoric" on various whimsical subjects, ". . . prepared the way for Greek romances."[39] Some fifty years earlier Bornecque had proposed that *controversiae*, colored speeches full of improbable situations or plots (similar, I must say, in improbability to the plots of some of the Greek novels) written for imaginary courtrooms, lay at the origin of the Greek novel.[40] Atkins and Bornecque are suggesting that these rhetorical practice devises are, in fact, the earliest forms of the novels and represent a kind of storehouse of ready plots. (Haight and Perry describe some of these *controversiae*, from which it is possible to judge their use as novel plots.[41]) Perry offers some caustic words about the likelihood of the novel having developed in this way.

A similar development, but from a different source, is postulated by Giangrande.[42] By focusing on the erotic elements in the novel and not on the episodes of adventure, the scholar, he believes, is closer to the heart and origin of the novel:

> the *Leitmotiv*, the essential nucleus of the romance is the story of two lovers, be it diluted and lengthened by means of adventurous accretions.[43]

Giangrande sees the love-elegy (e.g., Callimachus' *Acontius and Cydippe*) as the probable ultimate source of the novel. The immediate source, he claims, is the prose paraphrases of these love-elegies. A large collection of mythological tales called *Erotica Pathemeta*, suitable as subject matter in elegies and so, according to Giangrande and Gaselee, for novels, written by Parthenius (first century B.C.), is extant today. "Take away the strictly mythological element (substitute, that is, the names of unknown persons for the semi–historical characters of whom the stories are related), and almost all might serve as the plots for novels. . . ."[44] All arguments to support this theory arise from within literary history without even a nod toward the possible influence of individual inspiration or social conditions.

Some scholars hold that new forms of literature arise on the ruins or in the breakup of previous forms. Among these scholars are Scholes and Kellogg who confine their inquiries into literature to generic studies and literary structuralism and, in applying their methodology to the ancient novel, have determined that its origin lay in the epic. Though the possible influence of epic on Xenophon is surely less than on Chariton, it might still be useful for a generic study to state this theory of origin:

. . . in the epic (there exists) a synthesis of elements which, destroyed, yields two antithetical kinds of narrative, the fictional and the empirical. When epic storytellers are no longer interested in the "traditional story" or the *mythos* but are concerned more with entertainment (fiction) or truth (history), they cease to produce epics, and the form dies . . . as the empirical (real) narrative emerges from the epic synthesis it assumes two forms: the historical and the mimetic; as the fictional (ideal) emerges it takes two forms: the romantic and the didactic (fables). The ideal (fictional) part of the epic synthesis is the part that concerns our study. The writer . . . breaks first with traditional stories (epics) and then sets his writing (the ideal) in opposition to the empirical (the real, history). His search for "truth" takes him along artistic roads not scientific, and his world is ruled by poetic and artistic justice, not the cold reality of law and cosmic order. The intent of the writer of fiction is to delight (romance) or edify (fable).[45]

The most comprehensive approaches to the origins of the ancient novel have been put forward by Lavagnini [46] and Perry. Perry himself provides the best comments and description of Lavagnini's work and his own approach:

With Lavagnini I find myself in almost complete agreement insofar as concerns the main points in his thesis . . . he emphasized the originally humble and demotic character . . . he identified the spiritual values embodied in these romances as something peculiar to the cultural outlook of Hellenistic times . . . he demonstrated . . . that the early erotic romances were in many cases built upon local historical legends or myths.[47]

The virtue of Perry's work stems, it seems to me, from his comprehensive view of the development of the ancient novel.[48] He does not exclude from his study any of the theories I have just surveyed. No single one of them, however, does he believe can account for the rise of the novel. The literary forms which preceded the novel surely had some influence, as did the nature of the content of those forms. Perry goes to great lengths, after acknowledging the influence of the past, to point out that the creative will and intent of a writer in a social condition is still needed to turn available forms and content into a novel: "every piece of literature, strictly considered, is *sui generis* and represents a distinct literary form of its own. . . ."[49] Though consideration of genre and origins takes up the first ninety-two pages of his great work on the ancient novel, Perry places the emphasis for the rise of the novel in antiquity on the needs and intentions of individual writers.

Simply put, Perry's thesis on the origin of the novel contains the following items: (1) the novel has an originator rather than an origin, (2) who for some reason intends to write a work to entertain an audience, (3) who is sensitive to currents of all kinds in the Hellenistic age but who purposely cuts his work loose from any particular historical or political setting or meaning, and (4) who makes use of literary works close at hand, particularly those of drama and history. In the years of the developing novel, the writing of history had turned toward fiction to help embellish the bare facts, and, as others have shown, the drama of the *polis* and a closed society had given way to the New Comedy of the individual.[50] The novel has the content of New Comedy and the form of a history.

"Now this outline of New Comedy is not very far from summarizing the standard plot of the Greek novel."[51] Using Reardon's observation as a point of departure, I would like to catalogue certain similarities I find between New Comedy and the ancient novel, which, while not responsible for the creation of the novel, was available to its creators.

Early in his standard work on New Comedy George Duckworth observes that "the basis of each play is a love story. . . ."[52] As it is in the novels, the basic plot is simple and straightforward: two lovers wish to get together. The plots, however, become complicated and confusing by the addition of numerous episodes and new characters. The young lovers are usually unmarried but trying to marry in New Comedy (and in Heliodorus, Longus, Achilles Tatius) and this determines the structure. In Menander's *Epitrepontes*, as in Chariton and Xenophon, the lovers are already married and then separated. After a series of episodes in both of the above plot variations, the lovers marry. The young lovers (they are never middle-aged) are frequently neighbors or from the same town, and do not discover each other on their wanderings in foreign places. Anthropologists tell us that primitive tribes frequently require their young people to marry within the tribe. The further the hero or heroine moves away from home and the familiar, the more exotic become the adventures. Whether male or female, one usually marries a neighbor.

The young persons in Greek novels and in New Comedy fall in love at first sight, and throughout each work protestations of love or faithfulness occupy an influential position. In both genres, moreover, it happens that the young fall in love at religious festivals, but the new lovers in New Comedy do not usually stop there. The young girl is seduced or perhaps raped, and when the baby is born, the hero consents to marriage. In all of this, the content and the structure of both the novels and of the New Comedies are built more on the episodes (between the unstable beginning and the denouement) consequent upon love rather than on love itself.

"But with all their faults, real or imaginary, there is one vice of which the wives in comedy are not guilty—infidelity." [53] Not all the wives in ancient novels are faithful, but all female protagonists certainly are, and in this respect they are parallel delineations. The heroes in Longus and Achilles Tatius resemble many of the young men who experiment sexually with several women but would not tolerate such actions among the girls they consider marrying. While there is no "double standard" in Xenophon, it is there in others. This double standard of New Comedy and some of the novels (and most of society) is described nicely by the courtesan Bacchis in a little talk to a proper young woman (*Heauton Tim.* 388–95, a comedy by the Roman playwright Terence, 195–159 B.C.):

It's to your advantage to be good. The men with whom we deal won't let us be; our lovers cherish us because they are won over by our beauty; when that is gone they transfer their affections elsewhere and, unless we've provided for ourselves meanwhile, we're left forlorn. But when you women have decided to spend your life with one man whose character is as like your own as possible, you find husbands devoted to you, and you are both bound so closely by mutual love that no disaster can ever separate you. [54]

This very positive view of the practical value of marriage is identical to the one Xenophon portrays in his novel, and about which I have spoken elsewhere in this chapter. The same attitude toward the practical value of virginity and chastity which the reader sees in Xenophon is also operative in New Comedy. The cries of outrage voiced so often by Anthia, who claims that her chaste life should warrant better treatment than shipwreck in the company of pirates are echoes from New Comedy (Palaestra, shipwrecked but freed from pirates, speaks in the *Rudens* of Plautus, 254–184 B.C., lines 187 ff):

> . . . What have I done
> That the gods should treat me thus? Cast me ashore
> Like this in an unknown country? Oh poor me,
> Is this what I was born for? What a reward
> For my good life!
> . . . .
> Now there's no hope, no help, no one to turn to. . . .
> . . . .

> Oh father and mother, if you only knew
> Where your poor daughter is, and what she suffers.[55]

And when difficulties multiply, the heroine of New Comedy, as Anthia does so often, threatens suicide (Palaestra in *Rudens* 674–75):

> If this must be our lot,
> If this our fate,
> 'Twere better far to die.
> Ay, death is best;
> In our great misery
> 'Tis best to die.[56]

New Comedy in Plautus' hands is a robust and lusty expression of life. Young men seduce virgin slaves and free girls with a good deal of abandon, though all can be set right through marriage in the last act. The opening encounters between the young man and woman show a lack of sensitivity and respect of the man for the woman. Terence refines Roman New Comedy and, in building on the model of the Athenian playwright Menander (342–291 B.C.), develops personal relationships, which much later we will call "courtly":

Charinus (a character in Terence's *Andria*) is the first example in·European literature of a youth pining with honorable affection for a maiden of equal station.[57]

It is exactly this courtly attitude between young lovers which appears in the Greek novel.

As I have pointed out earlier, the slaves of Anthia and Habrocomes, Rhode and Leucon, are better able to cope with difficulties in life than are their masters. The *servus callidus* (clever slave) is an important motif in New Comedy, and frequently he is a leading character giving life to the story. An analysis of Xenophon's novel demonstrates that Rhode and Leucon are vitally important to the reunion of the young lovers. Slaves in both Xenophon and in New Comedy are usually "types," fairly predictable role-players rather than well-pointed individuals.

Much of what little direct speech there is in Xenophon is given over to monologues. Duckworth calculates that monologues in Roman New Comedy are likewise page-consuming: 17 percent in Plautus and 12 percent in Terence.[58] Monologues in both New Comedy and in Xenophon are frequently complaints about (supposed) injustices, not a few of which are directed to deities. In both literary genres monologues open up the inner character to the audience's view. Unfortunately, once opened to view, these characters reveal only their persecution complex. Each of the characters in New Comedy and in the novel knows certain facts of the plot, misunderstands others, and is unaware of still others. The audience of New Comedy like the reader of Xenophon knows all, and the ensuing superiority is a form of irony.

Finally, I would like to mention for New Comedy, as I have in chapter 2 and in section II of this chapter for Xenophon, the pervasive use of pairs:

> Contrasting pairs of characters appear with great frequency in the comedies of Plautus . . . two *senes*, two young men, two sweethearts, or two slaves serve as foils to each other. . . . The use of such balanced pairs is even more characteristic of Terence. . . .[59]

The whole question of the relationship between the ancient novel and the mystery religions is taken up in section VII of this chapter.

IV   *Novels and Romances*

When I ask myself, "What is that literary creation?" I believe that I am searching not so much for a definition as a distinguishing name: "That literary creation is a novel." But I do the same thing in other spheres of life. While walking through a field or woods I ask, "What is that animal?" and I seek something like, "That animal is an otter." This approach helps me to learn the distinguishing names of animals, trees, and flowers; through it, however, I can avoid defining. I believe, nevertheless, that there is a need to find a distinguishing name, a designation, because in that search a common experience or perception is realized: we learn from each other's search that something exists and that we can share in the appreciation of that existence. We have established some order, a shared order, and following from that an aesthetic.

Throughout these pages I employ the term "novel" for Xenophon's work and avoid the term "romance" because of the negative connotations attached to the latter. Nowadays romances are generally viewed as belonging to a subliterary genre of "lightweight commercial fiction deliberately written to flatter day dreams. Such 'romances' batten on the emotionally impoverished."[60] On the other hand, the "very word 'novel' has become a term of praise when applied to earlier narratives." [61] In addition simply to being a descriptive term, novel, like realism, has become an evaluative one. Critics do not *describe* Xenophon as unrealistic and Petronius as realistic, they *evaluate* them with those terms. The influence of Auerbach [62] and others to convince us that the whole of Western literature can be summed up as a striving for realism has been so great that we now jumble descriptive and evaluative terms.

The term romance was attached first to narratives written in the vernacular languages (as opposed to Latin) and from these passed over, on the Continent, to mean long prose fiction, as opposed to short (*nouvelle*). The problem of the terms novel–romance exists only in English. In German, for example, a novel is called *ein Roman*. The novel is surely the most widely read genre in literature today, but what publishers call novels might be further subsumed under mysteries, science fiction, westerns, spy thrillers, satire, historical novels, Gothic novels, or detective stories. What is usually meant by applying the word novel to a work is the same as applying realistic. A problem arises if we establish the realistic novel as a kind of perfect Platonic Form, since such action would cut us off from the narrative literature of the past even as "it cuts us off from the literature of the future and even from the advance guard of our own day." [63] Many of the finest novelists of this century, like Joyce, Nin, and Faulkner, have broken away from the recent traditions of realism and begun to experiment with techniques alien to the standard realists.

Perhaps the spectrum of narrative prose fiction is a wide band with the relatively unrealistic variety occupying the left wing and realistic naturalism (the potato with dirt on it) the right. The difference between romance and novel is, then, one of intensity not kind. What strikes us as unrealistic in Xenophon probably offended some of his audience as being too realistic in the second century A.D. The difference lies in the perspective more than in the fact. In the *Art of Fiction* Henry James illustrates "clumsy separations" by pointing to the "celebrated distinction between the novel and the romance." No less a literary pathologist than Northrop Frye can dissect the beast no further than to say: " 'Pure' examples of either (i.e. novel or romance) form are never found. . . . The forms of prose fiction are mixed . . . a romantic novel just romantic enough for the reader to project his libido on the hero and his anima on the heroine, and just novel enough to keep these projections in a familiar world." [64] But Frye can articulate differences much more carefully than that and, when he does, shows an appreciation for the "unrealistic": "The essential difference between novel and romance lies in the conception of characterization. The romance does not attempt to create 'real people' so much as stylized figures which expand into psychological archetypes. . . . That is why the romance so often radiates a glow of subjective intensity that the novel lacks, and why a suggestion of allegory is constantly creeping in around the fringes." [65]

While wrestling with the problems of categorizing the various types of prose fiction, Gillian Beer admits that "There is no single characteristic which distinguishes the romance from other literary kinds. . . ." [66] Beer is not concerned with putting Xenophon into a slot but with characterizing a kind of prose fiction. Romance, according to Beer, should exhibit a "cluster of properties": themes of love and adventure; a certain withdrawal of reader and hero from their own societies; simple—but with allegorical significance—heroes; mix of the unexpected with the usual; series of episodes without any climaxes; a happy ending; an enforced code of conduct. I find this a helpful list and a good point of departure for discussing ancient prose fiction. Some of the ancient novels exhibit these properties and others do not. That is a problem with lists.

Using an approach and criteria articulated by Paul Turner for establishing that Longus' *Daphnis and Chloe* was a novel and not something else, I would like to argue the same points for Xenophon.[67]

1.   The plot of Xenophon is quasi-historical (the record of it is taken, we are led to believe, from the temple of Artemis in Ephesus) rather than traditional (the plot, while including traditional elements, is drawn more from life than from literature—a record of universal fact of human experience).

Xenophon writes a stylized and patterned story, yet by adding names of specific government officials and specific geographical information he tries to make it believable and to keep it within the limits of the possible. While the hero, heroine, and their slaves are modeled to a certain extent on earlier literary creations, there are individual elements and experiences which Xenophon adapts from things he knows or has heard about. This is particularly true for characters like Hippothous, Aigialeus, and Bitch and for the scenes of violence and cruelty. Many experiences are specific, unusual, and do not appear as motifs in earlier literature.

2.   Record of the experience, often private, subjective experience of individuals.

The names of the characters in Xenophon are not common names: Anthia, Habrocomes, Hippothous, Perilaus, Manto, Bitch. Some of the names are used to indicate the character or physical description of the one named, but they are not stock names. Xenophon is clearly attempting to convey to his readers that the girl named Anthia (little bud, the fresh one) and Habrocomes (soft-haired) are doomed to have trouble with a lecherous and mean woman named Bitch. If any characters conform to stock characters, the hero and heroine come closest. The most individualistic and in a way the most cleverly delineated actors are those in minor or supporting roles. One of them, Hippothous, shows a kind of character development. Feeling that he had been mistreated by society, he became a brigand, more interested in harming the establishment than in acquiring its wealth by stealing. By the good example and faithfulness of Habrocomes he returns to his former law-abiding nature and makes peace with the world. The role of model human beings, examples of what young people can be, is perhaps a function Xenophon has in mind for his leading characters. There is an area for character development among minor players, who can be drawn as differently from each other as Xenophon wishes. The result is most interesting: we get a fisherman who sleeps with his dead wife; a heterosexual and his homosexual friend who agree to divide up, each according to his taste, Anthia and Habrocomes; a wife who kills her husband (in a love triangle) in order to run off with a younger and more handsome man; a doctor who delivers a simple sleeping potion to a young girl to protect her, although he knows she wants a poison for suicide.

Xenophon relates for us the very private and particularized experiences of the hero and heroine on their wedding night, and until the very end of the novel has his characters give voice in monologues to their innermost fear, doubts, and anxieties, and sometimes even their schemes.

3.   The action unfolds in a context of particularized time and place.

There is never any question about the exact location of the action of the story. Xenophon is very careful, it seems, to tell the reader exactly where all his characters are, from where they have come, and where they are headed. In the opening chapters Xenophon goes so far as to give exact distances of journeys. Likewise there is no doubt that the date of writing is some time after Anthia and Habrocomes had returned from their journeys and told all about their trials. We are, it seems, to understand that Xenophon got his story from the temple in Ephesus, and that it is in a way a true personal adventure with the usual fictional embellishments, acceptable and encouraged as additions to make the story more interesting.

4. Realistic particularity appears both in the narrative and in the characterization.

Xenophon appears to be interested in realistic description at almost every point, even when he is weaving a tale which some would describe as science fiction, and others as a miracle. Habrocomes is saved from crucifixion by a wind which blows his cross down and into the Nile, which then carries him to a kind of safety. Next, Habrocomes is condemned to be burned but is saved by the Nile river which rises, floods the bank, and puts out the fire. The episode in which Xenophon relates the murder of Araxus by his wife, Bitch, and her attempts to seduce Habrocomes, who is absolutely repelled by what she has done and by the thought of betraying Anthia, is set out in realistic detail.

The characters remain constant and true to form in what might be termed almost a tragic scene. We know that Habrocomes must refuse Bitch and that the lecherous woman will attack Habrocomes, especially after she has killed her husband. The swift and inhumane punishment of Bitch by the authorities is also graphic. In scenes like this characters are portrayed with the detail and particularity necessary to make them almost memorable.

Beginning at 1.15 Anthia and Habrocomes are entangled in a web of erotic attachments, the complexity of which is not very probable. These incredibly complicated sexual relations strike the reader at first as far-fetched and far from the reality of a novel; but biographies of modern, famous people make Xenophon's characters seem almost believable. I quote below from Sandra Darroch's *Ottoline: The Life of Lady Ottoline Morrell* (square brackets contain notes of the present writer):

But serene in mind at that moment Ottoline was not. She had gone down to Studland to await the arrival of Russell [Bertrand Russell, third Earl Russell, Nobel laureate 1950, who at this time, 1911, was still married to Alys], with whom she was maintaining an emotion-charged correspondence. Henry Lamb [an English portrait painter who gave his mistress Dorelia McNeill to his teacher Augustus John only to have Dorelia move into John's house which was still occupied by his wife and children; John's wife died and Dorelia took charge of John's children by his wife as well as those by herself. At this juncture Lamb's official mistress was still Helen Maitland, who would later become Boris Anrep's (a friend of Ottoline) mistress and then wife, before running off with Roger Fry, a friend and sometimes lover of Ottoline's] was hovering nearby at Corfe and Philip [Philip Morrell, Ottoline's husband] was due as soon as Russell's promised three days were up. Logan Pearsall Smith [a friend of Philip's and Ottoline's, an American, and homosexual; his sister Alys was married to Russell and, upon learning of Russell's affair with Ottoline, tried to ruin him] was also in the vicinity, as yet unsuspecting. Now, to further complicate a tangled skein of relationships, here was Fry [Roger Fry, noted art critic, member of the "Bloomsbury Group," fresh from a short affair with Ottoline and about to enter a long liaison with Vanessa Stephen, wife of Clive Bell and sister of Virginia Woolf] pouring out love letters from the East. No wonder Ottoline complained of headaches.[68]

The affairs of Ottoline and her friends, which were very real, would make fantastic reading, were they set into a novel. The basic events, then, surrounding Anthia and Habrocomes, if placed in a proper perspective, are not at all outside the circumference of the novel.

5.   The narrative structure is founded not on coincidence but on causal connection.

If one believes that there is no deity or guiding principle who directs in some fashion or other the affairs of men, nature, or the universe, then it follows that much of what happens in life (and hence in realistic novels) happens by chance. And one chance happening may set off a whole string of events connected causally to each other. One of the marks of contemporary novels as opposed to ancient prose fiction is that causal relationships in a series of events are substituted for chance happenings and coincidences. This is seen as an aspect of reality. But if one believes that some kind of deity or an anthropomorphized type of Fate has a directing influence on life and actions, then apparently chance events are not really fortuitous, but the results of the will of some mover. This latter world is the one that Xenophon writes about. I do not believe that he sees his novel as a form containing a sequence of fortuitous happenings. There is a direction and purpose. It must be added, however, that this approach yields for us only an outer cohesiveness and that an inner linking is missing from much of the narrative.

It may be that Xenophon, sensing that he needs something to bind the work into a kind of whole, places the response of the oracle, which outlines in some detail the course of future events, at the very beginning of the story. If an oracle can foresee and tell a series of events leading from sorrow at the beginning to happiness at the end, the characters in the story and the reader (or listeners) are able to perceive at least a kind of relationship, if not a cohesiveness, among the events.

6. The language is mostly referential rather than ornate.

The language of Xenophon is so inornate that as Turner points out "Xenophon . . . gives the impression of being almost illiterate." If Xenophon has any skill in the verbal arts, it does not come through in his novel, e.g., according to Scobie's count Chariton has forty-nine similes, Achilles Tatius one hundred and ten, and Xenophon only four.[69] I would hazard a guess that an ancient author is forced to make a special effort in suppressing traditional impulses, if he is to use only four similes in a piece of creative fiction.

In one of his studies on the ancient novel Scobie compares the ancient novel with the modern.[70] He is not as positive about the narrative qualities of Greek prose fiction as Turner is or I am. Scobie begins his study by classifying the works of ancient prose fiction. What I call novels, he terms romances:

I.   Short Stories
     A.   Comic, realistic: Aristides' *Milesiaca* and Sisenna's Latin transla-
          tion (adaption?) thereof in thirteen books or more
     B.   Tragic, sentimental: Parthenius' *Erotica Pathemata*; Pseudo-
          Plutarch's *Narrationes Amatoriae*
     C.   Marvellous: Lucian's *Philopseudes*
II. Romances:
     A.   Romances of marvels: Antonius Diogenes' *Wonders Beyond Thule*;
          "Lucius of Patrae's" *Metamorphoses*; Apuleius' *Metamorphoses*;
          Pseudo-Lucian's *Asinus*
     B.   Sentimental romances: Chariton, Iamblichus, Xenophon of Eph-
          esus, Achilles Tatius, Heliodorus
     C.   Pastoral romances: Longus
     D.   Rogue romances: Petronius
     E.   Epistolary romances: Chion of Heraclea

While I disagree with Scobie's use of the term romance, I cite above his outline of the works of ancient prose fiction because he has arranged them very neatly into subcategories which are illustrative of the thrust of each work. To compare and contrast contemporary novels with ancient prose fiction, Scobie chooses Achilles Tatius and Hemingway's *A Farewell to Arms*. The observations he makes about the sentimental ancient novel, after comparing it with the modern, are enlightening, though somewhat too generalized and not repre- sentative of all the novels.

1.   rigid story-pattern in all examples
2.   love is not an end product of growth, but always love at first sight

3. heroine must be a virgin
4. episodic structure with plot not tightening as climax nears
5. narratives do not reflect contemporary social conditions
6. moral viewpoint sees only good or bad
7. dearth of sustained dialogues
8. protagonists are wealthy, beautiful, and morally flawless
9. all characters use the same level of speech
10. ancient novelist is always a teacher of values

Because of these narrative elements Scobie feels confident in calling the production which uses them a romance; a production which employs the opposite is a novel.

V   *The World of Xenophon*

This section is a kind of *Anhang* or codicil to the previous section, which discussed whether the work of Xenophon was representative (and so a novel) of the real world or illustrative (and so a romance) of it. The discussion and arguments for or against either position were almost exclusively literary, i.e., within the context of literature and its own world.

Of all the extant writings from the ancient world, the histories, political speeches, biographies, letters, inscriptions, and graffiti are generally considered the *Realien*, the life and thought from antiquity. Most scholars hold that the ancient novels are meaningless because they "shortcircuit meaning by keeping [the] referential potential within the context of the narrative."[71] Since Classical scholarship is generally in pursuit of the history of the ancient world and only tangentially of the criticism of its creative literature, the ancient novels have been dismissed as useless—the equivalent term among historians to the literary critics' meaningless.

A few scholars (B. P. Reardon, A. Scarcella, E. L. Bowie), however, will argue that there is something beyond literary merit in Xenophon's work:

The Greek novels are very distinctly an expression of the society of the times; they are far from being, as sometimes seems to be thought, inexplicable and insignificant outcrops of subliterary material related to nothing in particular.[72]

The world of Xenophon is the eastern Mediterranean area of the Roman Empire, an Empire so vast as to be incomprehensible to the

average person. There had never before been anything like it, and
individual men paled before its power. Xenophon on some level
appreciates this vast empire and responds to it by writing a novel
about two lovers, who, unable to influence any part of the complex
system, ignore it and turn inward.

It is only in a relatively small world that the individual man can be thought of
as poetically great and heroic. . . . The hero . . . must represent ideal
values that no one questions. . . . This is possible and natural in a relatively
closed society. . . . In the vastly expanded world of Hellenistic and Roman
times the individual lost nearly all his quondam importance . . . having
become too tiny to be tragic, or heroic, or symbolical of anything more than
himself. . . . Faced with the immensity of things and his own helplessness
before them, the spirit of Hellenistic man became passive . . . and he
regarded himself instinctively as a plaything of Fortune. All this is conspi-
cuous from first to last in the Greek romance. [73]

Xenophon's response to this situation comes in the form of a novel.
One man in a room writes a novel; another in his room reads the
novel. The writer in Ephesus can be fully appreciated by the reader
in Alexandria. Unlike Greek epic, tragedy, and Old Comedy, the
novel of Xenophon serves no tribal or civic function. Xenophon's two
lovers are unconcerned for the welfare of Ephesus. While Sophocles'
Antigone is written for an audience which appreciates the *polis*
(city-state), Xenophon writes for a group which sees the Empire only
darkly. If Xenophon's novel conveys to us little hard evidence of
second century society, it at least reports Xenophon's perception of a
society "interested in private more than in public affairs." [74]

Habrocomes and Anthia return to Ephesus at the end of the novel,
not out of any love for or commitment to Ephesus, but because their
parents were there. Xenophon returns the lovers to Ephesus because
it is required by the novel's symmetry. Habrocomes and Anthia seem
at home in every city and country they visit and comfortable with
every new deity they encounter. They are citizens of any place in the
Empire, worshipers of any of its gods, with allegiance only to each
other. When they are separated from each other, they are each
absolutely isolated, though in fact constantly in the company of
others. These "others," however, provide no more meaningful society to the lovers than the desolate rocks and crags of Lemnos did to
Philoctetes.

Reardon makes the observation that fifth century B.C. Greek
tragedy and comedy function as a kind of political (i.e., of the *polis*)

expression, while the later New Comedy, at home in the *polis*, is, nevertheless, apolitical.[75] The Greek novel, in plot and sentimentality a type of descendant of New Comedy, is not only not at home in the *polis*, it is apolitical, personal, and representative of alienated man in the great Empire. The protagonists go through the plot surrounded by total strangers of many nationalities but always as individuals isolated from a political unit. In New Comedy the leading actors are surrounded by friends and relatives. The lovers in the novel wandering all over the eastern Mediterranean are symbolic of politically unattached individuals who can find no way to feel allegiance to an Empire. Travel and love are the two most dominant elements in the Greek novel: travel emphasizes the isolated and wandering lover, beset by strangers and separated from friends; love emphasizes the personal attachment at the expense of the political. Thus the genre of the novel with its elements of travel and love is appropriate for the story Xenophon wishes to tell his audience. The components of the ancient novel fit the tone. As New Comedy is "social myth," so the Greek novel is "personal myth." [76]

Habrocomes and Anthia receive little external personal protection and concern from the larger society and so turn to each other and form their own little society. As Reardon puts it, "unaccommodated man . . . lacking a social identity . . . seeks to create . . . a personal one. . . ." [77] and does so with a woman and transcendental gods. The *Zeitgeist* (mood of the times) which shines through Xenophon's eyes is that of a pair of lovers, aheroic and passive. Habrocomes is far more "resourceless" than Jason in Apollonius of Rhodes' (Greek epic writer in Alexandria who lived in the late third, early second centuries B.C.) *Argonautica*, because Jason has Medea, is, in addition, surrounded by other acquaintances, and is expected by all to be heroic. Society, as set out by Xenophon, encourages Habrocomes to be passive. The passive nature of Habrocomes is apparently something prized by Manto and Bitch—to judge from their eagerness to possess him. Habrocomes aspires to nothing higher than to love Anthia and to live long enough to realize that wish. He is no leader of men, worshipped as some sort of cultural, national hero; in the face of threats, whether from men or women, he regularly grovels and surrenders. He remains, however, the object of erotic attraction, and for that reason acquires importance in the story. Xenophon's chief character is concerned with small matters only, and only as they concern himself. Heroes, by definition, must take into account the opinions of others. Other than preserving himself chaste

for Anthia, Habrocomes has no general, moral principles from which
he speaks or draws guidance. Though he acts shamefully (1.13–1.14)
while his crew and old tutor perish, he feels no pangs of conscience or
guilt for betrayal. What the outside world might think or what the
gods might see does not concern him. It is as if for Habrocomes (and
Xenophon) there were no outside world before whom he should be
ashamed, or collection of deities who would hold him accountable for
his actions.

It is not particularly enlightening to read what acts the various
deities perform. There is such confusion toward the deities, though
the record is straight as to who does what, that attribution of discrete
duties is not always possible. This confusion can also be understood as
caprice: the gods do not offer an ordered world, but rather deal
whimsically with man, whenever they bother to notice at all.
Xenophon's characters, if they could be made to answer readers'
questions, would probably complain that their deities are capricious
and they themselves confused as to what to believe. The modern
reader, recognizing that Xenophon's ancient world is governed too
frequently by chance, will agree with Reardon that "Xenophon's
gods . . . have a penchant for melodrama. . . ." [78]

From the novel of Xenophon we can conclude that the characters,
at least, believe in a pleasant life after death, which lovers could enjoy
together. Both Anthia and Habrocomes pray for death in order to
remain chaste for each other and so to enjoy a better relationship in
the afterlife. While Xenophon does not spell it out, and his characters
do not articulate it in any consistent method, it is clear that there is
some faith in an overall, guiding providence, which, if it does nothing
else, rewards the good (which frequently equates with the chaste) and
punishes the evil (unchaste). The chastity of Anthia is clearly rewarded by reuniting her with a chaste Habrocomes, while the unfaithful Bitch is executed. The emphasis which Anthia and Habrocomes, while separated, place on the afterlife (as it were, almost a
medieval preoccupation with "otherworldliness"), makes them
almost Christian-like, turning the other cheek and awaiting the day
they can join their gods.

When the characters get into trouble, they pray for help from their
gods. They have not abandoned their gods, but are confused as to
which gods can help at which times. In the world of Xenophon's novel
the characters believe the gods can help them here on earth, though
it is not clear that belief in any god or initiation into any rite is a

prerequisite to a happy afterlife. All people seem to be headed for the Elysian Fields—certainly all lovers are.

Xenophon's lack of organization in dealing systematically with distinct deities suggests that (1) he does not understand the nature of ancient religion, (2) he understands it, but it is in such disarray that it defies organization, (3) he handles the material well and subtly in allowing the breakup of ancient religion to speak for itself throughout the story. "Xenophon's . . . gods may be beneficent, but they are singularly crude in their guidance of human affairs, and there is no telling what they will do next." [79]

The novel begins with a religious procession to the temple of Artemis, where the goddess is first honored, then rapidly set aside in favor of Eros. Surely Artemis and Eros are almost opposite forces, and a change from one to the other is not a change of emphasis; it is a radical movement. After Eros has complete control of Habrocomes and Anthia, Apollo, the brother of Artemis, is consulted by the fathers of the young lovers. While this appears to be a somewhat confused chain of events, one might argue that this is a clear and meaningful procession of events: Artemis (goddess of chastity) = thesis; Eros (god of erotic love) = antithesis; Apollo (god of reason) = synthesis and governor of the above two passions.

The puzzling proliferation of deities with important roles to perform continues. We learn from the oracle (1.6) that the Egyptian goddess, Isis, will bring an end to the sufferings of the young lovers and become, in effect, their savior. This deity becomes the fourth one with a major role in the first couple of pages of the novel. A curious parallel to the request for an oracle and the subsequent reply in Xenophon's novel exists in Aeschylus' *Prometheus Bound*. Io and the chorus beg Prometheus, who here has prophetic powers, to disclose the future wanderings of Io. Prometheus agrees and (in lines 786ff) lays out the preordained course of events, which will conclude in Egypt, where Io will find an end to her troubles. Both in Aeschylus and in Xenophon the actors obtain peace in Egypt.

At 4.2 we see Habrocomes rescued from the cross after praying to the Nile and to the sun, and in 5.4 Anthia receives help from Isis. While in the temple of the Sun (5.10) Habrocomes is first recognized; the people of Rhodes, whose patron deity is the sun, gather at the temple of Isis, who is then, for no real reason, praised for the lovers' reunion. The novel concludes (5.15) with the lovers back in Ephesus in the temple of Artemis, giving thanks to her.

Xenophon's characters place a great, almost single-minded, emphasis on chastity. This theme is present whenever either protagonist is on the stage, and before very long the reader understands it properly as an obsession rather than as a virtue. Habrocomes and Anthia are kind, honest, faithful and caring, but only when these approaches are connected to their striving for chastity. They do not see chastity as a quality related to building character. Obsessions with chastity and virginity are to be found in all the other extant ancient Greek novels as well. Xenophon's representation of this aspect of second century A.D. life is quite in keeping with what we can learn from popular Christian documents of the same time (see chapter 6, section I for further discussion). Much of the so-called apocryphal literature is consumed with fierce arguments preaching the celibate life for both men and women. Opinions regarding sexual relations held by St. Paul seem moderate and liberal when compared to those found in the likes of the *Acts of Thomas*. The cardinal virtue (as well as the *sedes doctrinae*) of much of this literature is faith in chastity. The protagonists in Xenophon's pagan novel could feel at home as actors in the *Acts of Thomas*.

This *Weltanschauung* (way of looking at life) of Xenophon and of apocryphal literature, in which chastity is a saving virtue and escape in death a constant wish, is in marked contrast with the pagan outlook of someone like Petronius, and it represents a major shift in view from the ancient world toward the medieval:

Man's hope is . . . the old pagan landscape, the radiance here and now, in which everything had *numen*, and nobody needed eternal life because life itself was good. . . . There is none of the Christian hatred of the body here. . . . [80]
A fitting epitaph for the Greek erotic romance was penned by Nietzsche: "Christianity," he says, "gave Eros poison to drink; he did not die of it, certainly, but degenerated to Vice." [81]

Because a basic ingredient of the plot of Xenophon's novel is travel, the plot takes on an episodic structure and the characters meet many different situations. The reactions of each character to certain situations may or may not reflect accurately fact or even popularly held opinions. Xenophon seems to be straightforward and not one to play games with his characters or his readers, and opinions and prejudices expressed by characters are probably those felt by Xenophon to represent the feelings of his audience. Above all else Xenophon wishes to entertain, but, to do so, he must make his audience feel comfortable and part of the story. Therefore I believe that his prejudices were also the prejudices of his world: Phoenicians are frequently pirates or at least sharp traders (1.13); Greek women are prettier than barbarian women, and barbarian men will regularly desert barbarian women if given a chance to follow Greek (2.2); Greeks are more rational than barbarians and do not have such terrible tempers (2.3–2.4); barbarians are superstitious (5.4; 5.7). Xenophon balances these views somewhat by observing that barbarians are manly and not afraid to fight, while Ephesians are shown to be soft and effete (1.13).

Recent scholars have begun to speculate whether or not they can see in Xenophon an "upper-class urban attitude" toward the nonurban countryside, forests, and (I would add) seas.[82] Scarcella observes that, for example, the countryside is held to be violent, dangerous, and full of brigands.[83] Cities are considered bastions for civilized people, who spend only the necessary traveling time in the countryside until they reach the next urban area. The seas are seen as a kind of countryside, inhabited by pirates and controlled by the violent forces of nature, which turn many voyages on them in Xenophon to disasters. Even when saved from a sea disaster, Habrocomes is not really saved, for as he comes ashore in a desolate spot he is captured by shepherds (cf. *boucoloi*) and sold into slavery (3.12). The sea and the countryside are no places for gentle people. Scarcella contends that, when Xenophon does pause to look at the countryside, he does not see cultivated farm land but rather the bucolic paradise of the big city dwellers who think that the earth on farms is not dirty. For Bowie, Xenophon's viewpoints betray him as "a rich city-dweller." [84]

If, in fact, the countryside were totally overrun by robbers and the sea-lanes subjected to nothing but pirates and shipwreck, commerce in the Roman Empire would never have developed. We know, however, that the economic health of the Empire in the second century A.D. was generally good. Through it all, Xenophon's picture of life in his own times must always be viewed as: selectively representative, within the realm of plausibility, and adding something to his story. "Capture by brigands may have been a rarity for second-century Greeks, but the statistical rarity of hi-jacking today does not make its exploitation in a story unrealistic." [85]

The creative writer chooses to report certain facts and conditions only. Each item of fact or condition may, as an isolated example, be true. It is an entirely different matter, however, to conclude that these facts or conditions are representative. While Scarcella has done much to correct earlier scholarly opinion that the Greek novels were totally useless for historical research, and for this should be complimented, he may have gone a bit too far in his attempt to balance the perspective.[86] In particular, I find his analysis of second century A.D. society from Greek novels somewhat unconvincing because of his application of modern Marxist economic principles to an agrarian society with few, small industries, no banking systems, and precious little capital in specie compared to land. Scarcella's observations are nevertheless interesting. Under "economic activity" he points out the booming slave trade; the large amount of interprovince trade; the fact that pirated goods are quickly recycled into the economy; the existence of a work force structured into free professionals, free small businessmen, and free hired laborers; the division of society into a wealthy class with time to pursue personal pleasures and a mass of workers whose lives are generally not pleasant. Under "fiscal matters" Scarcella is taken by what he considers to be large amounts of mobile wealth, i.e., gold, and the economic stability of the state; people working in the state bureaucracy and soldiers (who also function as police) are respected and hold jobs with hope for advancement. Under "social structure" Scarcella cites the advancement of Leucon and Rhode from the status of slaves to that of owners of wealth as an example of social mobility from the bottom to the middle rung; though there is plenty of violence portrayed in Xenophon, there are neither signs of rebellion of oppressed classes nor of social tensions.

VI   *The Characters: A Study of Passivity*

The only emotion people feel nowadays is interest or the lack of it. Curiosity and interest and boredom have replaced the so-called emotions we used to read about in novels or see registered on actors' faces. Even the horrors of the age translate into interest. Did you ever watch anybody pick up a newspaper and read the headline "Plane Crash Kills Three Hundred"? How horrible! says the reader. But look at him when he hands you the paper. Is he horrified? No, he is interested.[87]

The title of this section applies to the two protagonists of this novel, for many of the "minor" actors take an active role in determining their own fate. I would like to examine here the ways in which the passivity of the young couple is presented to the reader and to speculate why they are so portrayed.

The point of view adopted by Xenophon gives his novel an artificial flavor and his characters doll-like qualities. The characters do not have a chance to become flesh-and-blood creatures with whom the reader can identify and empathize. The reader is told about the characters, who then have few opportunities and little time to speak directly to the reader.

When first the reader meets Habrocomes and Anthia, it is through the intermediary of the author. The reader is separated at least one remove from communicating directly with the young protagonists, as they take their first halting steps into love. Xenophon, an interpreter for people not allowed to speak, tells us, and the crowds at Ephesus second the opinion, that Habrocomes and Anthia are lovely. A vivid sense of this beauty is never conveyed to the reader; no single distinguishing mark of identification is passed on by the author.

When Xenophon finally switches the point of view to the dramatic observations of Habrocomes and Anthia, these lovers are allowed only to complain about the pains connected with falling in love. Xenophon so restricts the lovers' point of view that the readers see none of the joys of the first awakenings of love. Inherent in the emotion of love must be at least some small element of pleasure, warmth, comfort, humor, excitement, erotic stirrings. The reader will not see any of this until the lovers' wedding night (1.9), when the emotional releases appear to be torrents—compared with what came earlier. At 1.9 the young lovers become characters of depth and draw the reader toward themselves, but Xenophon has already done much damage.

Since Xenophon has chosen to tell us about Habrocomes and Anthia instead of allowing them to tell us or show us about themselves, they appear unable to do things for themselves. The oracle informs the fathers about the nature of the illness, who promptly arrange the necessary wedding. The lovers apparently are never consulted whether or not they wish to marry each other. The author's exercise of power over the fate of his characters is inversely proportional to the characters' power; the more the reader learns from the author, the less important the actions and feelings of the characters. The net result of authorial domination of the point of view is the development of extremely passive characters, who seem to float through life unable to exert any control on forces about them. (See section V above for the difficulties imposed on the chief actors by Xenophon's theological system.)

What a refreshing treat it is then to meet Hippothous and

Aigialeus. Almost from the first moment when each is introduced, the reader learns about them from their own point of view. They control their own destinies and seem to influence fate; they suffer but do not complain to any great extent; they are not passive. The extreme passivity of Xenophon's main actors disappoints the reader who has certain ideas about what heroic characters in classical literature can be.

Xenophon's description of Habrocomes and Habrocomes' own words show him to be a plaything of fate, a complainer, and one full of self-pity. This picture is, however, somewhat inconsistent with Habrocomes' day-to-day activities. Though he suffers much in various prisons, survives attempts to burn him alive and crucify him, and withstands the onslaughts of Manto and Bitch, he stubbornly searches the Eastern Mediterranean for Anthia. In monologues Xenophon has Habrocomes feel sorry for himself and complain bitterly about his fate, but then, within a few words and with a point of view changed back to the author, Xenophon has Habrocomes travel hundreds of miles under real hardships, as he searches for Anthia (5.8). Xenophon passes rapidly over Habrocomes' manly achievements, as though he were embarrassed that his hero would show any initiative or perseverance. Even Anthia's passivity and lack of initiative are balanced by her "obstinate resistance" [88] to yield to any lover.

The irony which Xenophon develops between the understanding of his characters and that of his reader is not subtle. Habrocomes and Anthia understand almost nothing that is transpiring and the reader absolutely everything. One of the pleasures a reader obtains from literature is the ability to participate in the action of a story without being required to suffer any of the consequences. Our superiority over Habrocomes and Anthia, however, is too great. It is almost the superiority of man over ventriloquist's dummy. The reader can see Xenophon's hand working the dummy and his lips moving, as the dummy speaks. What should be pleasurable for the attentive reader is all too often painful—as though he were watching a bad ventriloquist and feeling embarrassed for him.

Perhaps I stress too much the passive role of Habrocomes and should instead emphasize that, like Jason in Apollonius' *Argonautica*, he is resourceless (*amēchanos*). Both men are unheroic; Jason is helped out of difficult situations by Medea who is resourceful, while Habrocomes receives aid from many sources. Apollonius' *Argonautica*, though in the epic genre, might have provided a pattern for the Greek novel: (1) the heroine is more resourceful than the hero;

(2) the length of the work is determined by the length of the travel; (3) the passion of women is likely to alter the course of the work; (4) the power of Jason is closer to human than to heroic, and like Habrocomes he frequently becomes despondent and arouses in the reader inordinate fear for the hero.[89]

Even among passive heroines, Anthia surely ranks near the top. Manto, Bitch, and Rhenaia all become aggressive in pursuit of what it is they want, and, in fact, all overstep the boundaries of propriety. Even the shy Psyche in Apuleius' *Metamorphoses* goes out in search of Cupid when she fears he will not look for her. Though Psyche (and other heroines) has her moments of weakness, she is a heroine of stern stuff. Through much of ancient literature (at least from Euripides' *Medea* to Xenophon) writers have enjoyed working with the "psychological portrayal of the irresolute heroine." [90] Like Medea, Manto (2.5) loses her resolve for action after having been spurned. But both women have enough inner reserves of courage at least for revenge. Except for the feelings of love for Habrocomes and for herself, Anthia seems incapable of other emotions: hate, vengeance, sorrow, joy, or even fear. In the characters of Manto, Bitch, and Rhenaia Xenophon shows that he can delineate a resolute female. All strong and aggressive women are not necessarily evil like Manto and Bitch, for we see in Rhenaia a peaceful woman stirred to intense and irrational emotions in order to save her marriage; Thelxinoe (5.1) has the courage and recklessness to defy convention (pre-marital sex) and then to defy the law and her parents (eloping with Aigialeus). Xenophon clearly approves of the aggressive actions of both Rhenaia and Thelxinoe and makes of them model women and minor heroines in the novel. The major heroine, however, remains Anthia who has to her credit (when compared to Thelxinoe) that she remains a virgin until her marriage and obeys her father in marrying Habrocomes, and that (when compared to Rhenaia) she is much more genteel (and ineffective) in her reactions to the "other woman" Manto. Unlike Manto, Bitch, and the slave Rhode, Anthia initiates no positive action (she does take *defensive* action in 3.6 against Perilaus, in 4.5 against Anchialus, and in 5.7 against the pimp) in the social world. It is as if she lives in the courtly world of the highest nobility, in which servants and knights do everything for her. The portrait of Anthia is surely one of *studied* passivity, and much the same could be said of the passivity of Habrocomes. It is a quality which distinguishes Anthia and Habrocomes from everyone else and seems in this novel to be equated with gentility.

In Section III above I list certain parallels which I believe exist between New Comedy and the novel of Xenophon. The young lovers from New Comedy seem to display a passivity similar to that of Anthia and Habrocomes, a similar helplessness, a similar dependence on a favorable nod from the gods to ensure happiness, a similar dependence on crafty slaves and helpful allies to act as go-betweens and help them cope with difficulties. The heroes of New Comedy and the novel are not mature characters out of the mold of the classic Greek heroes.[91] Under pressure, the new heroes of comedy and the novel yield to powerful forces and survive to live happily ever after. The classic Greek hero does not yield; he breaks.[92]

The character, i.e., the moral, intellectual, and substantive person of Anthia and Habrocomes, is fixed by the time they leave home for their marvelous adventures. By that time they have developed and learned all they ever will. Suffering a lengthy series of tribulations will not affect either protagonist more adversely than enduring the first one; the bitterness toward life or outrage at the unfairness of Fortune does not increase. It appears that Xenophon sacrifices his actors and their development to the working out of a structure dependent on a formal compact. The characters appear passive because as individuals they are unimportant. The compact dominates. At 1.6 the oracle, in response to desperate pleas from two fathers to save their children, makes a contract for the young lovers: they will be saved, allowed to marry and to enjoy some happiness; for this privilege they must undergo a series of ordeals; and, if they remain chaste and faithful to each other, they will after all be reunited and live happily. The ordeals and the compact are almost medieval in flavor. Xenophon uses the characters to develop the structure instead of the structure to develop the characters. Anthia and Habrocomes are the poorer for it.

Scarcella puts the actors in Xenophon's novel into an historical setting and explains their passivity as a condition or result of the social milieu.[93] There is little or no evidence of social tension, he feels, and the masses exhibit in general a passive attitude which indicates that there is no contention over conflicting values. This view is valid up to a point but does not apply in all instances. Only Anthia and Habrocomes are inexplicably passive.

Beer would suggest that these lines of inquiry are really quite useless since literary works such as Xenophon's are essentially subjective, and the reader-analyst is forced "to depend entirely on the narrator . . . (who) remakes the rules . . . (and consequently) our enjoyment (of the work) depends on our willing surrender to his power."[94] Writers like Xenophon who live in or write in "the world of the imagination and of dream"[95] should not be held to externally applied norms. The reader must be as indulgent as the writer is self-indulgent.

Many of the minor characters have no real substance because their role is limited to that of informing the reader how beautiful and desirable Anthia and Habrocomes are. Into this category fall Corymbus, Euxinus, Moeris, Psammis, Anchialus, Amphinomus, and Polyidus. Another group of characters appearing in the novel serves the same function as furniture on a stage setting: the four parents of Anthia and Habrocomes, Chrysion, Araxus, the governor of Egypt, the pimp, and Althaea. A third group is slightly less shadowy than the first two, and its function is to convey to the reader the high moral quality and goodness attendant on the beauty of Anthia and Habrocomes and to serve as a complement to group one above. With a little effort and care Xenophon could have made flesh and blood actors of these: the tutor, Rhode and Leucon, Apsyrtus, Lampo, Perilaus, Eudoxus, and Clytus. A fourth group of characters, consisting of Manto, Bitch, Aigialeus, and Rhenaia, is nicely sketched out, but the role of each is so limited in scope that none is important for the whole story. Each is a clearly defined individual, most probably drawn from life and not from tradition, who enlivens the story while he is on the stage. The character of each is so strong that each upstages the nominal hero or heroine in every confrontation. These four actors are not by any definition passive; each tries to remake the world to suit himself.

If the novel has a hero, it is Hippothous. Similar in many ways to those actors in group four, Hippothous is also not passive. He shares with them personality traits which encourage illegal actions and defiance of society in order to pursue personal pleasure. But Hippothous is important also for the structure of the plot; he appears from almost the beginning of the story to the end and acts as a "common factor" to keep Habrocomes and Anthia in touch with each other. By means of strong-arm tactics and numerous dangerous exploits Hippothous moves between the young lovers and unites the bifurcated plot.

Quite apart from the life and problems of Anthia and Habrocomes, Hippothous has his own past history and leads his own life. His joys and sorrows are unconnected to the young lovers'. He enters the story as an outlaw, having turned to a life of crime because of sup-

posed injustices done to him by society. In the novel he develops
once again into a pillar of society, abandoning his earlier life-style.
Alone of all the actors in this novel, Hippothous shows development
of character.

Hippothous comes very close to meeting the definition of a picaresque hero.[96] Xenophon's *picaro* is almost a dashing hero who twice
tries to kill Anthia, and, then in a sudden change of heart, falls in love
with her. His instability of inner character is matched by the instability of his profession and the chaotic condition of the world he lives in.
He travels widely in fits and starts, dogged at every turn by established authority intent on subduing him. Through all his evil deeds,
however, he keeps the sympathy and interest of the reader, who
enjoys the rogue hero exuding great energy and a fair amount of
charm. He is Xenophon's best character.

VII   *The Novel as Mystery Religion*

One of the most interesting problems the modern reader encounters with Xenophon and his novel is the one of intent. Why did
Xenophon write it? and why did he write in the form and style that he
did? Perhaps the most intriguing answer, and, in a way, appealing
because it provides a coherent explanation for the novel from beginning to end, is the one articulated so very carefully by R. E. Witt in
1971 in a chapter entitled "Xenophon's Isiac Romance." Witt contends that Xenophon writes a kind of aretalogy of Isis, a novel whose
intent is to praise the virtues of the goddess Isis:

The *Ephesiaca* of the novelist Xenophon is a typical Isiac romance of imperial
times. The plot is built on a deeply religious basis. The heroine Anthia
undergoes adventures reminiscent of Isis. At all times Artemis and Isis are
treated as two aspects of a single divinity. The novel . . . shows a hand . . .
which feels the influence of the heliolatry characteristic of the age. . . .[97]

The evidence marshaled by Witt to support his thesis is truly impressive. Looking at the several parts in isolation from the whole, I
could be convinced that he is right. Reading Xenophon's novel
through from beginning to end several times militates against Witt's
theory. It seems to me that the novel refuses to be listed categorically
as an "Isiac romance." There is no denying the substantial influence
of the cult of Isis on Xenophon. If we grant that Xenophon lived and
wrote about the life and times of the second century Eastern Roman

Empire, Isis would be the most logical choice of deities to use to unify a novel which makes its characters wander all over the eastern end of the Mediterranean world. Isis had a kind of pervasiveness, whether by syncretism or not, which rivaled even Christianity, and I should be surprised not by Xenophon's use of her in the novel; rather I would have been suspicious had she been left out. Each of Witt's arguments and proofs is by and large valid, but the parts do not constitute a whole. Nevertheless, what he has to say about Isis and Xenophon's novel is always illuminating and sheds valuable light on the sense of the work.

The illuminating points which Witt's background in ancient religion enables him to bring to our work in Xenophon are taken up in the paragraphs that follow. It seems clear—in Xenophon's mind, at least—that Artemis and Isis could be aspects of the same deity. In the opening scenes of the novel we see Anthia leading the procession to the temple of Artemis and greeted as the earthly substitute or human form of Artemis. This procession of virgins is under the protection of Artemis, but, at the same time, Artemis is making the young girls available to the view of young men. We learn later (3.11) that Anthia's father had consecrated her to Isis until the day of her wedding. This may, however, have been a ruse of Anthia to avoid marrying Psammis; if so, she had tried the same trick a little earlier (2.13) with Perilaus. How can a young woman be consecrated to Isis, at the same time be a leading priestess of Artemis, an adherent to the cult of Apollo, and a believer in the dominance of Helius unless (1) there is a great degree of syncretism in religion or conversely confusion bordering on anarchy or (2) Xenophon is an unbelievably sloppy writer? Some of the latter is obvious throughout the novel, but more of the former is, I believe, the case here.

In the early centuries of our era there was a considerable amount of conscious amalgamation of Isis and Artemis. Witt makes the interesting observation that in the third century A.D. the city of Ephesus, where the novel begins and which was the leading center of the worship of Artemis, and the city of Alexandria in Egypt, which was a center of Isis worship, signed a treaty which was commemorated by a coin containing the images of both Artemis and Isis. The great antiquity of Egypt, its amazing monuments, its impressive religious bureaucracy, and general mysteriousness, all gave special emphasis in spreading the Isis cult. It seems, however, that Xenophon might have had a very logical and ulterior motive for introducing Artemis and then writing about Isis in other parts of the novel. Perhaps right from the beginning Xenophon intended to write a novel in which Isis was the principal deity, and he introduced the story using Artemis to close the cultural gap between Greek and Egyptian worship. Wherever he writes Artemis we can thus read Isis. The connections and ties between the two deities had been there for some time. Xenophon is merely building a firm stage-scene, setting in order (for his readers) the names and roles of all the actors, so that he can get on with the main object of his writing, the telling of a good story. Since most ancient novels have scenes set in Egypt, we can assume that either the literary tradition of taking the novel to Egypt was very strong or else the reputation of Egypt as a kind of fairyland was such that it appealed to the romanticist-sentimentalists who read novels. Xenophon guides the Greek readers from the known to the unknown, and (most important for our study of the novel) from the common to the exotic. Such a procedure is spelled out quite literally in Heliodorus 2.27. By placing Anthia at the head of a procession of young girls and inviting the crowd of bystanders to mistake her for Artemis and by extension Isis (a mysterious goddess), Xenophon gives early indications of the kind of story he is about to tell us. The heroines of ancient novels are famous for only one thing, their erotic attraction, and Anthia (now Isis) is surely one of the most beautiful heroines. Anthia's deeds, thoughts, and actions would never make her memorable; her beauty, however, would. This is a kind of graphic analogue to the beauty, excitement, power, and mysteriousness of Isis. But I believe that Witt and Merkelbach have misplaced the emphasis of the story on Isis, making of the novel an aretalogy, when Xenophon meant it to be an enthralling story.

It would be inconceivable that in structuring his novel Xenophon did not have the myth of Isis (and thence the ritual of the Isiac cult) in mind, and he could be confident that his audience also knew the myth. Isis is married to Osiris, king of Egypt, who is responsible for civilization in Egypt. Osiris is killed by his brother Typhon, dismembered, and thrown piece by piece into the Nile. Isis then conducts a long search for her husband, recovers his body piece by piece, and by her life-giving powers helps to restore a kind of life into the body of Osiris. With the help of Horus, their son, Isis defeats Typhon and reestablishes legitimacy in Egypt. The parallels between Xenophon's novel and the myth (or cult practice) of Isis are not very exact. Anthia is buried alive and then delivered from a sure death; Habrocomes is first crucified and then burned on a pyre, only to be rescued both times by the Nile river. These life-death (*Scheintod*)-resurrection motifs parallel in a very general way the ritual of the Isis-Osiris cult in Egypt. But then, these rituals are not infrequent in the Mediterranean world, and they bear directly on Xenophon's novel only because some of the episodes take place in Egypt.

At least for Xenophon and probably also for his audience Artemis and Isis, as Witt has pointed out, have "interchangeable roles." Each goddess has a merciless side to her character which makes her someone to be feared and alternately respected. In competition with Artemis, however, Isis is in a better position to attract serious followers, for not only does she promise to protect her devotees here on earth, she pledges to take care of them in decent fashion in the next life. While Artemis is apparently always associated with purity, chastity and other such intangible notions, Isis comes to be associated with this idea also, and statements that there is temple prostitution connected with the cult of Isis in Egypt or Asia Minor are not necessarily supported by the evidence. If Xenophon can be believed, and I do not detect any place in his novel where he knowingly alters popularly held beliefs or items of common knowledge, Isis is the goddess of virgins *and* of chaste married women (3.11). In fact, Xenophon is supported by Achilles Tatius (5.14) in describing Isis (Artemis) as the goddess responsible for bringing chaste young lovers together and her temple as the place to meet. Even the early Christian apologist Tertullian concedes that some female devotees of Isis carry chastity to extremes and remain virgins all their lives. Little does Tertullian know of the extremes yet to come.[98] The chastity ordeals that Anthia and Habrocomes undergo will make a fine model for later avid Christians, and I suspect that the chaste nature of the people in Xenophon contributes to the survival of a copy of Xenophon's novel through the Christian dark ages.

A reading of the complete novel at one sitting will, I think, convince the reader that Xenophon lacks the intensity of an evangelist; the sections in which the name of Isis appears do not differ in tone or feeling from sections without her name, nor is there any excitement generated for conversion to the Isis cult. While it is clear that it is a good thing to be on the right side of Isis, the reader is not convinced that Isis is really much different from an opinionated force, kindly disposed to Anthia and Habrocomes, and other assorted people. Nor is Isis pictured by Xenophon in such a light that the uninitiated and uncommitted would be encouraged to add Isis to their list of favorites or, if Isis represents a kind of monotheism, to convert to the cult.

If, on the other hand, a purpose behind Xenophon's novel is to

create a kind of tension which will sustain the reader's interest for
seventy-five or so pages of Greek, then Isis' position in the novel is
supportive only. The tension of which I speak is created by turning
loose into a big, bad, lascivious world two innocent and chaste young
people. Can they withstand the temptations, threats, and entice-
ments? One or the other of the young people is beset by temptations
on just about every page—all of which proves that sex was on the
mind of everyone in the ancient world, except Anthia and Habrocomes.

It would be fair, I think, in many instances to call Xenophon a slave
to Chariton because he borrowed so much from Chariton—including
the entire pattern of his novel. Curiously, to my mind, Xenophon
chooses not to borrow the episode which played such a major role in
Chariton, namely the birth and education of the hero and heroine's
child. Xenophon follows Chariton in placing the marriage of the two
lovers at the beginning of the novel before their separation and
lengthy journeys. Achilles Tatius, Longus, and Heliodorus place the
marriages at the very conclusion of the work. The heroines of these
three writers not only remain chaste to the last page, but also virgins.
(A sidelight here: the heroes in Achilles Tatius and Longus experiment in sex with other women before they are married.) While
following the structure of Chariton, Xenophon does not have the
union of Anthia and Habrocomes result in a child. Xenophon shies
away from the physical aspect of love, and, though Anthia is married,
she is always portrayed as a type of virgin, a type of Artemis/Isis who
stands aloof not from love and loving, but from physical sex and its
resultant issues. Chariton's heroine not only has a child, a realistic
result of earlier actions, but to save herself and unborn child, she
marries another man, Dionysius, and convinces him that the child is
his.

Xenophon's lack of interest in realism can be explained by following Merkelbach and Witt who contend that his intention is not to
write realistic fiction, but to compose a work for the greater glory of
Isis.

Witt also suggests that the plot which Xenophon uses is in effect the
structure of the Io myth of Greek ritual. At 4.3 we learn that Anthia is
in Memphis, sacrificing first at the temple of Isis and then at the
shrine of Apis. The Egyptian bull deity Apis is equated by Herodotus
with the Greek Epaphus, son of Io and Zeus, and Io is considered a
form of Isis (Herodotus 2.41), an aspect of the all-powerful Isis. Isis
assumes the functions and myths of Io (Ovid, *Ars Amatoria* 3.393).

Myth of Io	Novel of Anthia
Io believed to be Hera	Anthia believed to be Artemis
Inachus consults Pythian Apollo	Her father consults the oracle of Apollo
Io captured by Phoenician pirates	Anthia captured by Phoenician pirates
Io prays for sweet death	Anthia prays for death as a release
Io is promised help at the Nile	Anthia is promised aid at the Nile

A story of Isis (Io) for Witt thus becomes the plot of Xenophon's story. While this could be a nice, clean solution to the origin of Xenophon's plot, it is more likely that he borrows much of what he has from Chariton, and does not really care much whether it has a natural origin or basis. The level of sophistication necessary to borrow plots from religion and use them in fiction seems to me to be out of Xenophon's range. But I give Witt's exact arguments:

. . . what we are dealing with is a species of sacred writing, a *hieros logos*, and the ordinary canons of literary criticism are not always relevant. For instance, when Anthia and Habrokomes had been married they could expect to live happily ever after: "Their life was all one holiday." So it would have been but for Apollo's prophecy and but for the hand of fate. Again, as Kerényi has observed, the behaviour of Anthia on the bridal night has to be judged by a cult criterion. We are told that she took the initiative. "She fastened her lips to his with a kiss, and through the lips all the thoughts that were in their minds were transmitted from one soul to the other." The active partner is Anthia. In her actions she copies Isis at the time when she embraced the dead Osiris. We may almost regard Anthia and her newly-wed husband as puppets in the religious drama of the Marriage and Death Chamber.[99]

Witt's arguments are almost seductive, but when he suspends for his study the "ordinary canons of literary criticism" he sets aside the only tools he has to dig into the meaning of the work. He does, however, speculate sensibly about the audience for whom Xenophon wrote his work, and sees in the population of Asia Minor a group of people to whom stories about the mercy of Isis and her protection of young lovers would appeal. While devout followers of the Isis cult might take readily to a novel which features their goddess as a benevolent and positive force for good in the world (and which might be used as a beginning handbook for new converts to put Isis in the best light), it seems to me that it should be impossible for any reader to see under the story a cult ritual of Isis.

The extraordinary story (5.1) of the fisherman Aigialeus, who, having had his dead wife embalmed in "the Egyptian style," consorts with her in bed as though she were alive, is taken by Witt to be not just another story designed to interest the reader, but rather it is a tale full of "unmistakable Isiac symbolism." It is much more likely that Xenophon remembers a similar episode in Euripides' play *Alcestis* (lines 348 ff), or he might be drawing on that common store of folk knowledge which preserves stories of necrophilia in many versions.

While all higher literary criticism rests ultimately on the informed opinion of individuals, and individuals do disagree, I cannot hold with Witt when he says that "Xenophon is not just a story-teller. He has a didactic and indeed a religious aim. His tale is that of the salvation of human lives through faith in divine powers that do intervene." Xenophon has been reduced to a writer of religious tracts, an evangelist. The problem with Witt's interesting observation is that very small sections or passing incidents have been made to appear to be the most important. A careful reading of Xenophon's novel will simply not support the interpretation that Witt and Merkelbach give it. Witt's opinions are also supported by Hadas, who feels that Xenophon's remarks about the power, glory, and concern of Artemis/Isis for her devotees "were written with high earnestness and may have been among the authors' prime motives in writing. . . ." [100]

What Witt, Merkelbach, Hadas, and others say about parts of ancient religion is that they can be understood and appreciated through the reading of certain novels like Xenophon's. After all, they could argue, much of what we know about ancient Greek religion comes from the narratives found in Homer, Aeschylus, Sophocles, and Euripides. The high seriousness of these works and their obvious intent allows critics to draw more than literary observations from them. What is fitting criticism for Greek tragedy, however, is not necessarily proper for ancient novels. Deeper meanings, moral truths, and explanations of an irrational universe should not be sought in Xenophon. Since it is clear from reading Xenophon that his intent is to entertain, I find that I must question Witt and Company as to the relevance of their criteria for judging this novel:

But if you're the writer, you have to decide, or feel, whether you're going to make your story to show their (the gods') power or to convert people to their cult, or write your story essentially in its own terms and bring on the Mothers or the Nile from time to time in prayers and miracles to show how serious it all is, to make it more thrilling. If you were going to preach a mystery cult, you'd have an initiation and show its good effects, and salvation would be more than going back home and living happily ever after in marriage. [101]

CHAPTER 5

Audience and Readers of Xenophon

> To whom specifically—that is, to what sort of reader—did the novelists writing in Greek or Latin direct what they wrote? Surely it is risky to extrapolate from modern mass-circulation novelistic fare and assume that the "best-sellers" of Graeco-Roman antiquity, produced in two different languages and varying widely in content and in style and in date of composition, were necessarily devoured in every instance by bored housewives and tired businessmen.[1]

THIS is the kind of question which should be asked more frequently by classical scholars and students of all ancient literature. Answers to this question will surely be more like speculations than like direct answers. To know such answers is acknowledged by all to be desirable, but the methodology involved in any inquiry along these lines will necessarily be suspect. The ancient novelists themselves offer scant evidence about their readership, ancient critics did not comment on the reading public of the novelists, and there seems to be no extant evidence from third parties in the ancient world about the number and kinds of readers of books. Xenophon would have been amazed by our copyright agreements, the percentage of royalties paid to authors, the commercial importance of the book trade industry, and the enormous numbers of common people who can and do read. Though Xenophon surely saw his work appear for sale in Ephesus, realized that people bought, read and then exchanged his book with other readers, and perhaps saw it appear even in the local libraries, he could never have imagined the number and size of modern libraries, or guessed at the paperback rights and movie or television sales.

The number of people in the twentieth century with reading skills is a factor which must be weighed, when we look back at Xenophon in the second century. Authors of today try to make, and some few even do, a decent living from writing. It is possible that Xenophon wrote under the patronage of one or more wealthy individuals, perhaps a public official, or (if Merkelbach and Witt are right) perhaps the wealthy priests and priestesses of the Artemis/Isis cult in Ephesus. In view of the ease and readiness with which he borrowed from Chariton, Xenophon would be very surprised to learn that today we frown on such borrowings and sometimes go to court in plagiarism suits. Chariton and Xenophon would have thought that the use by the latter of the former was a special kind of praise. And indeed it was.

It is likely that Xenophon appealed to a less sophisticated audience than Chariton. The latter's frequent quotations from Homer and various literary allusions and devices demanded an audience acquainted with a respectably wide range of literature. Where Chariton appealed to those lovers of historical fiction or biography, Xenophon would appeal more to the devout and religious.

Since 1974 I have altered somewhat my view about the intended audience of Chariton and, by extension, Xenophon:

But with the rise of prose fiction, and for us Chariton's romance in particular, we enter a literary creation built for the middle–class by a middle–class writer. The literature here is not intellectual but sentimental.[2]

While it is clear to the reader that Xenophon is ostensibly writing a novel with characters from the privileged classes, people with great political power, family influence, and vast amounts of money, he has created members of the aristocracy without knowing them. In fashion similar to the other Greek novelists Xenophon portrays the "socially remote."[3] The reader moves with Xenophon's characters among royalty and the privileged few, as though he were one of them. As children identify with heroes and spacemen, so adults fantasize that they can walk with socially remote royalty. (There is no need to dream about fraternization with average people.) The quality of royalty, when added to a character, universalizes that character to such an extent that he or she is no longer limited by racial identification or other frailties of mere mortals. Xenophon, however, fails to appreciate the possibilities inherent in the genre and portrays royalty as though they were commoners, a condition which does not universalize them. In 1974 I offered the following observation:

The middle-class in which centurions lived was able to, and apparently did, purchase books. And it is this middle-class audience to whom Chariton directed his novel. We might suggest that Chariton wrote what the middle-class wanted to read, or even that his work struck a respondent chord in the

middle-class. Though Chariton writes about characters in the upper class
who are above himself and his readers in station . . . in action and emotional
development and discipline they are actors very much like the author and the
reader . . .[4]

Chariton's delineation of the King Artaxerxes was almost absolutely con-
ditioned by his personal conception of the oriental despot, and he was almost
certainly mistaken. Artaxerxes was an oriental despot who had no need to
scheme to get Callirhoe; he would have simply taken her. Chariton pictured
for us a rather kindly, middle-class, nonregal despot.[5]

Now, some years later, I have modified this position. My use of the
term middle-class was fairly broad and agreed with nonscientific,
popular usage. I believe that I can speak more precisely about
Xenophon's intended audience, if I refer to it as a sentimental group,
i.e., one which suspends its intellectual judgments and appreciation
for reality and adopts a view that events in life are simple, rather than
as a middle-class audience. Connotations of the term are frequently
economic, and I do not mean necessarily to point to an economic
class.

In his splendid little book, *Criticism and Personal Taste*, R.
Peacock addresses the general problem of identifying an audience by
suggesting that each reader in himself has at least three different
"tastes" and thus constitutes three audiences:

For each of us there is an outer ring of works, of which . . . one can
acknowledge the power . . . but one may not be able to respond to them
with any great warmth. There is, next, a middle belt of works for which one
has an understanding. . . . Finally, however, there is the inner ring, the
pieces that we choose, or that choose themselves, because of some intuitive
sympathy, some correspondence between them and either our nature, or our
present needs, or phase of development. . . .[6]

There is a story of a philospher at Cambridge into whose rooms in
college no one had for years entered. When he died, the college
officials found the rooms stuffed with mystery novels. There are many
sophisticated and sensitive scholars in the field of literature who
rarely read so-called good literature at home in the evening when
they are relaxing. They choose from Peacock's "inner ring," those
works which they like but which would hardly be acceptable in a
college course offering. I might add that several intelligent and
cultured persons I know devote many hours each month to reading
the worst sort of romantic and gossipy trash which has been pur-

chased in grocery and drug stores. Xenophon would appeal to them, as he would to those parents who shudder at what their children read in adult bookstores.

Many writers of fiction along with not a few cinema directors have resorted to extreme forms of realism in order to represent or imitate everyday life. It is generally recognized that acts of violence and brutality among men and beasts are frequent and representative of contemporary living. The stimulus in writers to imitate or represent these acts is set off from another stimulus in other writers to transcend them. Each of these two groups of writers finds an audience for its work.

The reader of Xenophon enters a world in which there is a modicum of violence, but the violent are properly punished. In general, however, it is an ideal world, to which the reader can escape and in so doing free himself from a realism that may be too familiar and too oppressive. Escape might be too strong a word; change is perhaps more appropriate, since the reader is not forced to spend his whole life in the novel's ideal world. In the same way that a person can drift into a daydream or a dream, a reader of Xenophon can change from the real world he cannot comprehend to Xenophon's simplified one. While the characters in Xenophon do not display a wide range of emotions, neither do they confuse the reader with numerous idiosyncrasies which render them radically different from the reader.[7]

The reader, not wanting to see a picture of the world which is already too much with him, opens the pages of Xenophon in order to discover a new world. Nor does the reader of Xenophon seek an interpretation of the world around himself. The reader is reaching out for a world he can enter only through the pages of Xenophon. Speaking in general about the romance, Gillian Beer makes these observations:

It absorbs the reader into experience which is otherwise unattainable . . . drawing us entirely into its own world—a world which is never fully equivalent to our own. . . . It is not an entire world; it intensifies and exaggerates certain traits in human behavior and recreates human figures out of this exaggeration. It excludes some reaches of experience in order to concentrate intently upon certain themes. . . .[8]

Such a world is called "mythic" by scholars like Wellek and Reardon:

The novel, then, is itself a form of myth, the late Hellenistic myth. . . . It is a story embodying racial experience. What is that experience? Briefly, it is the isolation of the individual in the world. If New Comedy is social myth, the novel is personal myth; Perry rightly describes it as "latter-day epic for Everyman," in a non-heroic world. The hero is removed from his bourgeois setting; and the figure we see on shipboard, sailing ever farther from his home and his beloved, is the late Greek version of unaccommodated man. That he is not an ephemeral and insignificant figure is proved by the fact that we possess . . . half-a-dozen novels, and know . . . that a good many more once existed.[9]

In his monumental study called *The Classical Tradition*, Gilbert Highet speaks eloquently about the audience of the ancient novel. He does not speak of the audience's social and economic class, but rather of their social perspective and of their feeling for what they read. The audience of Xenophon according to Highet would be made up of young people and those whose fantasies are romantic:

Now although the pastoral . . . and although the romances with their absurd melodrama and stilted speeches and exaggerated emotions are practically unreadable, they are not intrinsically worthless. Both serve a real purpose. They are obsolete because the purpose is now served by something else. They are not high literature, as tragedy or epic is high literature, employing all the mind and all the soul. They are escape-literature, they are wish-fulfillment. And, as such, they fulfilled . . . the useful function of idealizing aspects of life which might have been gross, and adding poetic fantasy to what is often dull or harsh prose. They are meant for the young, or for those who wish they were still young. All the leading characters in them are about eighteen years old, and think almost exclusively about their emotions. No one plans his life, or works toward a distant end, or follows out a long-term career. The hero and heroine are buffeted about by events without deserving it—as young people always feel that they themselves are buffeted—and yet no irremediable damage happens to them, they are united while they are still fair and young and ardent and chaste. In these, as in modern romantic stories, the Cinderella myth is one of the chief fantasies: a typical wish-fulfillment pattern, in which one does not have to work for success or wealth, but is miraculously endowed with it by a fairy godmother and the sudden passion of a prince. (A pathetic note in the *Aethiopica*, which tells us something about the author and the audience he expected, is that the heroine, although the daughter of coloured parents, is miraculously born white.) Even the style reflects youth: for the commonest devices are antithesis and oxymoron. Everything in youth is black or white, and these devices represent violent contrast and paradoxical combination of opposites. The idealistic tone of the romances often had a real effect. Many a young man exposed to vice in the roaring metropolitan cities of the late Roman empire, or the corrupt courts of the Renaissance and baroque era, was drawn for a time to think more highly of love, by imagining himself to be the faithful shepherd and his beloved the pure clean Chloe. The manners of all the chief characters, even the shepherds, are intensely courtly: no one speaks gross rustic patois, everyone has fine feelings, and speaks gracefully, and behaves nobly—because youth has sensitive emotions.

The same yearning is satisfied to–day by fantasies about other milieux and by different social customs. Instead of reading about nymphs and shepherds in Arcadia, we read about idyllic peasants or idealized countrymen outside our own megapolitan cities: sometimes we even create them and support them. The Swiss; the Indians of the south-western United States . . . Steinbeck's drunken but angelic paesanos . . . the cowboys of Wyoming; and the fishers of the Aran Islands—all these, and many more, and the modern works of art made out of them . . . and the innumerable converted farm-houses and rebuilt cottages and primitive pictures and rustic furniture which we covet—all are products of a real need, which is becoming more poignantly felt as city life becomes more complex, difficult and unnatural.[10]

Ben Perry concurs with Highet's judgment that the ancient novel was intended for and probably read by young people in the ancient world. Because of the monuments which survive from the ancient world, almost all of which are the product of mature men, and because of the relatively inferior position of teenagers (compared to their importance today), we tend to overlook their presence:

There is such a thing as juvenile literature even in our own highly sophisticated age; and in ancient times the ideal novel must have catered to that obscure but far-flung literary market long before it became adapted in some measure to the taste and outlook of mature and educated minds.[11]

Moses Hadas speculates about an audience, a readership, and the intent of the authors of the ancient Greek novels, from an entirely different point of view. For Hadas the economic class, reading ability, and age of the audience are unimportant. What matters is the intent of the author, which Hadas implies is also the intent of the reader:

A motive central to the shaping of ancient fiction was the desire to defend and perpetuate cultural values which were in danger of being lost. . . .[12]

I suppose that cultural values, if there really are things identifiable as such, are always in danger of being lost, i.e., changed. People who are conscious of being part of a culture or who can identify a culture from afar might be able to sense that that culture is in danger of being

lost. St. Augustine senses the end of a culture, when in 410 he learns
that the Visigoths under Alaric have sacked Rome. I doubt that many
of the readers of the ancient novels had the same lofty perspective as
St. Augustine. Hadas develops this interesting perspective after
assuming several other interesting things: (1) the ninth century B.C.
poet of the *Iliad* was concerned with preserving the values of the age
of Greek heroes and passing on those values by way of example to the
next generation, (2) Herodotus in the fifth century B.C. said that he
wrote his history to keep fresh the record of the Greek-Persian wars,
(3) in the time of Alexander the Great when the Macedonian general
dictated Greek affairs, the writers of the age withdrew their interest
from politics of all kinds and, turning inward, wrote of the private
concerns of middle-class people, (4) the Jews of Alexander's empire
were particularly interested in preserving Jewish culture and things
Jewish, and the literature they produced was intended as propaganda
to ensure cultural survival; historical romances belong here and
"form a link to the surviving (Greek) romances."

It would be very important for the study of ancient prose fiction, if
Hadas's four-part historical object lesson were applicable. If it were,
we could then say that Xenophon wrote his novel and his audience
read it because they wished to ensure certain cultural values. The fact
is that I cannot identify a cultural value in Xenophon which he is
trying to propagate. Quite the opposite seems to be the case. A
careful reading of Xenophon teaches us, as Highet believes, that this
novel is intended to be escape-literature. I find that I must agree with
Ben Perry's judgment about the composition of the audience for the
ancient novel and also concur with Alex Scobie: ". . . they are written
for middle-class readers who enjoy reading fiction which mirrors
their own ideals and unfulfilled longings." [13]

In comment on the nature and audience of Greek novels, Elizabeth
Haight compares them to mystery stories: "The best escape-
literature which I know consists in Greek Romances and in mystery
stories." [14] Xenophon's novel is compared to John Buchan's *The
Three Hostages*. Buchan does not borrow anything from Xenophon
that I can identify; they both borrow from a like store. After making a
series of comparisons, Haight concludes her essay with a statement
that the ancient readers of Greek novels and modern mysteries have
common interests: "Human beings, however sceptic, still wish to
believe in romantic love, new adventure, and saving grace; and these
stories, old and new, which convey such faith may find a place in a
revival of the true romance." [15] Had Miss Haight lived a few more

years she would have seen millions of people turn to unadulterated
sentimental romance in Erich Segal's *Love Story*. While it is difficult to understand how simple writings can appeal to
sophisticated readers, we know that such situations are not infre-
quent. I need only cite T. E. Lawrence ("Lawrence of Arabia") and
his fascination for childlike medieval romance:

It is difficult to see how this medieval literature, had it not served strong
personal needs in Lawrence's psychology, could have compelled so fully the
attention of someone of his critical ability. For no matter how fine the style
. . . the *chansons de geste* . . . are fairy stories, often lovely ones, that appeal
to the childlike and unrealistic mind, a mind that needs to be nourished on a
glorious and idealistic conception of the world that is not bound by the
limitations of actuality.[16]

That there was some substantial readership for the Greek ancient
novels is substantiated by a remark of Julian (A.D. 361–63), the last
pagan Roman emperor, that fiction must be avoided. Had readers not
been attracted to Greek novels in large numbers, Julian would not
have been concerned with what they read:

It would be suitable for us to handle histories composed about real events: but
we must avoid all the fictions written of old in the style of history, love
subjects and everything in fact of that type [translation by A. D. Nock].

CHAPTER 6

Nachleben: The Influence of Xenophon on Later Literature

I The Ancient World

COMPARED to the Homers and Vergils, Xenophon had little influence on later literature; ancient prose fiction, under which genre Xenophon's work is placed, did, however, have a considerable influence.[1] I believe that much of the later influence realized by ancient prose fiction was exerted by the total corpus of ancient novels and not so very much by individual works. At the time of the novels' composition in later antiquity, their audiences, with the exception of Petronius' *Satyricon*, Apuleius' *Metamorphoses*, and Longus' *Daphnis and Chloe*, seem to have been made up of sentimental members of the reading public. Because of this, ancient novels apparently never became standard works in imperial libraries or libraries of wealthy aristocrats, thus further assuring a narrow readership.

Unlike Chariton's novel,[2] the earliest of the extant ancient Greek novels, there is yet no evidence that Xenophon's work enjoyed wide circulation. Within a short period after its publication the novel of Chariton, an inhabitant of Aphrodisias in Caria in southwestern Turkey, was read as far away as Egypt, where partial copies were recently unearthed.

The first writer[3] to show some influence of Xenophon's novel is Heliodorus, one of the most popular ancient novelists, who wrote in the early decades of the third century of the Christian era. Alexander Riese,[4] among others, has noted similarities between Xenophon's work and the so-called *Historia Apollonii Regis Tyri*, a very popular Latin romance of the fourth century, which was later included as chapter 153 of the influential, fourteenth century *Gesta Romanorum*, and which was used by Shakespeare for his *Pericles*. If Shakespeare knew the work of Xenophon, it was probably via the *Historia Apollonii*, whose author apparently borrowed elements from Xenophon.

139

The problems associated with the date, origin, and authorship of the *Historia Apollonii* are so monumental that I would prefer to defer any further comments about it.

Heliodorus shows some specific influences of Xenophon. We can see this clearly in the case of Thyamis, who plays a major role in Heliodorus' novel, and who was patterned after Hippothous: like Hippothous, he falls in love with the heroine of the story; like Hippothous, he becomes a friend and ally of the hero; like Hippothous, he steps aside and does not interfere with the love affair of hero and heroine, once he understands the situation. Both Hippothous and Thyamis begin life as upstanding citizens, but turn quickly to banditry because of real or imagined unpunished offenses against them; both then renounce their evil ways and once again become credits to society. The scene in Xenophon (1.15ff) where Corymbus falls in love with Habrocomes and Euxinus with Anthia, and the two robbers extol the virtues of each other to each other's intended lovers, and advise them to give in to superior power, finds an echo in Heliodorus (7.17) where Cybele tries to win Theagenes for her mistress Arsace, and Arsace tries to arrange a union between Chariclea and Cybele's son. Also Heliodorus seems to have borrowed the scene from Xenophon (5.1), where Habrocomes arrives in Syracuse and lives with a fisherman who had just lost his wife, for his own novel (5.18), where his hero Theagenes finds a room in a private house of a fisherman whose wife had just died. Xenophon's use of an oracle's prophecy (1.6) to provide the reader with an outline of the remainder of the story is repeated by Heliodorus (2.35).

Apart from Heliodorus and the *Historia Apollonii Regis Tyri*, Xenophon does not seem to have had any specific influence on other ancient novelists that we could not also attribute to Chariton. Under the direct influence of teachers of rhetoric, with some side influences from the genre of the novel, epistolography evolved into a genre distinct from that of the novel, but, nevertheless, retaining a strong similarity in subject matter. Certain rhetoricians with an interest in prose fiction, or storytelling in general, channeled their talents into epistolography, the art of writing letters to display the talent of the writer, not necessarily intended to convey any information. It was surely a parallel genre to the ancient novel and owed much to it for its own development. Among the practitioners of this genre we find Philostratus (love letters), Aelian (*Peasants' Letters*), and the second-century Alciphron (*Letters of Fishermen, Letters of Peasants, Letters of Parasites, Letters of Prostitutes*), the supreme writer of the *genus*.

Epistolography, like the novel, owes much to New Comedy. This point cannot be stressed too much. By and large the most predominant topoi in these letters are erotic, as they are in ancient prose fiction; one difference being that the efficient motif in the novels (except for Longus' *Daphnis and Chloe*) is the "marvellous journey." [5] The most interesting epistolographer for this study is Aristaenetus, who wrote books of *Love Letters*, perhaps in the fifth century. Like the *Erotica Pathemata* of Parthenius (first century B.C.), the *Love Letters* of Aristaenetus offer us a most complete collection of erotic story-plots, an expanded erotic motif-index, if you will. Aristaenetus almost certainly knew of Xenophon and borrowed from him in at least five, and perhaps seven instances, though all of the items of influence come from the first book of Xenophon. In this way Xenophon's writing, or at least sections of it, became part of the vast influence classical literature exerted, and, intermingled with much of ancient writing, Xenophon continues to move through world literature. [6]

Because the ancient novel was written for middle-class audiences and responded to their sentimental interests, it became an available vehicle for the propagandistic literature of the early Christian church.

If the characters and events in the work are wholly fictitious, it will be an imaginative romance. If the writer's aim is to depict the life and spirit of a saint honored by the Church by means of a series of happenings that are partly real and partly imaginary, then the work may be called a hagiographical romance. . . . Romances of this last kind are very numerous, and some of them go back to very early times: for example, the Acts of Paul and Thecla, and that collection of apocryphal Acts of the Apostles which had so long and remarkable a vogue. And there are the Clementine romances (*Homiles* and *Recognitions*). [7]

The early Church was interested in edification of its people and determined, whether consciously or not, to do so with fictional works of a religious character, designed to inspire devotion.

Except for one episode of sexual intercourse between unmarried persons in Longus' *Daphnis and Chloe* and one or two in Achilles Tatius' novel, ancient Greek prose fiction is remarkably moralistic and contains many scenes which can be used for edification. The ancient novels appealed to the same audiences in which the early Church found its members and in which it sought its converts. The format of the ancient novel was then apparently borrowed by the Church for its popular tales of saints' lives: the two main elements of the ancient novel, love and travel, were taken over completely. Erotic love easily became Christian love, because the erotic love in the ancient novels was already so pure that the transformation was really quite simple. It can, of course, be argued that the "marvellous journey" is such an integral part and common heritage of all people that the source of the ancient novel and of the saints' lives is one and the same, and both derive from one source rather than saints' lives from ancient novels. The fact that ancient novels cease to be written about the time that saints' lives and hagiographic romances begin supports the notion that the latter grew out of the former.

Hippolyte Delehaye has identified certain aspects of hagiographic romances which bear a striking resemblance to the ancient Greek novels: a tendency to simplify, poverty of imagination, and an artificial grouping of persons and happenings.[8] Interventions by God which deliver martyrs from terrible persecutions are a frequent motif in hagiographic romances and appear to be parallel events with those in Xenophon (4.2), where Habrocomes is saved from crucifixion and being burned alive. The marvellous journey of the hero and heroine in ancient novels becomes in Christian romances the "miraculous travels of crucifixes, madonnas, and images of saints." [9] The *deus ex machina* of Greek tragedy, used by the ancient novelists apparently was passed on by those novelists to the Christian writers, who made miracles a way of life, an almost daily happening. The vision of chaste women like Anthia, and Tarsia in the *Historia Apollonii Regis Tyri*, who are placed into brothels and preserve their chastity by miraculous means, lives on in the lives of Christian saints, saved from carnal knowledge by acts of God. Habrocomes, the chaste hero, finds a counterpart in innumerable saints who ward off all female temptresses like Manto (2.3). To my knowledge the only Western literature to rival the virginity mania of Greek novels is Christian.

The single piece of Christian writing which shows the greatest influence of Xenophon is, I believe, the so-called *Recognitions* of Clement, dated variously from the first to the fifth centuries A.D.: the third century is an easy compromise. In days gone by when scholars knew more and were surer of their facts, it was thought that Clement I, the fourth Pope (A.D. 91–100), was the author of the *Recognitions*. But on soberer reflection scholars now date this work after the novel of Xenophon. I would like to suggest that (at best) the author of the *Recognitions* was influenced by Xenophon's novel or, if this cannot be so, was (at least) influenced by numerous works in the genre of ancient prose fiction.[10]

The *Recognitions* are so named because by certain means Clement is able to *recognize* the previously lost members of his family. The motif is the same one used much earlier by Greek tragedians and comedy writers, and became a commonplace in New Comedy, where it was necessary to make use of it in order to end complicated plays. Between New Comedy and the *Recognitions* of Clement stand the ancient novels.

Right from the first page religious considerations, propagation of the faith, and the like take primacy in the *Recognitions*. But by the seventh book the writer must have become aware that his "message" was being applied with a too heavy hand, because in the eighth chapter of the seventh book, the necessity for Christian conversion is downgraded in the narrative, and we meet the interpolated narrative which speaks of Clement's family problems. Though Clement and the Apostle Peter are the main interlocutors of the *Recognitions*, it is not until we come to Book Seven that we learn anything about Clement. This Clement might be the famous pope; he might also be a figment of the anonymous author's imagination. It seems certain that Clement's family history is a figment of prose fiction imagination.

After enduring a long lecture from Peter, Clement interrupts: "When I was five years old my mother saw a vision in which she was advised to leave the city for ten years to avoid a terrible death." We have seen this motif before in Xenophon: some divinity advises a sea voyage in order that someone might live happily. Clement's father, Faustinianus, puts his wife, Matthidia, and their other sons Faustinus and Faustus on a ship for Athens: "Faustinianus put them on board ship with plenty of servants and money, but kept me at home as a comfort for himself." This is reminiscent of the scene in Xenophon where Habrocomes and Anthia leave their parents and sail for Rhodes. But Clement's wealthy mother is shipwrecked and separated from her sons. Again a similar motif. Matthidia finds refuge with a recently widowed, poor woman whose husband had been a sailor, an episode surely parallel to the scene in Xenophon (5.1ff) where Habrocomes stays with Aigialeus, a poor fisherman who had recently lost his wife. At one point in her story (7.19) Matthidia claims to come from Ephesus, an interesting remark in the context of our study of Xenophon. As Artemis and Isis are responsible for reuniting Anthia and Habrocomes, so Peter (as God's representative) brings Clement's family together again. Both narratives thus speak of religious miracles and become kinds of aretalogies. The reunion of Clement's family, like that in Xenophon, takes place piecemeal: all the family members are reassembled one at a time, and there follow several scenes of fainting and of crowds gathering to wonder at the proceedings. All of this clearly out of Greek novels, perhaps the novel of Xenophon.

Before this episode in the *Recognitions* ends, we hear much about chastity and its rewards, and are reminded once again of Anthia's struggle against all forces to preserve herself for Habrocomes. Though the emphasis on chastity in the *Recognitions* has all the elements of Christian religious fervor, the thematic echoes of chastity from Xenophon's pagan work are apparent in several statements. We also hear about the conversion to Christianity of Clement's family, an initiation into the Christian mysteries. Such a denouement of the novellike episode in the *Recognitions* cannot help but remind us of the final scene in Xenophon when Habrocomes and Anthia enter the temple of Artemis and affirm their faith in the ancient gods who advised them to leave Ephesus on a dangerous journey and then delivered them safely home again after duly testing their character.

In the so-called "Apocryphal New Testament" there is a collection of five "Acts" (John, Paul, Peter, Andrew, and Thomas) that M. H. James calls the "five primary romances." [11] Apparently this collection was put together by Manichaeans (a gnostic sect, developed from the old dualistic system of the Persians, one of whose tenets is a despising of matter, the body, and thus of all sexual relations) who therefore held to strict ascetic rules in favor of chastity. Cults of virginity among both men and women were very popular in the early centuries A.D., and these popular beliefs are probably reflected in the Greek novels, which do not often show double-standards in sexual behavior for men and women.

The *Acts of Thomas* (third century A.D.), divided into 170 chapters, are quite lengthy because the hero Thomas (like Habrocomes) travels a good deal. One of the places to which he journeys, is India, an exotic place like Egypt or the East, to which heroes and heroines from Greek novels regularly travel. The structure of the *Acts of Thomas* is tripartite and, in broad outlines, similar to the novel of Xenophon: (1) prelude: Thomas is sent to India because the Lord makes the lots fall in that direction (an oracle of Apollo sends Anthia and Habrocomes); (2) "filler" episodes revolving around miracles; Thomas associates with royalty; (3) final union of Thomas and God in martyrdom.

I have put together below a series of similarities between the *Acts* and Xenophon and other ancient novels. The case can be made, I believe, that the writer of these acts, if not influenced by Xenophon, was surely influenced by one or more writers in that genre. (Chapter

4) Thomas visits Andrapolis where the king's only daughter is about to marry: Apollonius in the *Historia Apollonii* (15) is invited to a reception where the king's only daughter falls in love with him. (Chapters 6–9) Like Apollonius, Thomas is singled out by a young girl, his appearance is changed, he is thought to be a god, and he sings a long song. (Chapters 22–23; 33; 54; 75) The motif of the *Scheintod* (apparent death) is employed in the *Acts* as it was in Xenophon (3.8), the *Historia Apollonii* (26), Apuleius, Achilles Tatius, and Heliodorus. (Chapter 2) Thomas is bought by the Indian Abbanes and taken in that direction: Anthia is bought by the Indian Psammis (3.11). (Chapter 43 and passim) Characters in the *Acts* would, like Anthia and Habrocomes, rather die than surrender their chastity. (Chapter 51) A young man, whom Thomas meets, tells an interpolated story very similar to that of Hippothous (3.1–2) and Aigialeus (5.1), in which his lover dies because he fears she will be taken by someone else. (Chapter 71) The narrator exaggerates the size of crowds which assemble to see a strange event. He claims, like Xenophon, that "the whole city turned out." (Chapter 91) Information is conveyed in dreams; so Xenophon (1.12; 2.8; 5.8). (Chapter 98) Mygdonia successfully convinces the panting Charisius that she cannot have sexual relations with him because she is dedicated to God. Polyidus believes the same kind of story when it is told to him by Anthia (5.4). (Chapter 140) A hot torture inflicted on Thomas is cooled by water miraculously springing from the earth: Habrocomes' pyre was extinguished by the rising Nile (4.2). (Chapter 141) When an official hears of Thomas' rescue, he orders him to prison "until I can consider what should be done to him": when Habrocomes is saved, the governor declares "he should be placed under guard . . . until we find out who he is and why this happened" (4.2). (Chapter 152) A woman, ordered to have intercourse, replies: "Over my body you have authority; so do what you wish. But I will not let my soul perish." When Habrocomes is pressured by Manto to desert Anthia and marry her, he replies: "I am a slave, but I know how to protect contracts; they have power over my body, but my soul I keep free" (2.4). (Chapters 159–70) Thomas dies a martyr's death, a form of suicide, rather than lose his chastity, because he believes he can rejoin his savior (lover, in a Christian sense) in the afterlife: Habrocomes and Anthia frequently threaten suicide both to rid themselves of present threats and to rejoin their lovers in the afterlife.

A famous story in the brief *Acts of Paul* (ca. A.D. 160) finds Paul and the virgin Thecla thrown together. Like Anthia (2.7), Thecla visits

Paul in prison, and, like Habrocomes (4.2), she is condemned to die on a pyre, only to have God put out the fire. The story also offers us yet another example of the *Scheintod* motif. And, finally, in a scene reminiscent of Anthia's captivity in a pit with two hungry dogs (4.6), we find Thecla, thrown to the beasts, who, however, only lick her feet.

II *Influence on Shakespeare*

In her nicely written and soberly documented *Shakespeare and the Greek Romance* Carol Gesner [12] takes up earlier suggestions [13] and speculates that certain episodes from Shakespeare have their origin in Xenophon. There are many *general* parallels between the adventures of Anthia and Habrocomes and *Romeo and Juliet*, but the specific episode in which Juliet drinks the sleeping draught, is buried alive, awakens in a tomb, and dies near her lover has a clear parallel in Xenophon (3.5 ff), where Anthia receives a potion of poison (so she believes) from Eudoxus (Friar Laurence in *Romeo and Juliet*), drinks it, falls into a deep sleep, is buried alive and awakens in a tomb. Habrocomes receives a false report that Anthia has died from poison, and he rushes off to Alexandria to kill himself on Anthia's body. Recognizing the improbability of Shakespeare's having read Xenophon (*Romeo and Juliet*, 1591–97; Xenophon's novel first published in Greek with Latin translation in 1726 and in English in 1727), Gesner suggests that Masuccio de Salernitano (Salerno 1415–75) in his *Mariotto Mignanelli and Gianozza Saracini* (1474) acted as an intermediary between the Greek humanists who knew of Xenophon's thirteenth century manuscript and Shakespeare, who knew Masuccio. Antonio di Tommaso Corbinelli (died 1425) gave the library of La Badia cloister in Florence the famous *codex unicus* of Xenophon, from which Angelo Ambrogine Poliziano quoted in his *Miscellaneorum Centuria Prima*, published in 1489 (thus available to Shakespeare) and frequently thereafter in Italy, France, and Switzerland. In his citation from Xenophon, however, Poliziano does not deal with the episode of Anthia's attempted suicide—a fly in Gesner's ointment—a link pin between Xenophon and Shakespeare.

Gesner also speculates about Shakespeare's borrowing scenes from Xenophon for *Cymbeline*. After taking a sleeping potion Imogen awakens and finds herself in a cave (a tomblike structure). In another scene Imogen, spared from death by Pisanio, seems to experience a fate similar to that of Anthia (2. 11), who had aroused the hatred of her mistress but was spared by the mistress' goatherd.

III   *Editions and Translations of Xenophon*

We owe the preservation . . . of Xenophon of Ephesus to a single manuscript of the thirteenth century, which remained the property of a small Florentine monastery until late in the eighteenth century, when it was transferred to the great Medicean library [the Laurentian Library in Florence].[14]

Since the text of Xenophon's novel did not move from handwritten manuscript to printed page until 1726, the novel's earlier lack of popularity is easily explained. Meanwhile, the novels of Achilles Tatius, Heliodorus,[15] and Longus had been known and appreciated for some two hundred years. The publication of the works of Xenophon and Chariton came upon the literary West as a new born baby comes upon a forty-five year old couple.[16] The Italian Antonio Cocchi, building on the work of a fellow countryman A. Salvini, edited the first printed text in 1726 in London—not in Italy. That century would see three more Greek editions of Xenophon, a fact which speaks more to the mania for printing anything from the Classics than it does about the intrinsic worth of Xenophon. The popularity of Longus, Heliodorus, and Achilles Tatius in the early eighteenth century [17] affected also the reception given to Xenophon, and by the nineteenth century Xenophon found himself included in the comprehensive German (Teubner) and French (Didot) collections of *Scriptores Erotici*. The Greek text of Xenophon has been readily available to scholars even in remote areas since the first years of the nineteenth century. Since the text of Xenophon is found in one manuscript only, little work of real importance, other than attempting to report accurately the one manuscript, has been undertaken. With the *editio princeps* of Cocchi in 1726 there has sprung up a slowly growing corpus of suggested manuscript emendations which are reported in each new edition. Until another manuscript is found from a different tradition from the one now extant or a papyrus of Xenophon is unearthed, nothing major can be done with the text. The controversy, for example, over the epitome theory will remain unresolved with proponents and opponents holding firm to their feelings about the text.

The twentieth century has witnessed the publication of three editions of Xenophon's Greek text. All have appeared in established series (Budé, Teubner, and Fundació Bernat Metge) that have some pressure on them to print all texts from the ancient world. It is difficult to say whether the intrinsic value of Xenophon's work brought him into these series, or the desire on the part of series' editors to be all-inclusive. At this time all three twentieth-century editions are still in print.

An Italian translation appeared in print in 1723, three years before the printed text. The translation was done by Salvini, who had seen the only extant manuscript in 1700 and had copied it. Over the succeeding century and a half this translation was frequently re-printed. The first English translation was worked up by Rooke in London, one year after the Greek text appeared. The eighteenth century also saw the first French (1736) and German (1775) translations. Indeed, that century, which produced a number of French and German translations of Xenophon, gives us more translations of our author than any other century.

The only other English translations were prepared by Moses Hadas in 1953 and by Paul Turner in 1957, and remain the ones used in schools today. While relatively few translations of Xenophon have appeared in our own time, 1956 records one done in Russian.

IV   *Influences on the Modern English Novel*

The English-speaking world became an audience for Xenophon's novel in 1727. The sequence in which the ancient Greek novels were translated into English is as follows:

> Heliodorus' *Aethiopica*, 1569
> Longus' *Daphnis and Chloe*, 1587
> Achilles Tatius' *Leucippe and Cleitophon*, 1597
> Xenophon's *Ephesiaca*, 1727
> Chariton's *Chaereas and Callirhoe*, 1764

Though many people in England during this period knew enough Greek to work with these texts even before they had been translated into English, it should not be assumed that they did. Even today, none of the above works is required reading at Oxford or Cambridge for classics scholars. Translation of these novels into English meant a wider audience and may, in fact, have created a secondary demand for original works patterned on the Greek models.

The influence of one work or one author on another author or his work is extremely difficult, if not impossible, to document. Then, too, because of the large number of similar episodes and motifs in the Greek novels, many of which might go back to a source common to all the novels, or which might simply be common to man-the-storyteller, it is risky to attribute a particular story or episode of a modern writer to the specific influence of this or that ancient work.

With the Greek edition of Xenophon of 1726 and the English translation of 1727 available to concerned parties, it is interesting to note the appearance in 1736 of the English romance of *Celenia: Or, the History of Hyempsol* by "Zelis," which contains an episode of striking similarity to Xenophon:

I have already noted the inset "Story of Antemora and Philarchus." . . . From it we learn that the parents of Antemora and her newly wed husband Busides, both of whom are only nine to ten years of age, separated them, apparently at the bidding of "Providence" as revealed by "some lines, which by way of Epithalamium, . . . we found in our wedding chamber." . . . This divinely ordained separation of the child couple is reminiscent of the critical episode in the *Ephesiaca* of Xenophon of Ephesus, where in response to the vague warnings of the oracle at Ephesus the parents of Habrocomes and Anthia send them abroad shortly after their wedding and thereby virtually ensure that they will encounter the hardships foretold. . . . Busides "adventures" for seven or eight years "with the thought of rendering . . . himself more worthy of " her, only to find her cold . . . because of her infatuation with Philarchus. . . . She and Philarchus then employ a physician to poison . . . Busides . . . but there now occurs the predictable pattern of the physician being forced to reveal all at the threat of having to drink the poison. Variations of this theme appear in . . . Xenophon of Ephesus.[18]

Paul Turner has illustrated how Henry Fielding, Charlotte Brontë, and the contemporary writer Nell Dunn have utilized materials or motifs which are found also in Xenophon.[19] While Turner notes that the two heroines of Samuel Richardson's (1689–1761) novels *Pamela* (1740) and *Clarissa* (1744) were, in the first place, created shortly after the first English translation of Xenophon's novel was made and, in the second place, bear striking resemblances to Xenophon's Anthia, he is cautious enough not to carry the argument one step further and state that Richardson borrowed the characters from Xenophon. If Anthia-like characters are in vogue while Richardson is composing his thoughts about the nature of his heroines, it is quite natural for him to be influenced or in some way to respond to such developments. We can speculate about such things, but will never be able with certainty to trace and itemize the borrowings. In despair, because she is being forced into illicit sex by the local squire, Pamela attempts suicide. Like Anthia (3.7), Pamela is saved in the attempt, and like Habrocomes (2.10), Pamela is set free from prison because her diary is properly understood by her captor. Clarissa, condemned to a whorehouse, is rescued temporarily by broken health—warmed over episode involving Anthia (5.5–7) and a bout with epilepsy. Richardson's *Clarissa* also shows some borrowings from Petronius' *Satyricon*, which was translated into English in 1694: e.g., Clarissa, like Trimalchio (*Satyricon* 78), asks that her funeral trappings be brought into her room while she is still alive.

Similarities between Xenophon and several English writers whom Turner identifies are worth restating because they illustrate that the building blocks of the ancient novel are the same ones used by modern novelists. Though the ancient novelists seem to use and reuse the same materials and language and to remain within a "closed field," it has been suggested by Professor Hugh Kenner "that for the narrative artist the limitations of language provide a 'closed field' in which a large but finite number of elements are susceptible to infinite combinations and permutations. He suggests that a preoccupation with the finiteness of the elements, the 'closedness' of the field, characterizes modern narrative." [20]

In writing *Joseph Andrews* (1747) Fielding parodied not only Richardson but also Richardson's source, Xenophon (Joseph Andrews is the supposed brother of Pamela). The following similarities between Xenophon's work and Fielding's *Joseph Andrews* are those selected by Turner. Habrocomes is set alongside Joseph: Habrocomes is captured and robbed by pirates (1.13) and later, after having escaped, is shipwrecked, robbed, and sold as a slave by the local inhabitants (3.12); Joseph is waylaid (1.12) by robbers. The importance given to pirates by Xenophon is natural enough because Habrocomes comes from the important port city (the end and beginning of important trade routes to the East) of Ephesus. What Northrop Frye said about fiction, "Of all fictions, the marvellous journey is the one formula that is never exhausted. . . ," [21] can easily be applied to the works of Xenophon and Fielding. While Habrocomes travels all over the eastern end of the Mediterranean, Joseph moves around Southern England. Neither protagonist would have been able to undergo and experience as many "slings and arrows of outrageous fortune," had he not frequently journeyed from place to place. Each location is seldom good for more than one experience. As Habrocomes has to fight off overly zealous women (and one or two men), so Joseph must withstand the advances of the amorous: Mrs. Slipslop is protrayed by Fielding as manly, and her attack ("rape") on Joseph (2.13) finds a parallel in the homosexual advances of Corymbus (1.14) on Habrocomes. Betty's pursuit of Joseph (1.18) reminds us of Manto's chase of Habrocomes (2.3), but where Manto precipitates a classic Potiphar motif, Betty acts clumsily and is herself dismissed instead of having Joseph thrown out. Finally, there is Bitch (3.12), the murderer of her husband (the only obstacle between herself and Habrocomes), whom Fielding changes into Lady Booby (1.5), a woman in hot pursuit of Joseph and delighted by her husband's timely death. (The episode also reminds us of Petronius' Widow of Ephesus.)

Attempts of varying degrees of seriousness to seduce Anthia are made by Euxinus (1.15), Moeris (2.11), Perilaus (2.13), Psammis (3.11), Anchialus (4.5), Amphinomus (4.6), Polyidus (5.4), and Hippothous (5.9). In *Joseph Andrews* we watch with bemused trepidation as Fanny eludes a seducer, only to fear her rescuer Parson Adams (2.10). But permanent safety is not coming to Fanny. Peter Pounce appears on the scene to rescue her again, but, as if according to some pre-arranged plan, he too falls under her spell of sex appeal and plots to seize her (3.12). Yet again, Fanny is attacked by a would-be raper, extricated by Joseph, and then given to fear over the less than honorable intentions of Joseph.

Jonathan Wild (1743) is another novel in which Fielding shows some influence of Xenophon's methods. Like Anthia, Mrs. Heartfree is married before she is separated from her husband, who, like Habrocomes, is imprisoned. Mrs. Heartfree travels by sea with a brigand named Wild, who is a type of Hippothous, and on this voyage, which takes her to Africa, where all ancient Greek novels except Longus' *Daphnis and Chloe* have episodes, she suffers shipwreck and capture by a group of pirates (2.9–10; 4.7–9, and 11)—an exact parallel to Xenophon. The following attackers strike at the feminine person of Mrs. Heartfree: (1) Wild, (2) a pirate, (3) a navy captain, (4) an unnamed gentleman, (5) a man who aided her to escape from the last named, (6) a magistrate, and (7) the ship captain who takes her home.

In both Xenophon and Fielding attempted seductions of the hero and heroine take place with great frequency, but do not cause any kind of development in the characters to anticipate, ward off, or handle future seductions. The only kinds of interest aroused in the reader are those of curiosity in learning how she will escape this time and of suspense in waiting until she recovers her husband, because there is some chance that the seducers will be successful. Seduction is to be expected because both hero and heroine are exceedingly lovely and attract the attention of everyone. While in language skill and description Fielding outstrips Xenophon handily, he owes a great deal to the plot structure of Xenophon and others and has learned from them how to extend a novel and keep up the interest of the audience: by staging one seduction scene after another Xenophon and Fielding play on the erotic emotions of the reader and keep him coming back for more, but avoid a charge of writing pornography by passing over clinical descriptions of seductions. As Chariton had done first and Xenophon followed, so Fielding uses the motif of the rescuer become seducer. Every time the heroine is saved from some plight, her rescuer at least falls in love with her or at worst tries to rape her. Petronius employs a variant of this motif where Encolpius sheds his friend Ascyltus because Ascyltus cannot keep his hands off Encolpius's lover Giton, only to get a more aggressive seducer as a friend in the person of Eumolpus. Such variants of this motif have been very popular in novel literature.

In Fielding's *Amelia* (1751) we see that the two lovers, who are married, are separated by sea voyages and by prison, and Booth is seduced by Miss Matthews, who, like Bitch in Xenophon, has murdered her husband. While separations caused by sea voyages and imprisonment are international and ancient motifs, and the murder of husbands by wives to give them the freedom to find a more suitable mate goes back to the earliest Western myths and stories, their combination in one work indicates some kind of influence of one author on the other.

In *Tom Jones* (1749) Fielding created one of his most enduring characters, a roguish *picaro*, skilled with a sword and in bedroom manners. With a zest for life in all its aspects, a sense of humor, and an attractive instability of personality, Tom bears almost no resemblance to Xenophon's hero, Habrocomes. Tom does seem, however, to be a latter-day version of Hippothous, who, with several characters from Petronius, represents the picaresque in ancient literature. Nevertheless, attention can be called to certain similar events in the episodic plots of *Tom Jones* and Xenophon. Like Habrocomes, Tom Jones is separated from Sophia by travels around England and also by his imprisonment on a charge of murdering his lover's husband. Xenophon gives us a similar episode in which Habrocomes is imprisoned for murdering Bitch's husband. Bitch claims that Habrocomes murdered her husband to remove him as a rival. Where Habrocomes finds a friend in a thief (Hippothous), so also does Tom Jones (12.14). Among other parallels we might list between *Tom Jones* and the work of Xenophon is the frequent attempt by women to seduce Habrocomes and similar attempts on Tom by Molly, Mrs. Waters, Mrs. Hunt, and Lady Bellaston. A radical difference, however, is that Tom surrenders where Habrocomes stands firm. Fielding's heroines, in that they can resist any temptation, resemble Anthia.

Turner sees possible influence of Xenophon in *Jane Eyre* (1847), by Charlotte Brontë. Manto comes back in the character of Blanche Ingram to separate the lovers, and the first Mrs. Rochester, who tried twice but failed to kill her husband, is a re-creation of Bitch. St. John Rivers, who wishes to marry Jane, makes a credible Perilaus. Like Habrocomes, who is saved by the rising Nile from being burned alive, so Rochester is rescued from certain death by the water Jane throws on his flaming bed.

Finally, Turner chooses a modern novel, *Poor Cow*, by Nell Dunn (London, 1967), who pictures for us a hero and heroine seduced by a long succession of lovers, as Habrocomes and Anthia had been. But in the 1967 novel both hero and heroine yield at every opportunity. From Xenophon, whose Anthia and Habrocomes remain under incredible pressure, through Tom Jones and Sophia, where only the female has to preserve herself chaste for her future husband, to *Poor Cow* we have shed our double standard and expect no moral character (in sexual matters) from either the hero or the heroine.

A contemporary writer who shows some knowledge of ancient prose fiction is Max Beerbohm in his *Zuleika Dobson* (1911).[22] Though out of fashion in this country, *Zuleika* does seem to have some strange power over the reading segment in England. Beerbohm, who was a fine Greek and Latin scholar, surely knew about the Greek novelists, and in particular Chariton and Xenophon, for it is from these two that he borrowed his descriptions of Zuleika and her admirer-lover, the Duke of Dorset. Like Callirhoe and Anthia, Zuleika makes instant lovers of every male who sees her, and instant enemies out of every female. Like the heroines of old, Zuleika renders every rejected male slightly suicidal because of his rejection. For those who know the ancient works as well as Beerbohm's marvelous tour de force of Oxford life, the comparisons are plentiful, but their mechanical listing here would not elucidate the ancient novels; it would detract, moreover, from the incomparable Max.

Appendix

(The material in this Appendix is added because of difficulty of the names and places, an aid to readers who do not have ready access to classical dictionaries and atlases.)

Dramatis Personae

(arranged according to dramatic chronology)

HABROCOMES.   Young man of Ephesus and hero of this novel.

LYCOMEDES.   Father of Habrocomes and resident of Ephesus. Appears in 1.1–1.11; dead by 5.6.

THEMISTO.   Mother of Habrocomes.

ANTHIA.   The most beautiful young woman in Ephesus and heroine of this novel.

MEGAMEDES.   Father of Anthia. Appears in 1.1–1.11; dead by 5.6.

EUIPPE.   Mother of Anthia.

TUTOR.   Teacher of Habrocomes. Appears in 1.14.

CORYMBUS.   Phoenician pirate (all Phoenicians are pirates, crooked merchants, or slave traders) who leads the band that captures Habrocomes and Anthia off Rhodes in 1.13 and imprisons them in Tyre in 1.14. Falls in love with Habrocomes in 1.14–2.2. No role in the novel after 2.2.

EUXINUS.   Fellow pirate and double of Corymbus. Falls in love with Anthia in 1.15.

LEUCON.   Slave of Habrocomes accompanying him from Ephesus, and imprisoned in Tyre in 1.14. A go-between for Manto in 2.3–2.5. Taken by Manto to Antioch in 2.9.

155

Sold as slave in Xanthus in Lycia in 2.10. Freed from slavery, and appears in Rhodes in 5.6 in anticipation of the arrival of Habrocomes and Anthia.

RHODE.   Slave of Anthia from Ephesus.

APSYRTUS.   Leader of the whole pirate band in Tyre in 1.14. Takes Habrocomes and Anthia as his share of the booty 2.2. Father of Manto 2.3. Tortures Habrocomes in 2.6, then appoints him manager of his estates in 2.10. Drops from the novel in 2.12.

MANTO.   Lecherous daughter of Apsyrtus. Falls in love with Habrocomes in 2.3, accuses him of rape in 2.5, and has him tortured in 2.6. Marries Moeris of Antioch in 2.7. Takes Anthia to Antioch, marries her to the goatherd Lampo in 2.9, and then in 2.11 has Lampo sell her to Cilician slavetraders. Drops from the novel in 2.12.

MOERIS.   Husband of Manto in 2.7. Returns home to Antioch with Manto in 2.9. Falls in love with Anthia in 2.11. Drops from the novel in 2.12.

LAMPO.   Goatherd of Moeris and husband (?) of Anthia in 2.9–2.11. Sells Anthia to Cilician slavetraders in 2.11.

HIPPOTHOUS.   Thief, cutthroat, murderer, from Perinthus on the Propontis (later called Heraclea), but otherwise, nice chap. Captures Anthia near her Cilician slavetraders in 2.11 and loses her in 2.13. Travels with Habrocomes in 2.14–3.10. Captures Anthia again in 4.3 from Psammis, and again loses her to Polyidus in 5.4, who forces him to flee to Sicily in 5.6. Marries an old, rich woman in 5.9. Buys Anthia from the pimp in Tarentum in 5.9, and escorts her to Rhodes in 5.11, where she meets Habrocomes.

PERILAUS.   Chief peace officer (*eirenarches*) of Cilicia. Rescues Anthia from Hippothous in 2.13, and takes her to Tarsus. Anthia agrees to marry him in 2.13; he prepares for the wedding in 3.3–3.6; buries her in 3.7. Perilaus drops out of the novel in 3.9.

HYPERANTHES.   Young man loved by Hippothous in 3.1. Not a character in this novel, but part of a flash-back told by Hippothous. Dies in 3.2.

ARISTOMACHUS.	Older man who steals Hyperanthes in 3.2, and is murdered by Hippothous in 3.2 in Byzantium (later called Constantinople).
EUDOXUS.	A physician of Ephesus who visits Tarsus and becomes Anthia's doctor in 3.4. He provides the "poison" for Anthia's suicide attempt in 3.5.
CHRYSION.	An old woman who appears in 3.9 in the role of a story teller near Tarsus, and informs Habrocomes of Anthia's proposed marriage to Perilaus, her death, burial, and the theft of her body.
PSAMMIS.	A prince of India, who in 3.11 buys Anthia from an Alexandrian slavetrader, and is killed in 4.3 by Hippothous in Ethiopia, as he attempts to take her to India.
ARAXUS.	A retired soldier, husband of Bitch, who in 3.12 buys Habrocomes from slavetraders after Habrocomes had been shipwrecked near Pelusium on his way to Alexandria.
BITCH.	Wife and murderer of Araxus in 3.12. Spurned by Habrocomes. Hanged by the Governor of Egypt in 4.5.
GOVERNOR OF EGYPT.	Punishes Habrocomes for the murder of Araxus in 4.2, but frees him and hangs Bitch in 4.5. Appoints Polyidus head of a (police) force to find Hippothous after his destruction of Areia in 5.3.
ANCHIALUS.	Robber friend of Hippothous. Killed by Anthia in 4.5.
AMPHINOMUS.	Robber in Hippothous's band. Guard and friend of Anthia 4.6–5.4.
AIGIALEUS.	A Spartan who lives in Syracuse in 5.1–5.2 and befriends Habrocomes.
THELXINOE.	Wife of Aigialeus in 5.1.
POLYIDUS.	Leader of a (police) force in Egypt which destroys Hippothous' band near Pelusium in 5.3. Falls in love with Anthia in 5.4–5.5.

RHENAIA.   Wife of Polyidus and rival of Anthia in 5.5.

CLYTUS.   Slave of Rhenaia, who sells Anthia to slavetraders in
                      Tarentum in 5.5.

PIMP.   Brothel keeper in 5.5; 5.7–5.9.

CLEISTHENES.   A young man from Syracuse who becomes the lover of
                      Hippothous in 5.9, and lives with him in Ephesus at
                      the end of the novel.

ALTHAEA.   An old woman of Rhodes who cares for Anthia in 5.11.

List of Places

(arranged according to dramatic chronology)

EPHESUS.   Home of Habrocomes and Anthia. Large and impor-
                      tant city in Asia Minor, near the Aegean Sea, about
                      thirty-five air miles south of Ismir, Turkey. Site of a
                      temple of Artemis, one of the seven wonders of the
                      ancient world. Habrocomes and Anthia leave Ephesus
                      at 1.11 and return at 5.15.

IONIA.   The district in Asia Minor which lies along the coast of
                      the Aegean sea from Smyrna (modern Izmir) in the
                      north to Miletus on the Meander river in the south
                      (i.e., from Izmir to a point about seventy-five air miles
                      south of Izmir). Ephesus is the chief city of this district.
                      Together with the area around Athens, Ionia is the
                      intellectual and artistic capital of Greece.

SAMOS.   A large island just west and south of the coast near
                      Ephesus. The home of fine painters and birthplace of
                      the philosopher Pythagoras. Visited by Habrocomes
                      and Anthia in 1.11.

RHODES.   Large island lying just off the southwest corner of
                      Turkey in the Carpathian sea. Once a seapower, later
                      famous for the Colossus. Visited by Habrocomes and
                      Anthia in 1.12, and the site of their final reunion in
                      5.11.

TYRE.   Ancient and famous city of Phoenicia, lying on the
                      Mediterranean coast of Palestine, some twenty miles

south of Sidon, and almost directly west of Damascus. Important commercial city in the time of King Solomon. Habrocomes and Anthia are held here by pirates at Apsyrtus' headquarters, 1.14 and 2.2. The lovers were separated here at 2.9.

PHOENICIA.   Roughly, the extreme eastern coastline of the Mediterranean, modern Lebanon and northern Israel. Important sea-trading district by the fifteenth century B.C.

ANTIOCH.   Founded by Seleucus in 300 B.C., as the capital of his Syrian Empire, which comprises much of modern day Palestine, i.e., Syria, Lebanon, Israel, Jordan, Iraq. Ancient Antioch is now Antakya, in southern Turkey, near the far northeast corner of the Mediterranean. Anthia is held prisoner here by Manto and later married to Lampo in 2.9. Visited by Habrocomes as he searches for Anthia in 2.12.

SYRIA.   See above, Antioch. It was the area of the Empire of Seleucus.

XANTHUS.   City in Lycia where Leucon and Rhode are slaves of a certain old man in 2.11 and 5.6. Lycia is a district in Asia Minor (Turkey), lying northeast of the island of Rhodes.

CILICIA.   District in Asia Minor (Turkey), lying immediately north of the island of Cyprus. It lies westward from the northeastern corner of the Mediterranean. Anthia is sold to slavetraders from Cilicia in 2.11, and taken captive in Cilicia by Hippothous in 2.11. Habrocomes visits Cilicia in 2.14 in search of Anthia and there meets Hippothous.

TARSUS.   Capital of Silicia, birthplace of St. Paul. Perilaus holds Anthia in Tarsus, after he has defeated Hippothous in 2.13. Habrocomes and Hippothous remain in Tarsus in 3.9 in search of Anthia.

MAZACUM.   Or Mazaca, in central Cappadocia; after A.D. 37 it is called Caesarea. Cappadocia lies immediately south of the eastern end of the Black Sea, and immediately north of Cilicia. Visited by Habrocomes and Hippothous in 3.1; Cappadocia is mentioned in 2.14.

ALEXANDRIA.

A major city in Egypt, on the Mediterranean, on the western edge of the Nile Delta, founded by Alexander the Great in 332 B.C. Major commercial and political center; site of the most famous library in antiquity. The grave robbers of Tarsus sell Anthia to merchants here in 3.9, and from here in 4.3 Psammis takes her toward India. Habrocomes is brought here in 3.12 to the governor of Egypt to stand trial for murder.

PELUSIUM.

City in Egypt, situated on the Mediterranean on the eastern edge of the Nile Delta. Habrocomes is sold here as a slave to Araxus in 3.12, after a shipwreck on his way to Alexandria.

MEMPHIS.

One of the great ancient cities of Egypt, located just south of the Nile Delta and a few miles above the Pyramids. Psammis and Anthia pass through it in 4.3 on their southern route to India, and Anthia and Polyidus on their northern route to Alexandria in 5.4.

COPTUS.

Large commercial city of Upper Egypt, lying some distance below (north of) Thebes. Important in the early history of Christianity. Visited by Anthia and Psammis in 4.3, by Anthia and Amphinomus in 5.2, and the site in 5.4 of Anthia's rescue by Polyidus.

INDIA.

The Greeks became familiar with India after its annexation by Alexander the Great. Important commercial ties existed between India and the West.

ETHIOPIA.

To the ancients Ethiopia is a rather vague area somewhere south of Egypt; however, there is no clear southern Egyptian border. To Homer and later to Herodotus and Strabo Ethiopia lies at the end of the world. Hippothous has his robber headquarters here in 4.1, and here in 4.3 captures Anthia from Psammis on their way to India. It seems clear that Psammis had gone this way so that he could employ also the easier sea route via the Red Sea and the Arabian Sea.

TARENTUM.

One of the early great Greek cities founded in Italy. Located in the heel of southern Italy. Here Clytus sells Anthia to a pimp in 5.5, and Hippothous buys her in 5.9.

SYRACUSE.   Surely the greatest and most influential Greek city ever established in Italy. Located on the eastern coast of Sicily, Syracuse was a powerful military state and a refined cultural center. In 5.1 Habrocomes leaves Alexandria and travels to Syracuse, where he stays with the necrophiliac Aigialeus. Habrocomes stops here again 5.10 on his way from Nucerium to Ephesus.

NUCERIUM.   Town in Italy where in 5.8 Habrocomes is destitute and takes employment as a stonecutter.

CYPRUS.   Large island in the far eastern part of the Mediterranean. Habrocomes pauses here in 5.10 on his way to Ephesus.

List of Named Deities

EROS.   The son of Aphrodite and Ares (or Zeus, or Hermes). Armed with bow and arrow and wearing a blindfold, Eros kindles love at random. When mortals try to reject his power, Eros becomes violent and strikes them down; if lovers are too happy, Eros becomes envious, and then envy (*phthonos*) spells doom for mortals. Seen in 1.1; 1.2; 1.3; 1.4; 5.1.

ARTEMIS.   Daughter of Zeus and Leto, twin sister of Apollo, virgin huntress, protectress of chastity. In pre-Hellenic Greece she was a type of earth-mother. Her temple in Ephesus was one of the wonders of the ancient world. Found in 1.2; 1.5; 1.10; 1.11; 5.15.

APOLLO   Son of Zeus and Leto, twin of Artemis, deity of law and
(of Colophon) of everything we generally subsume under civilization. His wishes come to man via his oracles, his most famous one being at Delphi; his oracle at Colophon, a city some few miles north of Ephesus, was his best attended oracle in Asia Minor. Has a role in 1.6.

ISIS.   Wife to Osiris, mother of Horus, Isis is the chief female deity in Egypt. Goddess of the earth and moon; clearly a fertility deity. Through a gradual process of syncretism she becomes the most powerful goddess in Egypt, then the East, and finally in the Roman Empire. All other female deities become mere aspects of her varied personality. From her role as earth mother she grows to become the savior deity and goddess of afterlife. She appears in 1.6; 3.11; 4.1; 4.3; 5.4; 5.13.

APHRODITE.   Goddess of love, related to the Eastern Astarte and Ishtar. Confused with her son Eros. Appears here in 1.8; 1.9.

ARES.   Bloodthirsty Greek god of war. Found in 1.9; 2.13; 3.3.

HERA.   Wife and sister of Zeus. Among the early Greeks she was the dominant female deity. In 1.11.

HELIUS.   Originally the sun, but slowly anthropomorphized into the god of the sun. Seen as the beneficent deity of light, sunshine, warmth, and all things good. Especially important at Rhodes where the Colossus was made in his image. Important here in 1.12; 4.2; 5.10; 5.11; 5.12.

NILE.   River and river god in Egypt. 4.2.

APIS.   Sacred bull god of Egypt, especially important at Memphis. Fertility god of life-death cycle. Appears in 5.4.

Notes and References

Chapter One

1. H. Gärtner, "Xenophon von Ephesos," *Real–Encyclopädie der classischen Altertumswissenschaft*, ed. Pauly-Wissowa et al., 2. Reihe, IX (Stuttgart, 1967), cols. 2055–89.
2. B. Lavagnini, "La patria di Senofonte Efesio," *Annali delle Università Toscane* 44 (1926): 239–49; see also Ben Perry, *The Ancient Romances* (Berkeley, 1967), p. 170.
3. Ben Perry, *The Ancient Romances*, p. 358.
4. See G. Schmeling, *Chariton* (New York, 1974), p. 17ff.
5. Cf. D. Magie, *Roman Rule in Asia Minor* (Princeton, 1950), p. 647ff. The office of Eirenarch could have existed earlier, but Magie's evidence seems to point to the reign of Trajan.
6. See G. Schmeling, *Chariton*, p. 17ff.; see also J. Oliver, "Xenophon of Ephesus and the Antithesis Historia–Philosophia," *Arktouros: Hellenic Studies Presented to B. W. Knox on the Occasion of his 65th Birthday* (Berlin, 1979), 401–6.
7. The Roman Emperor Julian (361–63) was set against reading ancient Greek novels: "It would be suitable for us to handle histories composed about real events: but we must avoid all the fictions written of old in the style of history, love subjects and everything in fact of that type" (translated by A. D. Nock). For a discussion of this together with primary evidence, see R. M. Rattenbury, "Chastity and Chastity Ordeals in the Ancient Greek Romances," *Proceedings of the Leeds Philosophical and Literary Society. Literature and History Section 1* (1926): 59–71.
8. See Ben Perry, *The Ancient Romances*, pp. 344–46, for the story of Xenophon's manuscript.

Chapter Two

1. Ben Perry, *The Ancient Romances* (Berkeley, 1967), p. 153ff.
2. T. Hägg, "The Naming of Characters in the Romance of Xenophon Ephesius," *Eranos* 69 (1971): 59.
3. Ibid., p. 26.
4. Ibid., pp. 39–40.
5. All citations in parentheses which include one letter plus one or more numerals refer to Stith Thompson, *Motif-Index of Folk–Literature*

163

(Bloomington, Indiana, 1955). It is a shame that this monumental research tool does not include any references to the Greek or Latin novels, since, of all the works from the ancient world, the novels represent the greatest store of motifs. Since the novel of Xenophon is nothing if it is not a carefully arranged collection of motifs, these parenthetical references will alert the reader to the pertinent information in Thompson. In her seminal study, *The Greek Novella in the Classical Period* (Cambridge, 1958), Sophie Trenkner includes the Greek and Latin novels when she writes of the survival of motifs.

6.   See also Arthur Heiserman, *The Novel Before the Novel* (Chicago, 1977).

7.   See T. Hägg, *Narrative Technique in Ancient Greek Romances* (Stockholm, 1971), pp. 227–33, on foreshadowing.

8.   Grundy Steiner, "The Graphic Analogue from Myth in Greek Romance," *Classical Studies Presented to Ben Perry* (Urbana, 1969), pp. 123–37. See also A. Scobie, *More Essays on the Ancient Romance and Its Heritage* (Meisenheim am Glan, 1973), p. 16f.

9.   In the ancient world many upper-class couples about to marry had little chance to let romance and love enter into their wedding plans; marriages were frequently arranged for family conveniences. Today this would be almost unthinkable—and today many marriages are grim. It might have been even worse in antiquity. Anthia and Habrocomes will have a marriage founded on love, and this will make it the envy of many readers whose marriages are extremely bad. These readers can, however, live vicariously in the love of this young couple.

10.   Ben Perry, *The Ancient Romances*, p. 98.

11.   G. Schmeling, *Chariton* (New York, 1974), pp. 49–51.

12.   E. Evans, *Physiognomics in the Ancient World* (Philadelphia, 1969).

13.   P. G. Walsh, *The Roman Novel* (Cambridge, 1970), pp. 73–74.

14.   See H. W. Parke, *Greek Oracles* (London, 1967), pp. 122, 139.

15.   P. Parsons, "A Greek *Satyricon*?," *Bulletin of the Institute of Classical Studies* 18 (1971): 53–68.

16.   T. Hägg, *Narrative Technique in Ancient Greek Romances*, pp. 55–63.

17.   Ibid., pp. 322–27.

18.   A. Scobie, *More Essays on the Ancient Romance and Its Heritage*, pp. 19–34.

19.   H. Gärtner, "Xenophon von Ephesos," *Real-Encyclopädie der classischen Altertumswissenschaft*, 2. Reihe, IX, (Stuttgart, 1967), cols. 2055–89.

20.   T. Hägg, *Narrative Technique in Ancient Greek Romances*, and H. Gärtner, *Real-Encyclopädie*.

21.   Ithaca, 1966.

22.   Dalmeyda sees here similarities to Vergil's Dido and Aeneas and Euripides' Admetus and Alcestis: G. Dalmeyda, *Xénophon d'Éphèse: Les Éphésiaques* (Paris, 1926 [1962]), p. xx.

23.   A. Heiserman, *The Novel Before the Novel*, p. 8.

24. In mythology the sea is regularly viewed as a place of monsters and grotesque beings. The unknown, the unpredictability, and the wildness of the sea make, by comparison, the land seem civilized. See M. Morford, *Classical Mythology*, 2nd edition (New York, 1977), pp. 91–97.

25. For a discussion of the barbarians in Greek literature one could consult the bibliography in A. Scobie, *More Essays on the Ancient Romance and Its Heritage*, p. 19ff. The best-delineated barbarian woman in Xenophon is Manto—sensuous, totally immoral, unscrupulous, and vicious when trapped. She represents, in short, the kind of woman every mother tells her son to avoid. She is a "foreign" woman, as Scobie so neatly puts it, and anyone who associates with her will suffer terrible consequences. Friends of Manto learn this quickly. The most memorable of all "foreign" women in the Greek novels is Arsace in Heliodorus.

26. P. G. Walsh, *The Roman Novel*, p. 206.

27. B. P. Reardon, "Aspects of the Greek Novel," *Greece and Rome* 23 (1976): 123.

28. S. Trenkner, *The Greek Novella in the Classical Period*, p. 45.

29. T. Hägg, *Narrative Technique in Ancient Greek Romances*, pp. 132–33.

30. G. Dalmeyda, "Autour de Xénophon d'Éphèse," *Bulletin de l'Association G. Budé* 13 (1926): 22, and E. Haight, *Essays on the Greek Romances* (New York, 1943), p. 58, compare the frequent scene changes to the modern motion picture.

31. George Devereux, "Greek Pseudo-Homosexuality and the 'Greek Miracle,' " *Symbolae Osloenses* 42 (1968): 69–92.

32. Otto Weinreich, "Kappadokōn phōnē," *Hermes* 55 (1920): 325. Citing ancient sources, Weinreich claims that the language of Cappadocia, which Hippothous claims to know, was a language distinct from Greek. Xenophon seems to know this fact about the language of Cappadocia; otherwise Hippothous' boast that he knows the language is meaningless. Either Xenophon was a better student of history and geography than we give him credit for, or perhaps he had visited Cappodocia and found himself in need of an interpreter.

33. G. Dalmeyda, *Xénophon d'Éphèse: Les Éphésiaques*, pp. xx, 40, sees parallels here with episodes in the lives of two other heroines, Dido and Alcestis. In Heliodorus (1.22ff), Chariclea tricks Thyamis into delaying their marriage by claiming she is consecrated to Artemis. She invents a story in which she states that she and Theagenes are shipwrecked travelers from Ephesus, where they left their elderly parents. This could be an echo from Xenophon or a parody of him.

34. Antti Aarne and Stith Thompson, *Types of the Folk–Tale* (Helsinki, 1961). For some reason the *Scheintod* motif is not indexed by Thompson in the *Motif–Index of Folk–Literature*.

35. See T. Szepessy, "The Story of the Girl Who Died on the Day of her Wedding," *Acta Antiqua Hungarica* 20 (1972): 341–57.

36.   A. Scobie, *Aspects of the Ancient Romance and Its Heritage* (Meisenheim am Glan, 1969), pp. 105–107.

37.   The travels of Hippothous in Egypt have been dealt with at some length by Henri Henne, "La géographie de l'Égypte dans Xénophon d'Éphèse," *Revue d'histoire de la philosophie et d'histoire générale de la civilisation* 4 (1936): 97–106. It is clear from this study that Xenophon knew something, but not very much, about Egyptian geography. I hardly find this small amount of knowledge about Egypt to be a fault. After all, what did Herodotus know about Egypt? And he devoted a whole book of his history to Egypt. In a world of fantasy like Xenophon's, we should not be amazed to find fantasy in his place descriptions.

38.   Xenophon is not alone among ancient writers in stretching his credibility as he explains how fires are extinguished by strange means. The Latin poet Statius (A.D. 45–95) in a serious poem about death tells us that a woman standing at her child's funeral pyre put out the smoldering ashes with the milk from her swollen breasts (Statius, *Silvae* V.5, lines 13–17). Herodotus (*Histories* 1.87) tells us that Croesus was saved from the pyre miraculously by a sudden change of heart in Cyrus. Another version of the story claims that in answer to Croesus' prayers the gods sent torrents of rain and put out the fire.

39.   P. G. Walsh, *The Roman Novel*, 159.

40.   Though there is very little explicit necrophilia in ancient literature, the subject is often just under the surface of the meaning. In his *Electra* (1144) Euripides has Electra say to Clytemnestra that, as she enjoyed sex with her husband on earth, so now she soon would enjoy it in Hades. The myth of Laodamia and Protesilaus has at least two aspects which might shed some light on the development of the necrophilia motif. After Protesilaus had been killed, Laodamia was given a special dispensation to spend three hours with her dead husband in the underworld. Rather than leave him after three hours, she killed herself. In an alternative version she was so in love with a statue of her husband that, when her father threw it away, she killed herself (see Ovid, *Heroides* 13). When Aeneas sees Dido in Hades in *Aeneid* 6, there are indications of erotic passions stirring in him—erotic for Aeneas, that is. In Euripides' *Alcestis* Admetus plans to make a statue of his wife, who has agreed to die for him, and indicates he will consort with the statuelike Alcestis. What we have here may be a motif and a variation: the motif would be the erotic attraction for someone or something inanimate—a statue or a dead person—because of that person's fear of real sex (Aeneas) or because of a sense of lost sex (Laodamia). In the myth of Pygmalion (Ovid, *Metamorphoses* 10.243–97) we see the hero fall in love with an ivory statue, which is turned into a lovely woman by Aphrodite and then into a stage play by G. B. Shaw. This latter "necrophilia" is quite innocent. On the subject of agalmatophilia (falling in love with a statue), see A. Scobie, "Perversions Ancient and Modern," *Journal of the History of the Behavioral Sciences* 11 (1975): 49–54. See also Herodotus 2.89.

41.   T. Hägg, *Narrative Technique in Ancient Greek Romances*, p. 327.

42. Otto Weinreich, "Haaropfer an Helios," *Hermes* 55 (1920): 326–28. Though hair is frequently offered as a votive to other deities, this offering appears to be the only recorded instance of hair dedicated to Helius.

43. R. M. Rattenbury, "Chastity and Chastity Ordeals in the Ancient Greek Romances," *Proceedings of the Leeds Philosophical and Literary Society: Literature and History Section* 1 (1926): 59–71.

Chapter Three

1. B. P. Reardon, "Aspects of the Greek Novel," *Greece and Rome* 23 (1976): 120.

2. Otto Weinreich, *Der griechische Liebesroman* (Zürich, 1962), p. 30, translated by G. Sandy, "Ancient Prose Fiction and Minor Early English Novels," *Antike und Abendland* 25 (1979): 44.

3. B. P. Reardon, "Aspects of the Greek Novel," p. 130. Ancient evidence for the low esteem in which ancient prose fiction was held is set out by C. García Gual, "Idea de la novela entre los griegos y romanos," *Estudios clasicos* 29 (1975): 111–44.

4. P. Turner, "Novels, Ancient and Modern," *Novel* 2 (1968): 15–24.

5. T. Hägg, *Narrative Technique in Ancient Greek Romances* (Stockholm, 1971), pp. 267–77, 296–300.

6. K. Bürger, "Zu Xenophon von Ephesus," *Hermes* 27 (1892): 36–67.

7. M. D. Reeve, "Hiatus in the Greek Novelists," *Classical Quarterly* 21 (1971): 514–39.

8. E. Haight, *Essays on the Greek Romances* (New York, 1943), 55.

Chapter Four

1. B. P. Reardon, "The Greek Novel," *Phoenix* 23 (1969): 292.

2. A. Scarcella, "La struttura del Romanzo di Senofonte Efesio," *La struttura della fabulazione antica* (Genoa, 1979), pp. 89–113. In a long and erudite compilation of materials F. Zimmermann, "Die *Ephesiaka* des sog. Xenophon von Ephesos. Untersuchungen zur Technik und Komposition," *Würzburger Jahrbücher für die Altertumswissenschaft* 4 (1949–50): 252–86, finds structure in the reunion scenes at the end of the story.

3. (New York, 1956 [1949]), Part 1, Chapter 4.

4. Analysis by T. Hägg, *Narrative Technique in Ancient Greek Romances* (Stockholm, 1971), pp. 272–73.

5. B. P. Reardon, "The Greek Novel," p. 303.

6. Ibid., p. 299.

7. Ibid., p. 298.

8. T. Hägg, *Narrative Technique in Ancient Greek Romances*, p. 169.

9. B. P. Reardon, "Aspects of the Greek Novel," *Greece and Rome* 23 (1976): 123.

10. Ibid.

11. R. Scholes and R. Kellogg, *The Nature of Narrative* (Oxford, 1966), p. 241. T. Hägg discusses at length point of view in his *Narrative Technique in Ancient Romances* (Stockholm, 1971).

12. R. Scholes and R. Kellogg, *The Nature of Narrative*, p. 245.

13. T. Hägg, *Narrative Technique in Ancient Romances*, pp. 132–33.

14. Ibid., p. 122.

15. Ibid., p. 233. Hägg has singled out this section as one with a particularly well wrought structure.

16. Moses Hadas, "Cultural Survival and the Origin of Fiction," *South Atlantic Quarterly* 51 (1952): 257.

17. (Harmondsworth: Penguin, 1954 [1929]), p. 222.

18. T. Hägg, *Narrative Technique in Ancient Greek Romances*, p. 158.

19. Ibid., p. 169.

20. Ibid., pp. 267–77, 327–32.

21. Ibid., p. 332.

22. Ibid., p. 99.

23. Ibid., p. 97.

24. R. Scholes and R. Kellogg, *The Nature of Narrative*, p. 88.

25. T. Hägg, *Narrative Technique in Ancient Greek Romances*, p. 99.

26. Cleanth Brooks, "The New Criticism," *Sewanee Review* 87 (1979): 599.

27. T. Hägg, *Narrative Technique in Ancient Greek Romances*, p. 99.

28. Cleanth Brooks, "The New Criticism," p. 598.

29. Ben Perry, *The Ancient Romances* (Berkeley, 1967), p. 9.

30. Ibid., p. 10.

31. Ibid., p. 12.

32. Ibid., p. 15.

33. B. P. Reardon, "The Greek Novel," p. 292.

34. E. Schwartz, *Fünf Vorträge über den griechischen Roman* (Berlin, 1896). See also G. Schmeling, *Chariton* (New York, 1974), pp. 51–56.

35. M. Braun, *History and Romance in Graeco-Oriental Literature* (Oxford, 1938).

36. G. Schmeling, *Chariton*, p. 52.

37. Ibid.

38. Ibid., p. 53.

39. (Oxford, 1949), p. 734.

40. H. Bornecque, *Les Déclamations et les Déclamateurs d'après Sénèque le père* (Lille, 1902).

41. E. Haight, *Essays on Ancient Fiction* (New York, 1936), pp. 125–50; Ben Perry, *The Ancient Romances*, pp. 331–33.

42. G. Giangrande, "On the Origins of the Greek Romance," *Eranos* 60 (1962): 132–59.

43. Ibid., p. 142.

44. S. Gaselee, *Parthenius* (London, 1916), p. 410.

45. G. Schmeling, *Chariton*, p. 43, summarizing the position of R. Scholes and R. Kellogg, *The Nature of Narrative.*

46. B. Lavagnini, *Le origini del romanzo greco* (Pisa, 1921), reprinted in his *Studi sul romanzo greco* (Florence, 1950).

47. Ben Perry, *The Ancient Romances*, p. 33.

48. Ibid., pp. 3–95.

49. Ibid., p. 18.

50. B. P. Reardon, "The Greek Novel," p. 292.

51. Ibid.

52. G. Duckworth, *The Nature of Roman Comedy* (Princeton, 1952), p. 28.

53. Ibid., p. 283.

54. Translation is by G. Duckworth, *The Nature of Roman Comedy*, p. 282.

55. *Plautus: The Rope and Other Plays*, translated by E. F. Watling (Harmondsworth, 1964).

56. Ibid.

57. W. Beare, "The Secret of Terence," *Hermathena* 56 (1940): 36.

58. G. Duckworth, *The Nature of Roman Comedy*, p. 103.

59. Ibid., p. 184.

60. G. Beer, *The Romance* (London, 1970), p. 1.

61. R. Scholes and R. Kellogg, *The Nature of Narrative*, p. 8.

62. E. Auerbach, *Mimesis: The Representation of Reality in Western Literature* (Princeton, 1953).

63. R. Scholes and R. Kellogg, *The Nature of Narrative*, p. 8.

64. N. Frye, *Anatomy of Criticism* (Princeton, 1957), p. 305.

65. Ibid., p. 304.

66. G. Beer, *The Romance*, p. 10.

67. P. Turner, "Novels, Ancient and Modern," *Novel* 2 (1968): 15–24.

68. (London, 1976), p. 100.

69. A. Scobie, *More Essays on the Ancient Romance and Its Heritage* (Meisenheim, 1973), p. 1ff.

70. Ibid., pp. 84–101.

71. R. Scholes and R. Kellogg, *The Nature of Narrative*, p. 99.

72. B. P. Reardon, "The Greek Novel," p. 304.

73. Ben Perry, *The Ancient Romances*, p. 48.

74. B. P. Reardon, "The Greek Novel," p. 292; see also G. Schmeling, *Chariton*, pp. 26–36.

75. B. P. Reardon, "The Greek Novel," pp. 292–93.

76. Ibid., p. 293.

77. Ibid., p. 294.

78. Ibid., p. 298.

79. Ibid., p. 303.

80. William Arrowsmith, "Luxury and Death in the *Satyricon*," *Arion* 5 (1966): 329–30.

81. Ben Perry, *The Ancient Romances*, p. 105.
82. E. L. Bowie, "The Novels and the Real World," *Erotica Antica: Acta of the International Conference on the Ancient Novel* (Bangor, Wales, 1977), p. 94.
83. A. Scarcella, "Les structures socio-économiques du Roman de Xénophon d'Éphèse," *Revue des études grecques* 90 (1977): 249–62.
84. E. L. Bowie, "The Novels and the Real World," p. 95.
85. Ibid.
86. A. Scarcella, "Les structures socio-économiques du Roman de Xénophon d'Éphèse," pp. 249–62.
87. Walker Percy, *Lancelot* (New York, 1977), pp. 21–22.
88. T. Hägg, *Narrative Technique in Ancient Greek Romances*, p. 174.
89. A. Heiserman, *The Novel Before the Novel* (Chicago, 1977), p. 55.
90. P. G. Walsh, *The Roman Novel* (Cambridge, 1970), p. 206.
91. G. Schmeling, *Chariton*, pp. 130–59.
92. T. B. L. Webster, *Philoctetes* (Cambridge, 1970), pp. 6–7.
93. A. Scarcella, "Les structures socio-économiques du Roman de Xénophon d'Éphèse," pp. 249–62.
94. G. Beer, *The Romance*, p. 8.
95. Ibid., p. 7.
96. S. Miller, *The Picaresque Novel* (Cleveland, 1967).
97. R. E. Witt, *Isis in the Graeco-Roman World* (Ithaca, 1971), pp. 243–54. The belief that the novel of Xenophon is somehow a disguised version of the rituals of the Isis cult and also a disguised aretalogy is not new with Witt—nor does he claim it is. This notion has been on the fringes of classical scholarship for some time, but only recently articulated by the brightest and best. For the imaginative reader interested in this line of inquiry, I would recommend Karl Kerényi, *Die griechisch-orientalische Romanliteratur in religionsgeschichtlicher Beleuchtung* (Darmstadt, 1973) and, especially, Reinhold Merkelbach, *Roman und Mysterium* (Munich, 1962).
98. R. M. Rattenbury, "Chastity and Chastity Ordeals in the Ancient Greek Romances," *Proceedings of the Leeds Philosophical and Literary Society. Literature and History Section* 1 (1926): 59–71; and the collections of the history of martyrs and saints' lives.
99. R. E. Witt, *Isis in the Graeco-Roman World*, p. 249.
100. Moses Hadas, "Cultural Survival and the Origin of Fiction," p. 258.
101. A. Heiserman, *The Novel Before the Novel*, pp. 67–88.

Chapter Five

1. Donald Levin, "To Whom Did the Ancient Novelists Address Themselves?" *Rivista di studi classici* 25 (1977): 18.
2. G. Schmeling, *Chariton* (New York, 1974). p. 33.
3. Gillian Beer, *The Romance* (London, 1970), p. 2.

4. G. Schmeling, *Chariton*, pp. 32–33.
5. Ibid., p. 119.
6. R. Peacock, *Criticism and Personal Taste* (Oxford, 1972), pp. 17–18.
7. Gillian Beer, *The Romance*, p. 9.
8. Ibid., p. 3.
9. B. P. Reardon, "The Greek Novel," *Phoenix* 23 (1969): 293; see also René Wellek and Austin Warren, *Theory of Literature* (New York, 1956 [1942]), p. 216.
10. Gilbert Highet, *The Classical Tradition* (Oxford, 1949), pp. 165–66.
11. Ben Perry, *The Ancient Romances* (Berkeley, 1967), p. 98.
12. Moses Hadas, "Cultural Survival and the Origins of Fiction," *South Atlantic Quarterly* 51 (1952): 253.
13. A. Scobie, *More Essays on the Ancient Romance and Its Heritage* (Meisenheim, 1973), p. 96.
14. E. Haight, "Ancient Greek Romances and Modern Mystery Stories," *Classical Journal* 46 (1950): 5.
15. Ibid., p. 45.
16. John E. Mack, *A Prince of Our Disorder: The Life of T. E. Lawrence* (London, 1976), pp. 46–47.

Chapter Six

1. A brief review of S. Wolff, *The Greek Romances in Elizabethan Prose Fiction* (New York, 1912), and W. McCulloh, *Longus* (New York, 1970), will show that Heliodorus, Longus, and Achilles Tatius had the greatest influence on later literature. The reader might care to consult also O. Weinreich, *Der griechische Liebesroman* (Zürich, 1962) on the influence of Heliodorus.
2. Discussed (with bibliography) by G. Schmeling, *Chariton* (New York, 1974), pp. 32, 160.
3. I am assuming that Chariton preceded Xenophon and not vice versa. The most convincing statements on the chronology of the ancient novelists are by H. Gärtner, "Xenophon von Ephesos," *Real-Encyclopädie der classischen Altertumswissenschaft*, 2. Reihe, IX (Stuttgart 1967), cols. 2055–89.
4. *Historia Apollonii Regis Tyri*, ed. Alexander Riese (Leipzig, 1893) p. xvi ff. See also the Introduction to Peter Goolden's *The Old English Apollonius of Tyre* (Oxford, 1958).
5. Northrop Frye, *Anatomy of Criticism* (New York, 1968 [1957]), p. 57.
6. H. Gärtner, op. cit., provides the specific references for this and for the earlier instances of influence.
7. H. Delehaye, *The Legends of the Saints* (London, 1962), p. 5.
8. Ibid., p. 12ff.
9. Ibid., p. 23.
10. Ben Perry, *The Ancient Romances* (Berkeley, 1967), compares the *Recognitions* to the anonymous *Historia Apollonii Regis Tyri*. This idea is picked up by Arthur Heiserman, *The Novel Before the Novel* (Chicago, 1977).

I would like to extend it back to Xenophon because of the use made of Xenophon's work by the anonymous author of the *Historia Apollonii*.

11.   M. H. James, *The Apocryphal New Testament* (Oxford, 1924), p. 364.

12.   Carol Gesner, *Shakespeare and the Greek Romance: A Study of Origins* (Lexington, Kentucky, 1970), p. 62ff.

13.   Francis Douce, *Illustrations of Shakespeare and of Ancient Manners* (London, 1807).

14.   Ben Perry, *The Ancient Romances*, p. 98.

15.   In his recent work on the influence of ancient novels, Gerald Sandy, "Ancient Prose Fiction and Minor Early English Novels," *Antike und Abendland* 25 (1979): 41, makes these observations:

Already in the early part of the seventeenth century Joseph Hall could declare: "What Schole-boy, what apprentice knows not Heliodorus?" Almost forty years earlier and a full five years before the complete *Aethiopica* was to be translated into English by Underdowne in 1587, Stephen Gosson reported that "the *Aethiopian historie*" had "beene throughly ransackt, to furnish the Playhouses in London."

16.   Ben Perry, *The Ancient Romances*, p. 96ff.

17.   See S. Wolff, *The Greek Romances in Elizabethan Prose*, passim.

18.   Gerald Sandy, "Ancient Prose Fiction and Minor Early English Novels," pp. 45–46.

19.   Paul Turner, "Novels, Ancient and Modern," *Novel* 2 (1968): 15–24.

20.   Hugh Kenner, "Art in a Closed Field," *Learners and Discoverers*, ed. R. Scholes (Charlottesville, 1964). Quotation comes from R. Scholes and R. Kellogg, *The Nature of Narrative* (New York, 1966), pp. 158–59.

21.   Northrop Frye, *Anatomy of Criticism*, p. 57.

22.   Max Beerbohm, *Zuleika Dobson* (Harmondsworth, 1971 [1911]).

Selected Bibliography

PRIMARY SOURCES

1. Greek Texts

COCCHI, A. *Xenophontis Ephesii Ephesiacorum libri V. De amoribus Anthiae et Abrocomae*. London: Typis Gulielmi Bowyer, 1726. This is the *editio princeps* of Xenophon, and was printed together with a Latin translation.

DALMEYDA, G. *Xénophon d'Éphèse. Les Éphésiaques ou le roman d' Habrocomès et d'Anthia*. Paris: Société d'Edition "Les Belles Lettres," 1926. Until 1973 the standard Greek text. Sensible notes but an unreliable text. Accompanied by a French translation.

HERCHER, R. *Xenophon Ephesius* in *Erotici Scriptores Graeci*, I. Leipzig: Teubner, 1858–59.

HIRSCHIG, G. A. *Xenophon Ephesius* in *Erotici Scriptores Graeci*. Paris; Didot, 1875.

KONTOU, POLYZOIS. *Xenophontis Ephesii amores de Anthia et Abrocome*. Vienna, 1793.

LOCELLA, A. E. *Xenophontis Ephesii de Anthia et Habrocome Ephesiacorum libri V*. Vienna: Blumauer, 1796. Together with a Latin translation. Locella added a commentary and Greek index. Considering the 1796 date, we find it a first-rate edition and a competent authority on the Greek text.

MIRALLES, C. *Xenophont d'Efes. Efesíaques*. Barcelona: Fundació Bernat Metge, 1967. Similar in quality to Dalmeyda's text. Accompanied by a Catalan translation.

MITSCHERLICH, C. W. *Xenophontis Ephesiacorum de amoribus Anthiae et Abrocomae libri V*. Zweibrücken: Ex Typographia Societatis, 1794.

PAPANIKOLAOU, A. D. *Xenophontis Ephesii Ephesiacorum libri V*. Leipzig: Teubner, 1973. Latest critical edition of the Greek. With Latin introduction, notes, and extensive bibliography. Reeve's review of this work in the *Journal of Hellenic Studies* 96(1976): 192–93, points out serious flaws.

PASSOW, F. *Xenophon Ephesius* in *Corpus scriptorum eroticorum Graecorum*, II. Leipzig: Teubner, 1833.

PEERLKAMP, P. H. *Xenophontis Ephesii de Anthia et Habrocome Ephesiacorum libri V*. Haarlem: Loosjes, 1818. Perhaps the most useful of the Greek texts (with Latin translation) of Xenophon. Excellent commentary (some borrowed from earlier works) and cross-references to other classical authors.

2. English Translations

HADAS, M. *Three Greek Romances*. Indianapolis: Bobbs-Merrill, 1953. This translation remains in print, and though dull at most points, it serves the purpose of translation.

ROOKE, M. *Xenophon's Ephesian History or The Love-Adventures of Abrocomas and Anthia*. London: J. Millan, 1727.

3. German Translations

BÜRGER, G. A. *Anthia und Abrokomas*. Leipzig: Weygand, 1775.

HÄUSLIN, J. A. *Etwas von Ephesus, oder Geschichte eines jungen Ehepaars*. Ansbach: Haueisen, 1771.

KRABINGER, J. G. *Des Xenophon von Ephesos Anthia und Habrocomes*. Munich: Fleischmann, 1820.

KYTZLER, B. *Xenophon von Ephesus. Die Waffen des Eros oder Anthia und Habrocomes*. Berlin: Propyläen-Verlag, 1968. The best translation into any modern language. It is the standard German translation.

4. French Translations

BAUCHE, P. (Publisher). *Les Éphésiaques de Xénophon Éphésien ou Les amours d'Anthie et d'Abrocomas*. Paris, 1736.

COURIER, P. *Habrocome et Anthia, Histoire Éphésienne*. Paris: Corréard, 1823.

DALMEYDA, G. *Xénophon d'Éphèse. Les Éphésiaques ou le Roman d'Habrocomès et d'Anthia*. Paris: Société d'Édition "Les Belles Lettres," 1926. This is the standard French translation of Xenophon, bound together with the Greek text.

JOURDAN, J. B. *Les amours d'Abrocome et d'Anthia. Histoire Éphésienne*. Paris: Bibliothèque Universelle des Dames, 1785.

5. Italian Translations

CATAUDELLA, Q. *Il romanzo classico. Il romanzo . . . di Senofonte Efesio*. Rome: Casini, 1958. The standard Italian translation. Very lively.

SALVINI, A. *Di Senofonte Efesio degli amori di Abrocome e d'Anzia libri cinque*. Florence, 1723. The earliest translation of this novel into any modern language.

6. Russian Translations

POLJAKOVA, S., and FELENKOVSKAJA, I. *Ksenofont Efesskij, Porovest'o Gabrokome i Antii*. Moscow: Institut des Belles Lettres, 1956.

7. Spanish Translation

MIRALLES, C. *Xenophont d'Efes. Efesíaques.* Barcelona: Fundació Bernat Metge, 1967. A translation into Catalan.

8. Dutch Translation

TRESLING, T. P. *Habrokomes en Anthia. Een Roman van Xenophon den Ephesier.* Groningen: M. Smit, 1829.

9. Translations of the Other Ancient Novels

BLAKE, W. *Chariton: Chaereas and Callirhoe.* Ann Arbor: University of Michigan Press, 1938.
GASELEE, S. *Achilles Tatius: Leucippe and Clitophon.* London: Heinemann, 1969.
HAIGHT, E. *The Romance of Alexander.* New York: Longmans, Green & Co., 1954.
LAMB, W. *Heliodorus: Ethiopian Story* London: Dent, 1961.
LINDSAY, J. *Apuleius: The Golden Ass.* Bloomington: Indiana Unversity Press, 1962.
SULLIVAN, J. P. *Petronius: Satyricon.* Harmondsworth: Penguin, 1965.
TURNER, P. *Apollonius Prince of Tyre.* London: The Golden Cockerel Press, 1956.
——— *Longus: Daphnis and Chloe.* Harmondsworth: Penguin, 1968.

SECONDARY SOURCES

1. Works with Extensive Bibliographies on Xenophon

HÄGG, T. *Narrative Technique in Ancient Greek Romances.* Stockholm: Acta Instituti Atheniensis Regni Sueciae, 1971.
HAIGHT, E. "Notes on Recent Publications about the Ancient Novel," *Classical World* 46 (1953): 233–37.
MAZAL, O. "Der griechische und byzantinische Roman in der Forschung von 1945 bis 1960: Ein Literaturbericht," *Jahrbuch der österreichischen byzantinischen Gesellschaft* 11–12 (1962–1963): 7–55; 13 (1964): 29–86; 14 (1965): 83–124.
PAPANIKOLAOU, A. D. *Xenophontis Ephesii Ephesiacorum libri V.* Leipzig: Teubner, 1973.
PERRY, B. E. *The Ancient Romances: A Literary-Historical Account of Their Origins.* Berkeley: University of California Press, 1967.
SANDY, G. "Recent Scholarship on the Prose Fiction of Classical Antiquity," *Classical World* 67 (1974): 321–59.
SCHMELING, G. L. *Chariton.* New York: Twayne, 1974.

ZIMMERMANN, F. "Zum Stand der Forschung über den Roman in der Antike: Gesichtspunkte und Probleme," *Forschungen und Fortschritte* 26 (1950): 59–62.

2. Miscellaneous Works

AVAERT, P. *Éléments de réalité chez Xénophon d'Éphèse*. Dissertation, Louvain, 1948. A work impossible to obtain.

BÜRGER, K. "Zu Xenophon von Ephesus," *Hermes* 27 (1892): 36–67. For reasons of narrative technique and constant alternation in settings, and because some material appears highly developed and other material a bare skeleton, Bürger suggests that the extant novel is in part an epitome of the tome written by Xenophon. He is supported in this by Zimmermann and more recently by the precise arguments of Gärtner. But Hägg's long article on the subject and his attack on the epitome theorists should carry the day.

DALMEYDA, G. "Autour de Xénophon d'Éphèse," *Bulletin de l'Association G*. *Budé* 13 (1926): 18–28.

GARIN, F. "Su i romanzi greci," *Studi Italiani di Filologia Classica* 17 (1909): 423–60. A careful comparison of Greek phrasing and sentence structure among the ancient novelists. Particularly useful for Xenophon and Chariton.

GÄRTNER, H. "Xenophon von Ephesos," *Real-Encyclopädie der classischen Altertumswissenschaft*, 2. Reihe, IX, (Stuttgart: Druckenmüller, 1967), cols. 2055–89. In this highly regarded German encyclopedia Gärtner has written a most comprehensive and illuminating essay on Xenophon. It is sensitive, and particularly appreciative of Xenophon and his work. Gärtner treats the narrative style, the language, characterization, Xenophon's date and debt to Chariton, and finally his later influence. Gärtner's essay is written in the difficult German for which this encyclopedia is famous. But reading it is worth the effort.

GIANGRANDE, G. "On the Origins of the Greek Romance: The Birth of a Literary Form," *Eranos* 60 (1962): 132–59. Alexandrian love-elegies are the source and origin of the Greek novel.

GUIDA, A. "Une nuova collazione del codice di Senofonte Efesio," *Prometheus* 1 (1975): 65–79, 279.

HÄGG, T. "Die Ephesiaka des Xenophon Ephesius—Original oder Epitome?" *Classica et Mediaevalia* 27 (1966): 118–61. Hägg opposes Bürger's theory that the extant novel of Xenophon is an epitome. He concludes that we cannot know one way or the other for sure, but that he is inclined to think that it is *not* an epitome.

————. "The Naming of the Characters in the Romance of Xenophon Ephesius," *Eranos* 69 (1971): 25–59.

————. *Narrative Technique in Ancient Greek Romances*. Stockholm: Acta Instituti Atheniensis Regni Sueciae, 1971. Clearly the finest analysis in print on the literary merits of Xenophon, Chariton, and Achilles Tatius. Every aspect of the narrative technique is discussed: temporal structures, parallel actions, linking phrases, point of view, characterization, motivation, first-person narrative, foreshadowing and suspense, and recapitulations.

HENNE, H. "La géographie de l'Égypte dans Xénophon d'Éphèse," *Revue d'Histoire de la Philosophie et d'Histoire Générale de la Civilisation* 4 (1936): 97–106.

KERÉNYI, K. "Der hellenistische Roman. Eine papyrologische Betrachtung über die alexandrinische Kultur," *Die neue Rundschau* 49 (1938): 393–405.

————. "Die Papyri und das Problem des griechischen Romans," *Actes du Vᵉᵐᵉ Congrès international de Papyrologie 1937* (Brussels, 1938), pp. 192–209.

————. *Die griechisch-orientalische Romanliteratur in religionsgeschichtlicher Beleuchtung.* Darmstadt, 1973. Like Merkelbach who came after him, Kerényi saw religious mystery ritual as the origin of the Greek novel, and the developed novel as the literary extension of that hidden mystery. Each novel then becomes a kind of aretalogy, or work in praise of some deity. It is not so much propaganda as praise. The form of the praise is at once literary and ritualistic.

LAVAGNINI, B. "Le origini del romanzo greco," *Annali della R. Scuola Normale Superiore Universitaria di Pisa* 28 (1921): 1–104.

————. "La patria di Senofonte Efesio," *Annali delle Università Toscane* 44 (1926): 239–49. Xenophon was not a native of Ephesus.

————. *Studi sul romanzo greco.* Messina: G. D'Anna, 1950. Contains the above two articles.

MANN, E. *Über den Sprachgebrauch des Xenophon Ephesius.* Kaiserslautern: Programm des Gymnasiums, 1896.

MERKELBACH, R. *Roman und Mysterium.* Munich: Beck, 1962. The Greek novel has its origin in the ritual of Greek mystery religions. According to Merkelbach Chariton was not aware of this origin, but Xenophon was.

MORESCHINI, C. "Un' ipotesi per la datazione del romanzo di Senofonte Efesio," *Studi classici e orientali* 19–20 (1970–1971): 73–75.

PERRY, B. E. *The Ancient Romances: A Literary-Historical Account of Their Origins.* Berkeley: University of California Press, 1967. The single best book on the reasons for the rise of prose fiction in antiquity. A sound grasp of the nature of Greek novels. It is the standard work on ancient prose fiction, but not to be tackled by the Greek-less or Latin-less reader.

REARDON, B. P. "The Greek Novel," *Phoenix* 23 (1969): 291–309. The age of the Greek novel is the age of the professional writer, prose fiction, and the rise of the individual. The best short discussion of the ancient novel. Recommended for all to read.

————. *Courants littéraires grecs des II ᵉ et III ᵉ s. après J. C.* Paris: Les

Belles Lettres, 1971. This book has one section set aside for Greek novels and does a thorough job of setting the stage and describing the literary circumstances in which the novel moved. It is a work of primary importance.

————. "Aspects of the Greek Novel," *Greece and Rome* 23 (1976): 118–31. Literary analysis for Xenophon.

REEVE, M. D. "Hiatus in the Greek Novelists," *Classical Quarterly* 21 (1971): 514–39. A study of the rhetorical device of avoiding juxtaposing words ending in a vowel before words beginning with a vowel. Reeve uses this to conclude, among other things, that the extant work of Xenophon is an epitome.

RHODE, E. *Der griechische Roman und seine Vorläufer.* Hildesheim: Olms, 1960. First published in Leipzig in 1876, this book was the standard reference work on the ancient novel until the publication of Perry's research. Though it was reedited and updated by the brilliant German scholar W. Schmid in 1941, it nevertheless contains some speculation and personal bias by Rhode which has subsequently been proved erroneous by papyri "finds" in Egypt, etc. Most of the book is solid scholarship.

SCARCELLA, A. "Noterelle al Romanzo di Senofonte Efesio," *Prometheus* 3 (1977): 79–86.

————. "Les structures socio-économiques du Roman de Xénophon de Éphèse," *Revue des Études Grecques* 90 (1977): 249–62. Analysis of the novel as a social, nonimaginative work.

————. "La struttura del Romanzo di Senofonte Efesio," *La struttura della fabulazione antica.* Genoa: Istituto di Filologia Classica e Medievale, 1979, pp. 89–113.

SCHISSEL VON FLESCHENBERG, O. "Technik der Romanschlüsse im griechischen Liebesroman," *Wiener Studien* 30 (1908): 231–42. An analysis of the way in which the various Greek novelists conclude their works by recapitulating the previous actions of the protagonists.

————. *Die Rahmenerzählung in den ephesischen Geschichten des Xenophon von Ephesus.* Innsbruck: Wagner, 1909. Schissel here studies the "frame narratives" at the beginning and end of the novel which frame the action in the body of the work. He contends that the novel displays fine classical unity.

————. *Entwicklungsgeschichte des griechischen Romanes im Altertum.* Halle: Niemeyer, 1913. A study not so much of development as of the form of the ancient novel.

SCHMID, W. "Der griechische Roman. Gegenwärtiger Stand unserer Kenntnis über seinen Begriff und Ursprung," *Neue Jahrbücher für das klassische Altertum* 13 (1904): 465–85.

SCHNEPF, M. *De imitationis ratione, quae intercedit inter Heliodorum et Xenophontem Ephesium, commentatio.* Kempten: Programm der Studienanstalt, 1887.

SCOBIE, A. *Aspects of the Ancient Romance and Its Heritage. Essays on Apuleius, Petronius, and the Greek Romances.* Meisenheim am Glan: Anton Hain, 1969. A clear, short introduction to the ancient Roman novels with a short appendix on Xenophon.

TRENKNER, S. *The Greek Novella in the Classical Period.* Cambridge: Cambridge University Press, 1958. Ms. Trenkner is convinced that the Greeks were among the greatest storytellers of all time and that the themes and motifs developed in preclassical times survived and became the subject matter of parts of the later Greek novels.

WITT, R. E. "Xenophon's Isiac Romance," *Isis in the Graeco-Roman World.* Ithaca: Cornell University Press, 1971, pp. 243–54.

ZIMMERMANN, F. "Aus der Welt des griechischen Romans," *Die Antike* 11 (1935): 292–316.

————. "Die *Ephesiaca* des sog. Xenophon von Ephesos. Untersuchungen zur Technik und Komposition," *Würzburger Jahrbücher für die Altertumswissenschaft* 4 (1949–1950): 252–86. Like Bürger, Zimmermann feels the extant novel of Xenophon is at least in part an epitome, and, like Schissel, he believes that Xenophon planned the form of his novel carefully and worked each of the apparently fortuitous episodes into a closely knit structure.

3. General Studies in the Ancient Novel

BARNS, J. "Egypt and the Greek Romance," *Mitteilungen aus der Papyrussammlung der österreichischen Nationalbibliothek* 5 (1956): 29–36. From the evidence of papyrus discoveries in Egypt Barns is led to believe that the Greek novel, or perhaps the proto-Greek novel, owes as much to Egyptian sources as to Greek.

BOOTH, W. C. *The Rhetoric of Fiction.* Chicago: University of Chicago Press, 1965.

BRAUN, M. *History and Romance in Graeco-Oriental Literature.* Oxford: Blackwell, 1938. Braun discusses the relationships between history and legends, and makes a strong case for the development of legend into history as well as the degeneration of history into legend.

CALDERINI, A. *Le avventure de Cherea e Calliroe.* Turin: Fratelli Bocca, 1913. The first 200-plus pages of Calderini's translation of Chariton's novel are taken up with an introduction to the Greek novel. Calderini's opening essay is very important for its analysis and organization of motifs in the novel, and for his search for similar motifs in earlier Greek literature.

FEUILLATRE, E. *Études sur les Éthiopiques d'Héliodore. Contribution à la connaissance du roman grec.* Paris: Presses Universitaires, 1966.

GÄRTNER, H., ed. *Beiträge zum griechischen Liebesroman.* Hildesheim: Olms, 1974. Announced.

GESNER, C. *Shakespeare and the Greek Romances*. Lexington: University Press of Kentucky, 1970.

VAN GRONINGEN, B. A. "General Literary Tendencies in the Second Century A.D.," *Mnemosyne* 18 (1965): 41–56.

HAIGHT, E. "Ancient Greek Romances and Modern Mystery Stories," *Classical Journal* 46 (1950): 5–10, 45.

———. *Essays on the Greek Romances*. New York: Longmans, Green & Co., 1943. A good solid review of the Greek novels, and appreciative remarks from a keen observer. If her judgment errs in any respect, it is in her inability to see some of the serious flaws in the whole extant production of ancient novels.

———. *More Essays on Greek Romances*. New York: Longmans, Green & Co., 1945.

HEISERMAN, A. *The Novel Before the Novel*. Chicago: University of Chicago Press, 1977. Literary history of the classical precedents of the novel. Written very sensitively by a professor of English who, while he does not command access through the original language, does appreciate the ancient novels. Good work, but lacking a treatment of Petronius' *Satyricon*.

HENRICHS, A. *Die Phoinikika des Lollianos*. Bonn: Habelt, 1972. The Greek edition of the surviving fragments of a popular, sensational, piece of ancient prose fiction.

KERÉNYI, K. *Der antike Roman*. Darmstadt: Wissenschaftliche Buchgesellschaft, 1971. Kerényi looks at the ancient novels from the standpoint of a scholar deeply involved in ancient religious studies.

KIRK, D. M. *The Digression: Its Use in Prose Fiction from the Greek Romance through the 18th Century*. Dissertation, Stanford University, 1960.

MCCULLOH, W. *Longus*. New York: Twayne, 1970. A study of Longus' use of his Greek predecessors, and of his influence on later writers.

MORTENSEN, P. *Structure in Spenser's Fairie Queen, Book VI*. *Primitivism, Chivalry, and Greek Romance*. Dissertation, Oregon State University, 1966.

PARSONS, P. "A GREEK *Satyricon*?" *Bulletin of the Institute of Classical Studies* 18 (1971): 53–68. Parsons has published an Egyptian papyrus which seems to contain a story in Greek similar to the *Satyricon*.

PHILLIMORE, J. S. "The Greek Romances," in *English Literature and the Classics*, ed. G. S. Gordon. Oxford: Oxford University Press, 1912, pp. 87–117. The Greek novel appears on the stage when the Greeks are no longer the intellectual giants of the West, but rather its senile inhabitants.

RATTENBURY, R. M. "Chastity and Chastity Ordeals in the Ancient Greek Romances," *Proceedings of the Leeds Philosophical and Literary Society. Literature and History Section* 1 (1926): 59–71. When the Greek novel no longer portrayed chaste heroines, the middle class readers rejected it, and it died.

_____. "Romance: Traces of Lost Greek Novels," in *New Chapters in the History of Greek Literature*, Third Series, ed. J. U. Powell. Oxford: Oxford University Press, 1933, pp. 211–57. Scholars must search early Egyptian writings if they wish to learn more about the sources of the Greek novel.

REARDON, B. P. "The Second Sophistic and the Novel," *Approaches to the Second Sophistic*. University Park, Pennsylvania: American Philological Association, 1974, pp. 23–29.

REITZENSTEIN, R. *Hellenistische Wundererzählungen*. Leipzig: Teubner, 1906.

SCHMELING, G. L. *Chariton*. New York: Twayne, 1974.

SCHOLES, R., and KELLOGG, R. *The Nature of Narrative*. New York: Oxford University Press, 1966.

SCHWARTZ, E. *Fünf Vorträge über den griechischen Roman*. Berlin: De Gruyter, 1943. A study of narrative literature in Greece; emphasis on the historical side of the Greek novel.

SCOBIE, A. *More Essays on the Ancient Romance and Its Heritage*. Meisenheim am Glan: Anton Hain, 1973. A varied, but excellent collection of essays on the ancient novel.

STEINER, G. "The Graphic Analogue from Myth in Greek Romance," *Classical Studies Presented to Ben Perry*. Urbana: University of Illinois Press, 1969, pp. 123–37. The use of myth universalizes the story situation in the Greek novel. Other novelists make better use of it than Xenophon.

SULLIVAN, J. P. *The Satyricon of Petronius: A Literary Study*. London: Faber and Faber, 1968.

TURNER, P. "Novels, Ancient and Modern," *Novel* 2 (1968): 15–24. The genre of the novel first appeared in Greece in the first century A.D., not in England in 1700. A defense of the quality of the Greek novel.

DE VRIES, G. J. "Novellistic Traits in Socratic Literature," *Mnemosyne* 16 (1963): 35–42.

WALSH, P. G. *The Roman Novel*. Cambridge: Cambridge University Press, 1970. An analysis of the mixed forms which led to the creation of the *Satyricon* and the *Metamorphoses*. Relevant statements about the Greek novel. Excellent treatment.

WATT, I. *Rise of the Novel*. Berkeley: University of California Press, 1960.

WEINRICH, O. *Der griechische Liebesroman*. Zürich: Artemis, 1962. Short history of the Greek novel, stressing particularly Heliodorus.

WELLEK, R. and WARREN, A. *Theory of Literature*. New York: Harcourt, Brace & Co., 1962.

WEST, S. "Joseph and Asenath: A Neglected Greek Romance," *Classical Quarterly* 68 (1974): 70–81.

WOLFF, S. *The Greek Romances in Elizabethan Prose Fiction*. New York: Columbia University Press, 1912. The influence of Longus, Heliodorus, and Achilles Tatius on early English fiction writers.

Index

182